1998

THE 100

BEST
MUTUAL
FUNDS
YOU CAN BUY

Gordon K. Williamson

Adams Media Corporation
Holbrook, Massachusetts

Also by Gordon K. Williamson

Big Decisions, Small Investor
Low Risk Investing
Making the Most of Your 401(k)

Dedication
This book is dedicated to all of my clients.
I would be nowhere without their trust and support.

Acknowledgments
Special thanks to Cynthia Shaffer for her computer skills. This is a truly
thankless job, and I appreciate everything she has done.

Published by Adams Media Corporation
260 Center Street, Holbrook, MA 02343

ISBN: 1-55850-754-X

Printed in the United States of America.

J I H G F E D C B A

While due care has been taken to ensure accurate and current data, the ideas, principles, conclusions, and general suggestions contained in this volume are subject to the laws and regulations of local, state, and federal authorities, as well as to court cases and any revisions of
court cases. Due to the magnitude of the database and the complexity of the subject matter,
occasional errors are possible; the publisher assumes no liability direct or incidental for any
actions or investments made by readers of this book, and strongly suggests that readers seek
consultation with legal, financial, or accounting professionals before making any investment.

This publication is designed to provide accurate and authoritative information with regard to
the subject matter covered. It is sold with the understanding that the publisher is not engaged
in rendering legal, accounting, or other professional advice. If legal advice or other expert
assistance is required, the services of a competent professional person should be sought.
— From a *Declaration of Principles* jointly adopted by a Committee of the
American Bar Association and a Committee of Publishers and Associations

This book is available at quantity discounts for bulk purchases.
For information, call 1-800-872-5627 (in Massachusetts, 781-767-8100).

Visit our home page at http://www.adamsmedia.com

Contents

I.

About This Book

There are 5.4 million business entities operating in the United States; 13,000 of these businesses are publicly held (meaning they have issued stock to the public). Of the 13,000 pubicly traded companies, 2,700 are listed on the New York Stock Exchange.

There are over 8,000 mutual funds. There are close to three times as many mutual funds as there are stocks listed on the New York Stock Exchange! The mutual fund industry is now the second largest financial institution in the nation, with assets approaching $4 trillion, up from $1 trillion in 1991. Over the past five years, the percentage of U.S. households that invest in mutual funds has risen from 25 percent to 37 percent.

Mutual funds are the *best* investment vehicle that has been developed in the twentieth century. When properly selected, these vehicles combine professional management, ease of purchase and redemption, simple record keeping, risk reduction, and superb performance, all in one type of investment. There are dozens of other types of investments, but none matches the overall versatility of mutual funds.

A mutual fund is simply one method of investing. When you invest in a fund, your money is pooled with thousands of other investors' monies. This large pool of money is overseen by the fund's management. These managers invest this pool of money in one or more types of investments. The universe of investments includes common stocks, preferred stocks, corporate bonds, tax-free municipal bonds, U.S. government obligations, zero-coupon bonds, convertible securities, gold, silver, foreign securities, and even real estate. The amount of money invested in one or more of these categories depends upon the fund's objectives and restrictions and on the management's perception of the economy.

The beauty of mutual funds is that, once the investor decides upon the *type* of investment desired, there are several funds that fulfill that criterion. As an example, someone who needs current income would be attracted to bond funds (or a series of equity-oriented funds coupled with what is known as a "systematic withdrawal plan"—a monthly income program described in Appendix D). A person interested in appreciation would focus on an aggressive growth, growth and income, and/or international stock fund. A person who wanted some current income plus some growth to offset the effects of inflation should consider a balanced fund.

The track records of these funds can easily be obtained, as contrasted to the track records of stockbrokers, who are not ranked at all. A few mutual fund sources even look at a fund's risk-adjusted return, a standard of measurement that has not been sufficiently emphasized in the past.

This book was written to fill a void. There are already several mutual fund books and directories, but none deals exclusively with the very best funds. More important, *none of these publications measures risk properly*.

This is the eighth edition of this book. If you have read one or more of the previous editions, you will notice that this edition includes funds not previously listed; several of the previous "100 best" are not included here. This does not mean that you should sell or transfer from a previous recommendation to one that appears in this edition. For the most part, mutual funds described in past editions are still excellent choices and should not be moved. There are a number of reasons why a fund no longer appears in this, or previous, editions. These reasons will be detailed in Chapter 10.

Moving from one fund to another can often spell trouble. Consider a recent Morningstar study that compared the performance of its growth fund index with the average investor's return during the five-year period ending 5/31/94. While the overall market gained, on average, 12.5 percent a year, the average investor *lost* 2.5 percent a year. Volatility can make it easy for investors to forget about the long-term case for stocks.

Other sources give almost endless numbers and performance statistics for hundreds and hundreds of mutual funds, leaving readers to draw their own conclusions as to what are the best funds. This book will save you a great deal of time because it has taken the over 8,000 existing funds and narrowed them down to the best 100, ranked by specific category and risk level. Even money market funds are included, a category rarely covered by any other publication.

Investors and financial advisors are not concerned with mediocre or poor performers; they simply want the best funds, *given certain parameters*. Personal investment considerations should include (in order of priority) your time horizon, risk tolerance, financial goals, existing portfolio, and tax bracket. Parameters within a given fund category include risk, performance, and consistency.

Current books and periodicals that cover funds focus on how a fund has performed in the past. Studies clearly point out that a fund whose performance is in the top half one year has a 50–50 chance of being in the bottom half the next year, or the year after that. Since there is little correlation between the past and the future when it comes to market returns, this book concentrates on consistency in management and the amount of risk assumed.

The model used to rank the 100 best is fully described in a later chapter. It is a logical, common-sense approach that cuts through the statistical jargon; it is also easy to understand. As my dad used to say, "There is nothing as uncommon as common sense."

II.
What Is a Mutual Fund?

A mutual fund is an investment company—an entity that makes investments on behalf of individuals and institutions who share common financial goals. The fund pools the money of many people, each with a different amount to invest. Professional money managers then use the pool of money to buy a variety of stocks, bonds, or money market instruments that, in their judgment, will help the fund's shareholders achieve their financial objectives.

Each fund has an investment objective, described in the fund's prospectus, that is important to both the manager and the potential investor. The fund manager uses it as a guide when choosing investments for the fund's portfolio. Prospective investors use it to determine which funds are suitable for their own needs. Mutual funds' investment objectives cover a wide range. Some follow aggressive investment policies, involving greater risk, in search of higher returns; others seek current income from more conservative investments.

When the fund earns money, it distributes the earnings to its shareholders. Earnings come from stock dividends, interest paid by bonds or money market instruments, and gains from the sale of securities in the fund's portfolio. Dividends and capital gains produced are paid out in proportion to the number of fund shares owned. Thus, shareholders who invest a few hundred dollars get the same investment return per dollar as those who invest hundreds of thousands.

Mutual funds remain popular because they are convenient and efficient investment vehicles that give all individuals—even those with small sums to invest—access to a splendid array of opportunities. Mutual funds are uniquely democratic institutions. They can take a portfolio of giant blue-chip companies like IBM, General Electric, and General Motors, and slice it into small enough pieces so that almost anyone can buy.

Mutual funds allow you to participate in foreign stock and bond markets that might otherwise demand too much time, expertise, or expense to be worthwhile. International funds make investing across national borders no more difficult than investing across state lines. Over the next decade, as securities markets develop in the former Iron Curtain countries, mutual funds will no doubt give investors many opportunities to participate in those markets as well.

Mutual funds have opened up a world of fixed-income investing to people who, until recently, had few choices apart from passbook accounts and savings bonds. Through bond funds, shareholders can tap into the interest payments from any kind of fixed-income security you can imagine—and many you have never heard of. The range goes from U.S. Treasury bonds (T-bonds) to collateralized mortgage obligations (CMOs), adjustable-rate preferred stock, floating-rate notes, and even to other countries' debts—denominated both in U.S. dollars and in other currencies.

What is heavily marketed is not necessarily what is appropriate for you to invest in. A global biotechnology fund may be a great investment, but it may not be the right mutual fund for you. Buying what is hot rather than what is appropriate is one of the most common mistakes made by investors and an issue that is addressed throughout this book.

III.

How to Invest in a Mutual Fund

Investing in a mutual fund means buying shares of the fund. An investor becomes an owner of shares in the fund just as he or she might be an owner of shares of stock in a large corporation. The difference is that a fund's only business is investing in securities, and the price of its shares is directly related to the value of the securities held by the fund.

Mutual funds continually issue new shares for purchase by the public. The price per share for existing fund investors is not decreased by the ongoing issuance of new shares, since each share created is offset by the amount of new money coming in. Phrased another way, new money that comes into the fund is used to purchase additional securities in order not to dilute the income or value for existing shareholders.

A fund's share price can change from day to day, depending on the daily value of the securities held by the fund. The share price is called the net asset value (NAV), which is calculated as follows. The total value of the fund's investments at the end of the day, after expenses, is divided by the number of shares outstanding.

Newspapers report mutual fund activity every day. An example from the *Wall Street Journal* is shown below.

Everett Funds:			
Evrt r	12.38	NL	−.01
MaxRtn	18.39	NL	+.06
ValTr	12.33	NL	−.01
LtdSl	17.71	NL	−.14
ExtrMid	2.82	2.95	−.02
ExJY p	7.24	7.60	+.01
FBK Gth t	11.06	11.06	..
FJA Funds:			
Capit f	14.67	15.69	−.02
NwHrz	9.65	10.10	..
Permt	12.91	13.81	..
Perrin	20.96	22.42	−.02

The first column in the table is the fund's abbreviated name. Several funds under a single heading indicate a family of funds.

The second column is the net asset value (NAV) per share as of the close of the preceding business day. In some newspapers, the NAV is identified as the sell or the bid price—the amount per share you would receive if you sold your shares. Each mutual fund determines its net asset value every business day by dividing the market value of its total assets, less liabilities, by the number of shares outstanding. On any given day, you can determine the value of your holdings by multiplying the NAV by the number of shares you own.

The third column is usually the offering price or, in some papers, the buy or the asked price—the price you would pay if you purchased shares. The buy price is the NAV plus any sales charges. If there are no sales charges, an NL for no load appears in this column. In such a case, the buy price would be the same as the NAV.

The next column shows the change, if any, in the net asset value (NAV) from the preceding quotation—in other words, the change over the most recent one-day trading period. Thus, if you see a "+.06" in the newspaper next to your fund, *each* of your shares in the fund went up in value by six cents during the previous day.

A *p* following the abbreviated name of the fund denotes a fund that charges a fee that is subtracted from assets for marketing and distribution costs, also known as a 12b-1 plan (named after the federal government rule that permits such an expense). If the fund name is followed by an *r*, the fund has a contingent deferred sales load (CDSL) or a redemption fee. A CDSL is a charge incurred if shares are sold within a certain period; a redemption fee is a cost you would pay *whenever* shares are sold. An *f* indicates a fund that habitually enters the previous day's prices, instead of the current day's. A *t* designates a fund that has both a CDSL or a redemption fee and a 12b-1 plan.

IV.
How a Mutual Fund Operates

A mutual fund is owned by all of its shareholders, the people who purchased shares of the fund. The day-to-day operation of a fund is delegated to a management company.

The management company, often the organization that created the fund, may offer other mutual funds, financial products, and financial services as well. The management company usually serves as the fund's investment advisor.

The investment advisor manages the fund's portfolio of securities. The advisor is paid for its services in the form of a fee that is based on the total value of the fund's assets; fees average 0.5 percent. The advisor employs professional portfolio managers who invest the fund's money by purchasing a number of stocks or bonds or money market instruments, depending on what type of fund it is.

These fund professionals decide where to invest the fund's assets. The money managers make their investment decisions based on extensive, ongoing research into the financial performance of individual companies, taking into account general economic and market trends. In addition, they are backed up by economic and statistical resources. On the basis of their research, money managers decide what and when to buy, sell, or hold for the fund's portfolio, in light of the fund's specific investment objective.

In addition to the investment advisor, the fund may also contract with an underwriter who arranges for the distribution of the fund's shares to the investing public. The underwriter may act as a wholesaler, selling fund shares to security dealers, or it may retail directly to the public.

V.
Different Categories of Mutual Funds

Aggressive Growth. The investment objective of aggressive growth funds is maximum capital gains, with little or no concern for dividends or income of any kind. What makes this category of mutual funds unique is that fund managers often have the ability to use borrowed money (leverage) to increase positions. Sometimes they deal in stock options and futures contracts (commodities). These trading techniques sound, and can be, scary, but such activities represent only a minor portion of the funds' holdings.

Because of their bullish dispositions, these funds will usually stay fully invested in the stock market. For investors, this means better-than-expected results during good (bull) markets and worse-than-average losses during bad (bear) market periods. Fortunately, the average bull market is almost four times as long as the typical bear market.

Do not be confused by economic conditions and stock market performance. There have been eight recessions since World War II. During seven of those eight recessions, U.S. stocks went up. During all eight recessions, stocks posted impressive gains in the second half of every recession. By the same token, do not underestimate the impact of a loss. A 20-percent decline means that you must make 25 percent to break even. A loss of 20 percent does not happen very often to aggressive growth funds, particularly on a calendar year basis, but you should be aware that such extreme downward moves are possible. Often brokers like to focus on the +45 percent and +50 percent years, such as 1980 and 1991, while glossing over a bad year, such as 1984, when aggressive growth funds were down almost 13 percent on average.

One of the great wonders of the stock market is how volatility of returns is reduced when one's holding period is increased. Because of this, aggressive growth funds should only be owned by one of two kinds of investors: those who can live with high levels of daily, monthly, quarterly and/or annual price per share fluctuations, and those who realize the importance of a diversified portfolio that cuts across several investment categories—the investor who looks at how the entire package is performing, not just one segment.

The top ten holdings of aggressive growth funds are: HFS, Wisconsin Central Transport, Rational Software, Cascade Communications, CBT Group, Papa John's International, Dura Pharmaceuticals, Apollo Group Class A, Microchip Technology, and McAfee Associates. The typical price-earnings (p/e) ratio for stocks in this category is 32, a figure approximately 20 percent greater than that found with S&P 500 stocks (which have an average p/e ratio of 26). This group of funds has an average beta of 1.0, making its *market-related* risk the same as the S&P 500 (which always has a beta of 1.0, no matter what market conditions or levels are).

The standard deviation for aggressive growth funds is 20 percent. This means that one's expected return for any given year may vary either way by 20 percent. In other words, since aggressive growth funds have averaged 20.5% over the past three years, annual returns are expected to range from −0.5 percent (20.5 − 20) to 40.5 percent (20.5 + 20). This would represent *one* standard deviation (20 percent in the case of aggressive growth funds). A single standard deviation accounts for what you can expect every two out of three months (67 percent of the time or roughly two out of every three years). If you are looking for greater assurance, then two standard deviations must be used (2 x 20 percent in this case). This means that returns for about 95 percent of the months (two standard deviations) would be 20.5 percent plus or minus 40 percent. In other words, a range of −19.5 percent to +60.5 percent.

Small-company stock funds are included in the aggressive growth category for the purposes of this book and other publications. The top ten holdings of small-company funds are: BancTec, Quantum, PXRE, ICN Pharmaceuticals, Marshall Industries, Keane, America Online, Expeditors International Washington, CalEnergy, and Magellan Health Services.

Small-company stocks have an average p/e ratio of 28. (The price-earnings ratio refers to the selling price of a stock in relation to its annual earnings. Thus a fund category that has a p/e ratio of, say, 10 is comprised of mutual funds whose typical stock in the portfolio is selling for ten times what the corporation's earnings are for the year.) Small-company stock funds have a standard deviation of 19 percent and a beta of 0.9 percent, figures that support the view that this category is slightly less volatile than aggressive growth funds.

Historical returns over the past three, five, ten, and fifteen years for aggressive growth and small-company stock funds are shown below. All of the figures shown are average *annual* rates of return (all periods ending 6/30/97).

category	3 years	5 years	10 years	15 years
aggressive growth	20%	17%	12%	15%
small-company stocks	22%	17%	13%	15%
S&P 500	29%	20%	15%	19%
T-bills	5%	4%	5%	6%
CPI (rate of inflation)	3%	3%	4%	4%

The aggressive growth fund category is dominated by technology stocks. This single group represents over 27 percent of the typical aggressive growth fund's portfolio. The other four top sectors are service, health, industrial cyclical, and financial stocks. Small-company stocks are also dominated by technology and service issues.

Balanced Funds. This kind of fund invests in common stocks and corporate bonds. The weighting given to stocks depends upon the fund manager's perception of, or belief in, the market. The more bullish the manager is, the more likely the portfolio will be loaded up with equities. Yet, no matter how strongly management feels about the stock market, it would be very rare to see stocks equal more than 75 percent of the portfolio. Similarly, no matter how bearish one becomes, it would be unlikely for a balanced fund to have more than 70 percent of its holdings represented by bonds. Often a fund's prospectus will outline the weighting ranges: The fund's managers must stay within these wide boundaries at all times. A small portion of these funds is made up of cash equivalents (T-bills, CDs, commercial paper, etc.) with a very small amount sometimes dedicated to preferred stocks and convertible securities.

Three other categories, "multi-asset global," "convertible," and "asset allocation" have been combined with balanced funds for the purposes of this book. This grouping together is logical; since overall objectives are largely similar, general portfolio composition can be virtually identical in many cases, and the fund managers in each of these categories have the flexibility to load up heavily on stocks, bonds, preferreds, or convertible securities.

Multi-asset global funds typically emphasize bonds more than stocks or cash. It is not uncommon to see a multi-asset global fund that has 60 percent of its holdings in bonds, with 10 to 20 percent in stocks, and the remainder in foreign equities, preferred stocks, and cash. For the *stock* portion of this category, the p/e ratio is 27 and the standard deviation 8 percent. On the bond side, the average maturity of debt instruments in the portfolio is nine years.

Convertible funds, as the name implies, are made up mostly of convertible preferred stocks and convertible bonds. The conversion feature allows the owner, the fund in this case, to convert or exchange securities for the corporation's common stock. Conversion and price appreciation take place during bull-market periods. Uncertain or down markets make conversion much less likely; instead, management falls back on the comparatively high dividend or interest payments that convertibles enjoy. The typical convertible fund has somewhere between two-thirds and three-quarters of its holdings in convertibles; the balance is in cash, stocks, and preferreds. For the stock portion of this category, the p/e ratio is 24 and the standard deviation is 8 percent. On the bond side, the average maturity of debt instruments in the portfolio is eight years.

Asset allocation funds, like other categories that fall under the broad definition of "balanced," are hybrid in nature, part equity and part debt. These funds have a tendency to emphasize stocks over bonds. A fund manager who wants to take a defensive posture may stay on the sidelines by converting moderate or large parts of the portfolio into cash equivalents. The average asset allocation fund has somewhere between 50 and 65 percent of its portfolio in common stocks, with the remainder in bonds, foreign stocks, and cash. For the stock portion of this category, the p/e ratio is 24 and the standard deviation is 8 percent. On the bond side, the average maturity of debt instruments in the portfolio is ten years.

The top ten holdings of balanced funds are: Philip Morris, General Electric, Bristol-Myers Squibb, Citicorp, American Home Products, DuPont, U.S. Treasury Bonds, Allstate, BankAmerica, and Royal Dutch Petroleum. The typical price-earnings (p/e) ratio for stocks in this category is 23, a figure that is lower than that of the S&P 500. This group of funds has an average beta of 0.7, making its *market-related risk* 30 percent less than the S&P 500. Keep in mind that beta refers to a portfolio's *stock market-related* risk—it is not a meaningful way to measure bond or foreign security risk. The typical bond in these funds has an average maturity of nine years.

The standard deviation for balanced funds is 8 percent, less than half the level of aggressive growth funds. This means that one's expected return for any given year will vary by 8 percent. (For example, if you were expecting an annualized return of 12 percent, your actual return would range from 4 percent to 20 percent most of the time.)

Historical returns over the past three, five, ten, and fifteen years for balanced, multi-asset global, convertible, and asset allocation funds are shown below. All of the figures shown are average *annual* rates of return (all periods ending 6/30/97).

category	3 years	5 years	10 years	15 years
balanced	17%	13%	11%	15%
multi-asset global	12%	11%	6%	16%
convertible	15%	13%	10%	14%
asset allocation	16%	12%	10%	13%
Corp./Gov't Bond Index	9%	7%	9%	11%

The equity portion of the balanced fund category is dominated by industrial and financial stocks. These two groups represent a third of the typical balanced fund's stock portfolio. The other four top equity sectors are: service, technology, health, and energy stocks.

Like other hybrid funds, balanced funds provide an income stream. The average yield of balanced and asset allocation funds is under 3 percent. The typical yield for both multi-asset global and convertible securities funds is about 3 percent. High-tax-bracket investors who want to invest in these funds should consider using tax-sheltered money, if possible. Balanced, multi-asset global, asset allocation, and convertible bond funds are particularly attractive within an IRA, other qualified retirement plans, or variable annuities. (For more information about both fixed-rate and variable annuities, see two of my other books, *The 100 Best Annuities* and *All About Annuities*.)

Corporate Bonds. These funds invest in debt instruments (IOUs) issued by corporations, governments, and agencies of the U.S. government. Perhaps the typical corporate bond fund should be called a "government-corporate" fund. Bond funds have a wide range of maturities. The name of the fund will often indicate whether it is made up of short-term or medium-term obligations. If the name of the fund does not include the words "short-term" or "intermediate," then the fund most likely invests in bonds with average maturities over ten years. The greater the maturity, the more the fund's share value can change. There is an inverse relationship between interest rates and the value of a bond; when one moves up, the other goes down.

The top ten holdings of corporate bond funds are: U.S. Treasury bonds, U.S. Treasury notes, FNMA, General Motors, Republic of Italy, Motorola, Ford Motor, Proctor & Gamble, General Electric Capital, and UPS. The weighted maturity date of the bonds within this group averages eight years, with a typical coupon rate of 7.4 percent. (The coupon rate represents what the corporation or government pays out annually on a per-bond basis.)

All bonds have a maturity date—a date when the issuer (the government, municipality, or corporation) pays back the *face value* of the bond (which is almost always $1,000 per bond) and stops paying interest. There are often hundreds of different securities in any given bond fund. Each one of these securities (bonds in this case) has a maturity date; these maturity dates can range anywhere from a few days up to thirty years. "Weighted maturity" refers to the time left until the average bond in the portfolio comes due (matures).

The standard deviation for corporate bonds is 4 percent, about half the level of balanced funds. This means that one's expected return for any given month, quarter, or year will be more predictable than almost any other category of mutual funds.

Using a beta measurement for bonds is of little value, since beta defines *stock market* risk and has nothing to do with interest-rate or financial risk. Historical returns over the past three, five, ten, and fifteen years for corporate bond funds are shown below. All of the figures shown are average *annual* rates of return (all periods ending 6/30/97).

category	3 years	5 years	10 years	15 years
corporate bond funds	7%	7%	8%	11%
government bond funds	7%	6%	8%	10%
municipal bond funds	7%	6%	8%	10%
world bond funds	9%	6%	8%	13%
CPI (rate of inflation)	3%	3%	4%	4%

Like income funds, corporate funds provide a high yield that is fully taxable and should be sheltered whenever possible. The average yield of these bond funds is just under 6 percent.

Global Stock. This category of mutual funds invests in equities issued by domestic and foreign firms. Fifteen of the twenty largest corporations in the world are located outside of the United States. It makes sense to be able to invest in these and other corporations and industries—to be able to take advantage of opportunities wherever they appear. Global, also known as world, stock funds have the ability to invest in any country. The more countries a fund is able to invest in, the lower its overall risk level will be; often return potential will also increase.

For the purposes of this book, the global stock category includes foreign and international equity funds. When it comes to investing in mutual funds, the words "foreign" and "international" are interchangeable. A foreign, or international, fund invests in securities outside of the United States. Some foreign funds are broadly diversified, including stocks from European as well as Pacific Basin economies. Other international funds specialize in a particular region or country. A global fund invests in domestic as well as foreign securities. The portfolio manager of a global fund generally has more latitude in the securities selected, since either U.S. or foreign securities can end up representing 50 percent or more of the portfolio, depending upon management's view of the different markets; whereas a foreign or international fund may not be allowed to invest in U.S. stocks or bonds.

To get an idea of the return potential of global stocks, take a look at how the United States has fared compared to stock markets in other countries. The table below shows the best-performing market for each of the past eleven years (ending 12/31/96), its total return in U.S. dollars, and performance figures for the U.S. stock market. All of the figures shown below are adjusted for any good or bad foreign currency swings (meaning that these percentage figures reflect those times when the U.S. dollar has been strong or weak).

year	best major market	best emerging market	U.S. returns
1986	Spain (123%)	n/a	+18%
1987	Japan (43%)	n/a	+5%
1988	Belgium (55%)	Indonesia (258%)	+17%
1989	Austria (105%)	Turkey (547%)	+31%
1990	United Kingdom (10%)	Greece (90%)	–3%
1991	Hong Kong (50%)	Argentina (405%)	+31%
1992	Hong Kong (32%)	Jordan (40%)	+8%
1993	Hong Kong (117%)	Poland (754%)	+10%
1994	Finland (52%)	Brazil (66%)	+1%
1995	Switzerland (45%)	Israel (24%)	+37%
1996	Spain (39%)	Venezuela (228%)	+26%

The top ten holdings of global (world) stock funds are: Cheung Kong Holdings, Telefonica de Espana, Philips Electronics, Philip Morris, ING Groep, Telecom Italia Mobile, Novartis, Bank International Indonesia, HSBC Holdings, and Elf Aquitaine. The typical price-earnings (p/e) ratio for stocks in this category is 26, a figure that is virtually identical to that of the S&P 500. This group of funds has an average beta of 0.7, meaning that its *U.S. market-related* risk is about 30 percent less than that of the general market, as measured by the S&P 500. The standard deviation for global stock funds is 11 percent, versus 14 percent for growth funds.

Foreign stock funds, which are exclusive of U.S. investments, have a p/e ratio of 26. Their standard deviation over the past three years has been 12 percent. Pacific Basin funds, a more narrowly focused type of foreign fund, have an average p/e ratio of 26 and a standard deviation of 16 percent. European funds, another type of specialized international fund, have a price-earnings ratio of 24 and a standard deviation of 11 percent.

Historical returns over the past three, five, ten, and fifteen years for global stocks are shown below. All of the figures shown are average *annual* rates of return (all periods ending 6/30/97).

category	3 years	5 years	10 years	15 years
global stock funds	15%	14%	10%	16%
foreign stock funds	10%	12%	9%	16%
S&P 500	29%	20%	15%	19%
world bond funds	9%	6%	8%	13%
CPI (rate of inflation)	3%	3%	4%	4%

The four areas that dominate world stock funds are the United States, Europe, Japan, and the Pacific Rim. Stocks from U.S. and European markets account for over two-thirds of a typical global equity fund's portfolio.

Government Bonds. These funds invest in securities issued by the U.S. government or one of its agencies (or former affiliates), such as GNMA, FHLMC, or FNMA. Investors are attracted to bond funds of all kinds for two reasons. First, bond funds have monthly distributions; individual bonds pay interest only semiannually. Second, effective management can control interest rate risk by varying the average maturity of the fund's portfolio. If management believes that interest rates are moving downward, the fund will load up heavily on long-term obligations. If rates do decline, long-term bonds will appreciate more than their short- and medium-term counterparts. Conversely, if the manager anticipates rate hikes, average portfolio maturity can be pared down so that there will be only modest principal deterioration if rates do go up.

Bond funds have portfolios with a wide range of maturities. Many funds use their names to characterize their maturity structure. Generally, "short term" means that the portfolio has a weighted average maturity of less than five years. "Intermediate" implies an average maturity of five to ten years, and "long term" is over ten years. The longer the maturity, the greater the change in the fund's price per share (your principal) when interest rates change. Longer-term bond funds are riskier than short-term funds but tend to offer higher yields. The top holdings of government bond funds are GNMAs and U.S. Treasury notes (T-notes) of varying maturities.

The weighted maturity date of the bonds within this group averages just under eight years, with a typical coupon rate of 7 percent (the coupon rate represents what is paid out annually on a per bond basis)—figures that are virtually identical to the corporate bond category. These funds have a standard deviation of 4 percent—again the figure is almost identical to that for corporate bonds. This means that corporate and government bonds have similar volatilities.

Historical returns over the past three, five, ten, and fifteen years for government bond funds are shown below (all periods ending 6/30/97).

category	3 years	5 years	10 years	15 years
government bond funds	7%	6%	8%	10%
high-yield bond funds	11%	11%	10%	12%
CPI (rate of inflation)	3%	3%	4%	4%
utility funds	15%	12%	10%	14%
convertible bond funds	15%	13%	10%	14%

Like corporate bond funds, government funds provide a high yield that is fully taxable on the federal level and should be sheltered whenever possible. Interest from direct obligations of the U.S. government—T-bonds, T-notes, T-bills, EE bonds, and HH bonds—are exempt from state and local income taxes. This means that a part of the income you receive from funds that include such securities is exempt from *state* taxes.

Corporate bonds are rated as to their safety. The two major rating services are Moody's and Standard and Poor's. By reading the fund's prospectus or by telephoning the mutual fund company, you can find out how safe a corporate bond fund is. The vast majority of these funds are extremely conservative and safety (default) is not really an issue. U.S. government bonds are not rated since it is believed that there is no chance of default—unlike a corporation, the federal government can print money.

Growth. These funds seek capital appreciation with dividend income as a distant secondary concern. Indeed, the average annual income stream from growth funds is just 0.5 percent. Investors who are attracted to growth funds are aiming to sell stock at a profit; they are not normally income oriented. If you are interested in current income you will want to look at Appendix D, "Systematic Withdrawal Plan."

Growth funds are attracted to equities from large, well established corporations. Unlike aggressive growth funds, growth funds may end up holding large cash positions during market declines or when investors are nervous about recent economic or market activities. The top ten holdings of growth funds are: Intel, Cisco Systems, GE, Citicorp, Pfizer, Merck, Philip Morris, Fannie Mae, Microsoft, and Boeing. The typical price-earnings (p/e) ratio for stocks in this category is 27, compared to 26 for the S&P 500. This group of funds has an average beta of 1.0, the same as the S&P 500.

The standard deviation for growth funds is 14 percent. This means that one's expected return for any given year will vary by 14 percentage points. As an example, if you were expecting a 15 percent annual return, annual returns would probably range between 1 percent and 29 percent (15 percent plus or minus 14 percent).

Historical returns over the past three, five, ten, and fifteen years for growth and small-company stock funds are shown below. All of the figures shown are average *annual* rates of return (all periods ending 6/30/97).

category	3 years	5 years	10 years	15 years
growth funds	23%	17%	13%	16%
small-company stock funds	22%	17%	13%	15%
S&P 500	29%	20%	15%	19%
growth & income funds	24%	17%	12%	16%
global stock funds	15%	14%	10%	16%

Technology, industrial cyclicals, financial, and service stocks dominate growth funds. The balance is fairly evenly divided up among health, utility, retail, and consumer staple issues.

Growth and Income. With a name like this, one would think that this category of mutual funds is almost equally as concerned with income as it is with growth. The fact is, growth and income funds have an average dividend yield of just one percent. This boost in income is due to the small holdings in bonds and convertibles possessed by most growth and income funds.

The top ten holdings of growth and income funds are: Philip Morris, Intel, IBM, DuPont, Chrysler, Allstate, Citicorp, General Motors, Exxon, and AT&T. The typical price-earnings (p/e) ratio for stocks in this category is 24, versus 26 for the S&P 500. This group of funds has an average beta of just under 0.9, meaning that its *market-related risk* is 10 percent less than that of the general market, as measured by the S&P 500.

The standard deviation for growth and income funds is 12 percent, about 15 percent less than that found with the average growth fund. This means that, as a group, growth and income funds have slightly more predictable returns than growth funds.

For the purposes of this book, a second category, "equity-income funds," has been combined with growth and income. Equity-income funds have a lower standard deviation (10 percent compared to 12 percent for growth and income funds), a higher yield (2.0 percent compared to 1.0 percent), and a lower beta (0.8 percent compared to 0.9 percent for growth and income funds).

The typical growth and income fund is divided as follows: 90 percent in common stocks (5 percent of which is in foreign stock), 6 percent in cash, 2 percent in bonds, and 2 percent in other assets. The average equity-income fund is divided as follows: 83 percent in common stocks (6 percent of which is in foreign stock), 6 percent in cash, 4 percent in bonds, and 7 percent in other assets. The typical price-earnings (p/e) ratio for stocks in this category is 22.

Historical returns over the past three, five, ten, and fifteen years for growth and income funds are shown below. All of the figures shown are average *annual* rates of return (all periods ending 6/30/97).

category	3 years	5 years	10 years	15 years
growth and income funds	24%	17%	12%	16%
equity-income funds	22%	16%	12%	16%
growth funds	23%	17%	13%	16%
balanced funds	17%	13%	11%	15%
foreign stock funds	10%	12%	9%	16%

Industrial cyclicals and financial stocks dominate growth and income funds, representing over a third of the typical portfolio. Service, health, technology, and consumer stocks represent the other major industry groups for this category.

High-Yield. These funds generally invest in lower-rated corporate debt instruments. Bonds are characterized as either "bank quality," also known as "investment grade," or "junk." Investment-grade bonds are bonds rated AAA, AA, A, or BAA; junk bonds are instruments rated less than BAA: BA, B, CCC, CC, C, and D. High-yield bonds, also referred to as junk bonds, offer investors higher yields in exchange for the additional risk of default. High-yield bonds are subject to less *interest-rate risk* than regular corporate or government bonds. However, when the economy slows or people panic, these bonds can quickly drop in value.

The top ten holdings of high-yield bonds funds are: Trump Atlantic City, Tenet Healthcare, TransTexas Gas, Revlon Worldwide, TeleWest Step, Echostar Comm. Step, PanAmSat Capital Step, Owens-Illinois, Gaylord Container, and SFX Broadcasting. The average weighted maturity date of the bonds within this group is eight years, a figure similar to that for high-quality corporate and government bond funds. The typical coupon rate is 9 percent. (The coupon rate represents what the corporation pays out annually on a per bond basis.) When it comes to high-yield bonds, investors would be wise to accept a lower yield in return for more stability of principal and appreciation potential. As with income funds, corporate funds provide a high yield that is fully taxable and should be sheltered whenever possible.

The standard deviation for high-yield bond funds is 4 percent, a figure very similar to that of corporate and government bond funds as a whole but 4 percent less than balanced and global bond funds. Historical returns over the past three, five, ten, and fifteen years for high-yield corporate bond funds are shown below. All of the figures shown are average *annual* rates of return (all periods ending 6/30/97).

category	3 years	5 years	10 years	15 years
high-yield bond funds	11%	11%	10%	12%
corporate bond funds	7%	7%	8%	11%
government bond funds	7%	6%	8%	10%
world bond funds	9%	6%	8%	13%
balanced funds	17%	13%	11%	15%

Metals and Natural Resources. Metals funds invest in precious metals and mining stocks from around the world. The majority of these stocks are located in North America; South Africa and Australia are the only other major players. Most of these companies specialize in gold mining. Some funds own gold and silver bullion outright. Direct ownership of the metal is considered to be a more conservative posture than owning stocks of mining companies; these stocks are more volatile than the metal itself.

Metals funds, also known as gold funds, are the most speculative group represented in this book. They are considered to be a sector or specialty fund, in that they are only able to invest in a single industry or country. Metals funds enjoy international diversification but are still narrowly focused; the limitations of the fund are what make it so unpredictable. Usually, fund management can invest in only three things: mining stocks, direct metal ownership (bullion or coins), and cash equivalents.

Despite their volatile nature, gold funds are included in the book because they can actually reduce portfolio risk. Why? Because gold and other investments often move in opposite directions. For example, when government bonds are moving down in value, gold funds often increase in value. What could otherwise be viewed as a wild investment becomes somewhat tame when included as part of a diversified portfolio.

The top ten holdings of precious metals funds are: Barrick Gold, Newmont Mining, Getchell Gold, Euro-Nevada Mining, Franco-Nevada Mining, Placer Dome, Freeport-McMoran Cop/Gold A, Santa Fe Pacific Gold, TVX Gold, and Homestake Mining. The typical dividend for these funds is 0.6 percent. The typical price-earnings (p/e) ratio for stocks in this category is 32, about 20 percent more than the p/e ratio for the S&P 500.

This group of funds has an average beta of 0.6, meaning that its stock market-related risk is modest—but do not let this fool you. We are only talking about *stock market risk*. Beta focuses on that portion of risk that investors cannot reduce by further diversification in U.S. stocks. Metals funds, as shown by their wild track record, are anything but conservative. A 0.6 beta indicates that movement in this category has a fair amount to do with the direction of the S&P 500, and therefore risk can be reduced by further diversification. The standard deviation for metals funds is 23 percent, higher than any other mutual fund category in this book.

Another category, natural resources, has been combined with metals funds for this book. As the name implies, natural resources funds are commodity-driven, just as metals funds are heavily influenced by two commodities, gold and silver. In the case of natural resources funds, the prices of oil, gas, and timber are the driving force. Natural resources funds invest in companies that are involved with the discovery, exploration, development, refinement, storage, and transportation of one or more of these three natural resources. The standard deviation for this group is 17 percent, beta is 0.7, and the p/e ratio is 26. The top ten holdings for natural resources funds are: Schlumberger, Royal Dutch Petroleum, Mobil, British Petroleum, Cooper Cameron, Newmont Mining, Halliburton, Transocean Offshore, DuPont, and Weatherford Enterra.

Historical returns over the past three, five, ten, and fifteen years for metals funds are shown below. All of the figures shown are average *annual* rates of return (all periods ending 6/30/97).

category	3 years	5 years	10 years	15 years
metals funds	-5%	4%	-2%	4%
aggressive growth funds	20%	17%	12%	15%
natural resources funds	17%	15%	7%	13%
emerging markets funds	7%	12%	7%	11%
CPI (rate of inflation)	3%	3%	4%	4%

Money Market. These funds invest in short-term money market instruments such as bank CDs, T-bills, and commercial paper. By maintaining a short average maturity and investing in high-quality instruments, money market funds are able to maintain a stable $1 net asset value. Since money market funds offer higher yields than a bank's insured money market deposit accounts, they are a very attractive haven for savings or temporary investment dollars. Like bond funds, money market funds come in both taxable and tax-free versions. Reflecting their tax-free status, municipal money market funds pay lower *before-tax* yields than taxable money market funds but can offer higher returns on an *after-tax* basis.

Since the price per share of taxable money market funds always stays at $1, interest is shown by the accumulation of additional shares. (For example, at the beginning of the year, you may have 1,000 shares and, by the end of the year, 1,050. The 50-share increase, or $50, represents interest.) There are no such things as capital gains or unrecognized gains in a money market fund. The entire return, or yield, is fully taxable (except in the case of a tax-free money market fund, where your gain or return would always be exempt from federal taxes and possibly state income taxes as well).

These funds are designed as a place to park your money for a relatively short period of time, in anticipation of a major purchase such as a car or house, or until conditions appear more favorable for stocks, bonds, and/or real estate. There has only been one, now defunct, money market fund that has ever lost money for its investors (most of whom were bankers).

There are approximately 900 taxable money market funds and 450 tax-exempt money funds. By far the largest money market fund is the Merrill Lynch CMA Money Fund ($41 billion). As of 6/30/97, the ten largest money market funds controlled close to $200 billion and had an average maturity of 64 days. The five highest-yielding taxable money market funds as of the middle of 1997 were: Strong Heritage Money Fund (5.7% over the past 12 months), OLDE Premium Plus MM Series (5.6%), Strategist Money Market Fund (5.6%), E Fund (5.4%), and Kiewit Mutual Fund/MMP (5.4%).

The standard deviation for money market funds is lower than any other category of mutual funds. Historical returns over the past three, five, ten, and fifteen years for taxable and tax-free money market funds are shown below. All of the figures shown are average *annual* rates of return (all periods ending 6/30/97).

category	3 years	5 years	10 years	15 years
money market funds	5%	4%	6%	7%
tax-free money market funds	3%	3%	4%	n/a
municipal bond funds	7%	6%	8%	10%
government bond funds	7%	6%	8%	10%
CPI (rate of inflation)	3%	3%	4%	4%

Municipal Bonds. Also known as tax-free, these funds are made up of tax-free debt instruments issued by states, counties, districts, or political subdivisions. Interest from municipal bonds is normally exempt from federal income tax. In almost all states, interest is also exempt from state and local income taxes if the portfolio is made up of issues from the investor's state of residence, a U.S territory (Puerto Rico, the U.S. Virgin Islands, etc.), or the District of Columbia.

Until the early 1980s, municipal bonds were almost as sensitive to interest rate changes as corporate and government bonds. During the last several years, however, tax-free bonds have taken on a new personality. Now when interest rates change, municipal bonds exhibit only one-half to one-third the price change that occurs with similar funds comprised of corporate or government issues. This decreased volatility is due to a smaller supply of municipal bonds and the elimination of almost all tax shelters, which has increased the popularity of tax-free bonds.

Three kinds of events may result in tax liability for every mutual fund except money market funds. The first two events described below cannot be controlled by the investor. The final event is determined solely by you, the shareholder (investor).

First, when bonds or stocks are sold in the fund portfolio for a profit (or loss), a capital gain (or capital loss) occurs. These gains and losses are passed down to the shareholder. Tax-free bond funds are not immune from capital gains taxes (or capital losses).

Second, interest and/or dividends paid by the securities within the fund are also passed on to shareholders (investors). As already mentioned, interest from municipal bonds is free from federal income taxes and, depending on the fund, may also be exempt from state income taxes. Municipal bond funds do not own stocks or convertibles, so they never throw off dividends.

Third, a taxable event may occur when you sell or exchange shares of a fund for cash or to go into another fund. As an example, suppose you bought into the fund at X dollars and cents per share. If shares are sold (or exchanged) by you for X plus Y, then there will a taxable gain (on Y, in this example). If shares are sold or exchanged for a loss (X minus Y), then there will be a capital loss. Municipal bond funds are subject to such capital gains or losses. Fortunately, you are never required to sell off shares in any mutual fund; the decision as to when and how much is always yours.

The standard deviation for municipal bond funds is 5 percent, meaning that this category's volatility is a little greater than that of high-yield bonds and government securities. Historical returns over the past three, five, ten, and fifteen years for municipal funds are shown below. All of the figures shown are average *annual* rates of return (all periods ending 6/30/97).

category	3 years	5 years	10 years	15 years
municipal bond funds	7%	6%	7%	10%
CA municipal bond funds	7%	6%	8%	9%
NY municipal bond funds	7%	6%	7%	6%
government bond funds	7%	6%	8%	10%
T-bills (90-day maturity)	5%	4%	5%	6%

Utilities. These funds invest in common stocks of utility companies. A small percentage of the funds' assets are invested in bonds. Investors opposed to or in favor of nuclear power can seek out funds that avoid or buy into such utility companies by reviewing a fund's semiannual report or by telephoning the fund, using its toll-free phone number.

If you like the usual stability of a bond fund but want more appreciation potential, then utility funds are for you. Since these funds are interest-rate sensitive, their performance somewhat parallels that of bonds, but is also influenced by the stock market. The large dividend stream provided by utility funds makes them less risky than other categories of stock funds. Recession-resistant demand for electricity, gas, and other utilities translates into a comparatively steady stream of returns.

Since a healthy portion of the total return for utility funds (dividends) cannot be controlled by the investor, these funds are best suited for retirement plans or as part of some other tax-sheltered vehicle. But even if you do not have a qualified retirement plan such as an IRA, pension plan, or TSA, utility funds can be a wise choice to lower overall portfolio volatility.

The standard deviation for utility funds is 9 percent, a figure that is about 30 percent lower than that of growth and income funds. Utility funds have a beta of 0.5.

The top ten holdings for this category are: GTE, CINergy, PanEnergy, FPL Group, SBC Communications, Texas Utilities, Ameritech, Sonat, Williams, and BellSouth.

Historical returns over the past three, five, ten, and fifteen years for utilities funds are shown below. All of the figures shown are average *annual* rates of return (all periods ending 6/30/97).

category	3 years	5 years	10 years	15 years
utility funds	15%	12%	10%	14%
convertible funds	15%	13%	10%	14%
multi-asset global funds	12%	11%	6%	16%
asset allocation funds	16%	12%	10%	13%
growth & income funds	24%	17%	12%	16%

World Bonds. Although the United States leads the world in outstanding debt, other countries and foreign corporations also issue IOUs as a way of financing projects and operations. As high as our debt seems, it is not out of line when compared to our GNP (now called GDP—gross domestic product). The ratio of our debt to GDP is lower than any other member of the group of seven. (The other G-7 members are: Germany, Japan, Canada, Italy, the United Kingdom, and France.)

International, also known as foreign, bond funds invest in fixed-income securities outside of the United States. Global, or world, bond funds invest around the world, including the United States. Foreign bond funds normally offer higher yields than their U.S. counterparts but also provide additional risk. Global bonds, on the other hand, provide less risk than a pure U.S. bond portfolio and also enjoy greater rates of return.

Global diversification reduces risk because the major economies around the world do not move up and down at the same time. As we climb out of a recession, Japan may be just entering one, and Germany may still be in the middle of one. When Italy is trying to stimulate its economy by lowering interest rates, Canada may be raising its rates in order to curtail inflation. By investing in different world bond markets, you ensure that you will not be at the mercy of any one country's political environment or fiscal policy.

The top ten holdings of world (global) bond funds are: Republic of Argentina, Currency (Fut) Germany, U.S. Treasury Notes, Currency (Fwd) Germany, Government of Japan Option (Call), U.S. Treasury Bonds, Republic of Germany, Government of Canada, Republic of Venezuela FRN, and Province of Quebec.

The weighted maturity date of the bonds within this group is seven years, about the same as U.S. government bond funds. Global bond funds have an average coupon rate of 8 percent. As with any investment that throws off a high current income, global and foreign bond funds should be part of a qualified retirement plan or variable annuity whenever possible.

The standard deviation for world bond funds is 8 percent, a low figure but one that is still about 50 percent higher than the typical U.S. government bond fund. Historical returns over the past three, five, ten, and fifteen years for world bond funds are shown below. All of the figures shown are average *annual* rates of return (all periods ending 6/30/97).

category	3 years	5 years	10 years	15 years
world bond funds	9%	6%	8%	13%
government bond funds	7%	6%	8%	10%
corporate bond funds	7%	7%	8%	11%
high-yield bond funds	11%	11%	10%	12%
global stock funds	15%	14%	10%	16%

All Categories. An inescapable conclusion drawn from these different tables is that patience pays off. The only single-digit performers over the past fifteen years have been emerging markets, metals, and money market funds. What the tables do not take into account, moreover, are the tax advantages of certain investments. Government bonds are exempt from state and local income taxes. (Note: this is only true with direct obligations of the United States, it does not apply to GNMAs, FNMAs, or other government-agency issues.) Municipal bonds are exempt from federal income taxes and, depending upon the type of tax-free fund as well as your state of residency, may also be exempt from any state or local taxes.

Money market funds should never be considered an investment. Money market funds, T-bills, and bank CDs should be viewed as places to park your money temporarily. Such accounts are best used to earn interest before you make a major purchase, while you are becoming educated about investing in general, or until market conditions change.

Average Annual Returns for the 15-Year Period Ending 6/30/97

category	15 years	category	15 years
aggressive growth	15%	growth & income	16%
asset allocation	13%	high-yield	12%
balanced	15%	metals (only)	4%
convertible bond	14%	money market	7%
corporate bond	11%	multi-asset global	16%
emerging markets	11%	municipal bond	10%
equity & income	14%	natural resources	10%
European (stock)	n/a	Pacific (stock)	15%
foreign	16%	small company	15%
global equity	16%	utilities	14%
government bond	10%	world bond	13%
growth	16%	average for all categories	13%

A common theme throughout this book is that, given time, equity (the different stock categories) always outperforms debt (the different bond categories). This does not mean that all of your money should be in the equity categories. Not everyone has the same level of patience or time horizon. It does mean that the great majority of investors need to review their portfolios and perhaps begin to emphasize domestic and foreign stocks more.

VI.
Which Funds Are Best for You?

When asked what they are looking for, investors typically say "I want the best." This could mean that they are looking for the most safety and greatest current income or the highest total return. There is no single "best" fund. The top-performing fund may have incredible volatility, causing shareholders to redeem their shares at the first sign of trouble. The "safest" fund may be devastated by risks not previously thought of: inflation and taxes.

As you have already seen, there are several different categories of mutual funds, ranging from tax-free money market accounts to precious metals. During one period or another, each of these categories has dominated some periodical's "ten best funds" list. These impressive scores may only last a quarter, six months, or a year. The fact is that no one knows what will be the *next* best-performing category or individual fund.

For some fund groups, such as international stocks, growth, growth and income, and aggressive growth, the reign at the top may last for several years. For other categories, such as money market, government bond, and precious metals, the glory may last a year or even less. Trying to outguess, chart, or follow a financial guru in order to determine the next trend is a fool's paradise. The notion that anyone has special insights into the marketplace is sheer nonsense. Countless neutral and lengthy studies attest to this fact. If this is the case, what should we do?

Step 1: Categories That Have Historically Done Well
First we should look at those generic categories of investments that have historically done well over long periods of time. A time frame of at least fifteen or twenty years is recommended. True, your investment horizon may be a fraction of this, but keep in mind two points. First, fifteen or twenty years includes good as well as bad times. Second, bad results cannot be hidden when you are studying the long term. Even the investor looking at a one- or two-year holding period should ask, "Do I want something that does phenomenally well one out of every five years, or do I want something that has a very good return in eight or nine out of every ten years?" Unless you are a gambler, the answer is obvious.

All investments can be categorized as either debt or equity instruments. Debt instruments in this book include corporate bonds, government bonds, high-yield bonds, international bonds, money market accounts, and municipal bonds. Equity instruments include growth, growth and income, international stocks, metals, and utility funds. Four other categories are hybrid instruments: asset allocation, balanced, convertible, and multi-asset global funds. In this book, these four categories are combined under the heading "balanced."

Throughout history, *equity has outperformed debt*. The longer the time frame reviewed, the better equity vehicles look. Over the past half century, the worst fifteen-year holding period performance for stocks (+4.3% a year) was very similar to the average fifteen-year holding period performance for long-term government bonds (+4.9% a year). For twenty-year holding periods, the worst period for common stocks has been more than 40 percent better than the average for long-term government bonds. Indeed, stocks have outperformed bonds in every decade. Look at it this way: would you rather have loaned Henry Ford or Bill Gates the money to start their companies, or would you rather have given them money in return for a piece of the action?

Step 2: Review Your Objectives

Decide what you are trying to do with your portfolio. Everyone wants one of the following: growth, current income, or a combination of growth and income. Don't assume that if you are looking for current income your money should go into a bond or money market fund. There is a way to set up an equity fund so that it will give you a high monthly income. This is known as a "systematic withdrawal program" and is discussed in Appendix D. The growth-oriented investor, on the other hand, should consider certain categories of debt instruments or hybrid securities to help add more stability to a portfolio.

Objectives are certainly important, but so is the element of time. The shorter the time frame and the greater the need for assurances, the greater the likelihood that debt instruments should be used. A growth investor who is looking at a single-year time frame and wants a degree of safety is probably better off in a series of bond and/or money market accounts. On the other hand, the longer the commitment, the better equities look. Thus, even a cautious investor who has a life expectancy (or whose spouse has a life expectancy) of ten years or more should seriously consider having at least a moderate portion of his or her portfolio in equities.

A retired couple in their sixties should realize that one or both of them will probably live at least fifteen more years. Since this is the case, and since we know that equities have almost always outperformed bonds when looking at a horizon of ten years or more, their emphasis should be in this area.

The conservative investor may say that stocks are too risky. True, the day-to-day or year-to-year volatility of equities can be quite disturbing. However, it is also true that the medium- and long-term effects of inflation and the resulting diminished purchasing power of a fixed-income investment are even more devastating. At least with an equity there is a better than 50–50 chance that it will go up in value. In the case of inflation, what do you think are the chances that the cost of goods and services will go *down* during the next one, three, five, or ten years? The answer is "not likely."

Step 3: Ascertain Your Risk Level

No investment is worthwhile if you stay awake at night worrying about it. If you do not already know or are uncertain about your risk level, contact your financial advisor. These professionals usually have some kind of questionnaire that you can answer. Your responses will give a good indication of which investments are proper for you and which should be avoided. If you do not deal with a financial advisor, try the test below. Your score, and what it means, are shown at the end of the questionnaire.

Test for Determining Your Risk Level

1. "I invest for the long term, five to ten years or more. The final result is more important than daily, monthly, or annual fluctuations in value."

(10) Totally disagree. (20) Willing to accept some volatility, but not loss of principal. (30) Could accept a moderate amount of yearly fluctuation in return for a good *total* return. (40) Would accept an *occasional* negative year if the final results were good. (50) Agree.

2. Rank the importance of current income.

(10) Crucial, the exact amount must be known. (20) Important, but I am willing to have the amount vary each period. (30) Fairly important, but other aspects of investing are also of concern. (40) Only a modest amount of income is needed. (50) Current income is unimportant.

3. Rank the amount of loss you could tolerate in a single *quarter*.

(10) None. (20) A little, but over a year's time the total value of the investment should not decline. (30) Consistency of total return is more important than trying to get big gains. (40) One or two quarters of negative returns are the price you must pay when looking at the total picture. (50) Unimportant.

4. Rank the importance of beating inflation.

(10) Factors such as preservation of principal and current income are much more important. (20) I am willing to have a slight variance in my returns, *on a quarterly basis only*, in order to have at least a partial hedge against inflation. (30) Could accept some annual volatility in order to offset inflation. (40) I consider inflation to be important, but have mixed feelings about how much volatility I could accept from one year to the next. (50) The long-term effects of inflation are devastating and should not be ignored by anyone.

5. Rank the importance of beating the stock market over any given two-to-three-year period.

(10) Irrelevant. (20) A small concern. (30) Fairly important. (40) Very important. (50) Absolutely crucial.

Add up your score from questions 1 through 5. Your risk, as defined by your total point score, is as follows: 0–50 points = extremely conservative; 50–100 points = somewhat conservative; 100–150 points = moderate; 150–200 points = somewhat aggressive; 200–250 points = very aggressive.

Step 4: Review Your Current Holdings

Everyone has heard the expression, "Don't put all your eggs in one basket." This advice also applies to investing. No matter how much we like investment X, if a third of our net worth is already in X, we probably should not add any more to this investment. After all, there is more than one good investment.

Since no single investment category is the top performer every year, it makes sense to diversify into several *fundamentally* good categories. By using *proper* diversification, we have an excellent chance of being number one with a portion of our portfolio every year. Babe Ruth may have hit more home runs than almost anyone, but he also struck out more. As investors, we should be content with consistently hitting doubles and triples.

Trying to hit a homer every time may result in financial ruin. Never lose track of the fact that losses always have a greater impact than gains. An investment that goes up 50 percent the first year and falls 50 percent the next year still has a net loss of 25 percent. This philosophy is emphasized throughout the book.

Step 5: Implementation

There is no such thing as the perfect time to invest. No matter how strongly you or some "expert" individual or publication believes that the market is going to go up or down, no one actually knows.

Once you have properly educated yourself, *now* is the right time to invest. If you are afraid to make the big plunge, consider some form of dollar-cost averaging (see Appendix C). This is a disciplined approach to investing; it also reduces your risk exposure significantly.

Reading investment books and attending classes are encouraged, but some people may be tempted to remain on the sidelines indefinitely. For such people, there is no perfect time to invest. If the stock market drops two hundred points, they are waiting for the next hundred-point drop. If stocks or bonds are up 15 percent, they say things are peaking and they will invest as soon as it drops by 10 percent. If the stock or bond market does drop by that magical figure, these same investors are now certain that it will drop another 10 percent.

The "strategy" described above is frustrating. More important, it is wrong. One can look back in history and find lots of reasons not to have invested. But the fact is that all of the investments in this book have gone up almost every year. The "wait and see" approach is a poor one; the same reasons for not investing will still exist in the present and throughout the future.

Remember, your money is doing something right now. It is invested somewhere. If it is under the mattress, it is being eaten away by inflation. If it is in a "risk-free" investment, such as an insured savings account, bank CD, or U.S. Treasury bill, it is being subjected to taxation and the cumulative effects of reduced purchasing power. Do not think you can hide by having your money in some safe haven. Once you understand that there can be things worse than market swings, you will become an educated investor who knows there is no such thing as a truly risk-free place or investment.

If you are still not convinced, consider the story of Louie the loser. There is only one thing you can say about Louie's timing: It is *always* awful. So it is no surprise that when he decided to invest $5,000 a year in New Perspective, a fund featured in this book, he managed to pick the *worst* possible times. *Every year* for the past twenty years (1977–1996), he has invested on the very day that the stock market *peaked*. How has he done? He has over $523,000, which means his money has grown at an average rate of 14.7 percent a year (a cumulative investment of $100,000; twenty years times $5,000 invested each year).

If, perchance, Louie had managed to pick the best day each year for the last twenty years (ending 12/31/96) to make his investments, the day the market bottomed each year, his account would have been worth $636,000 (16.1 percent a year) by the beginning of 1997. Yet even by picking the *worst* possible days, Louie still came out way ahead of the $218,000 he would have had if he had put his money in U.S. Treasury bills each year. Even though his timing was terrible, he still fared much better than if he had done what many people are doing today: waiting for the "perfect" time to invest.

After asking you a series of questions, your investment advisor can give you a framework within which to operate. Investors who do not have a good advisor may wish to look at the different sample portfolios below. These general recommendations will provide you with a sense of direction.

The Conservative Investor
- 15 percent balanced
- 10 percent utilities
- 10 percent growth & income
- 10 percent world bond
- 15 percent international equities
- 10 percent money market or short-term bonds
- 30 percent intermediate-term municipal or government bonds
  (depending upon your tax bracket)

This portfolio would give you a weighting of 43 percent in equities (stocks) and 57 percent in debt instruments (bonds and cash equivalents). Investors who are not in a high federal income tax bracket may wish to avoid municipal bonds completely and use government bonds instead.

If your tax bracket is such that you are not sure whether you should own tax-free or taxable bonds (if, that is, the after-tax return on government bonds is similar to what a similarly maturing, high-quality municipal bond pays), lean toward a municipal bond fund—they are almost always less volatile than a government bond fund that has the same or a similar average maturity.

The Moderate Investor
    10 percent small-company growth
     5 percent balanced/convertibles
    15 percent growth
    15 percent growth & income
    15 percent high yield
    10 percent world bond
    25 percent global equities
     5 percent natural resources

This portfolio would give you a weighting of 75 percent in equities (common stocks) and 25 percent in debt instruments. The figures are a little misleading since high-yield bonds are more of a hybrid investment—part stock and part bond. The price, or value, of high-yield bonds is influenced by economic (macro and micro) news as well as interest rate changes. Whereas government, municipal, and high-quality corporate bonds often react favorably to bad economic news such as a recession, increases in the jobless rate, a slowdown in housing starts, and so on, high-yield bonds have a tendency to view such news positively. Thus, taking into account that high-yield bonds are about halfway between traditional bonds and stocks, the weighting distribution is more in the range of 82.5 percent equities and 17.5 percent bonds.

The Aggressive Investor
    20 percent aggressive growth
    10 percent small-company growth
    10 percent growth
     5 percent growth & income
    30 percent international equities
    15 percent emerging markets
    10 percent natural resources

This portfolio would give you a weighting of 100 percent in equities. Bond fund categories, with the possible exception of high-yield and international, are not recommended for the aggressive investor because they usually do not have enough appreciation potential.

Readers of the previous editions of this book may notice that this edition weighs equities (the different stock categories) more heavily than it has in the past. This is because bonds cannot experience the appreciation or total return for the balance of the 1990s that they saw in the 1980s and very early 1990s. For the most part, bonds increase in value because of falling interest rates. In 1981, the prime interest rate briefly peaked at 21.5 percent; for more than a dozen years this benchmark figure dropped. During the balance of the 1990s, it would be literally impossible for prime to drop 13 points (it cannot drop below zero).

Stocks, on the other hand, could end up doing worse than bonds, the same, or better. At least conceptually, however, equities have the possibility of exceeding their performance over the past ten years. The 1980s and early 1990s (whatever ten-year period you wish to use during this time horizon) were not the best ten years in a row for stocks. It is certainly possible that the next ten years, or the ten years beginning in 1998 or 1999, will be the best. When you look at the state of the world, the conditions certainly seem more favorable now for tremendous economic and stock market growth for the next several decades.

Step 6: Review

After implementation, it is important that you keep track of how you are doing. One of the beauties of mutual funds is that, if you choose a fund with good management, managers will do their job and you can spend your time on something else. Nevertheless, review your situation at least quarterly. Once you feel comfortable with your portfolio, only semiannual or annual reviews are recommended.

Daily or weekly tracking is pointless. If a particular investment goes up or down 5 percent, that does not mean you should rush out and buy more or sell off. That same investment may do just the opposite the following week or month. By watching your investments too closely, you will be defeating a major attribute of mutual funds: professional management. Presumably these fund managers know a lot more about their particular investments than you do. If they do not, you should either choose another fund or start your own mutual fund.

Step 7: Relax

If you do your homework by reading this book, you will be in fine shape. There are several thousand mutual funds. Some funds are just plain bad. Most mutual funds are mediocre. And, as with everything else in this world, a small portion are truly excellent. This book has taken those thousands of funds and eliminated all of the bad, mediocre, and fairly good. What are left are only excellent mutual funds.

If you would like help in designing a portfolio or picking a specific fund, telephone the Institute of Business & Finance (800/848-2029). The institute will be able to give you names and telephone numbers of Certified Fund Specialists (CFS) in your area. To become a CFS, one must complete a rigorous, one-year educational program, pass a comprehensive exam, adhere to a professional code of ethics, and meet annual continuing education requirements.

VII.
Fund Features

Advantages of Mutual Funds

Listed below are some of the features of mutual funds—advantages not found in other kinds of investments.

Ease of Purchase. Mutual fund shares are easy to buy. For those who prefer to make investment decisions themselves, mutual funds are as close as the telephone or the mailbox. Those who would like help in choosing a fund can draw upon a wide variety of sources.

Many funds sell their shares through stockbrokers, financial planners, or insurance agents. These representatives can help you analyze your financial needs and objectives and recommend appropriate funds. For these professional services, you may be charged a sales commission, usually referred to as a "load." This charge is expressed as a percentage of the total purchase price of the fund shares. In some cases, there is no initial sales charge, or load, but there may be an annual fee and/or another charge if shares are redeemed during the first few years of ownership.

Other funds distribute their shares directly to the public. They may advertise in magazines and newspapers; most can be reached through toll-free telephone numbers. Because there are no sales agents involved, most of these funds, often called "no loads," charge a much lower fee or no sales commission at all. With these funds it is generally up to you to do your investment homework.

In order to attract new shareholders, some funds have adopted 12b-1 plans (named after a federal government rule). These plans enable the fund to pay its own distribution costs. Distribution costs are those costs associated with marketing the fund, either through sales agents or through advertising. The 12b-1 fee is charged against fund assets and is paid indirectly by existing shareholders. Annual distribution fees of this type usually range between 0.1 percent and 1.25 percent of the value of the account.

Fees charged by a fund are described in the prospectus. In addition, a fee table listing all transactional fees and all annual fund expenses can be found at the front of the prospectus.

Access to Your Money (Marketability). Mutual funds, by law, must stand ready on any business day to redeem any or all of your shares at their current net asset value (NAV). Of course, the value may be greater or less than the price you originally paid, depending on the market.

To sell shares back to the fund, all you need to do is give the fund proper notification, as explained in the prospectus. Most funds will accept such notification by telephone; some funds require a written request. The fund will then send your check promptly. In most instances the fund will issue a check when it receives the notification; by law it must send you the check within seven business days. You receive the price your shares are worth *on the day* the fund gets proper notice of redemption from you. If you own a money market fund, you can also redeem shares by writing checks directly against your fund balance.

Disciplined Investment. The majority of funds allow you to set up what is known as a "check-o-matic plan." Under such a program a set amount of money is automatically deducted from your checking account each month and sent directly to the mutual fund of your choice. Your bank (or credit union) will not charge you for this service. Mutual funds also offer such programs free of charge. Automatic investment plans can be changed or terminated at any time, again at no charge.

Exchange Privileges. As the economy or your own personal circumstances change, the kinds of funds you hold may no longer be the ones you need. Many mutual funds are part of a "family of funds" and offer a feature called an exchange privilege. Within a family of funds there may be several choices, each with a different investment objective, varying from highly conservative funds to more aggressive funds that carry a higher degree of risk. An exchange privilege allows you to transfer all or part of your money from one of these funds to another. Exchange policies vary from fund to fund. The fee for an exchange is nominal, five dollars or less. For the specifics about a fund's exchange privilege, check the prospectus.

Automatic Reinvestment. You can elect to have any dividends and capital gains distributions from your mutual fund investment turned back into the fund, automatically buying new shares and expanding your current holdings. Most shareholders opt for the reinvestment privilege. There is usually no cost or fee involved.

Automatic Withdrawal. You can make arrangements with the fund to automatically send you, or anyone you designate, checks from the fund's earnings or principal. This system works well for retirees, families who want to arrange for payments to their children at college, or anyone needing monthly income checks. See Appendix D for a more detailed example as to how a systematic withdrawal plan (SWP) works.

Detailed Record Keeping. The fund will handle all the paperwork and record keeping necessary to keep track of your investment transactions. A typical statement will note such items as your most recent investment or withdrawal and any dividends or capital gains paid to you in cash or reinvested in the fund. The fund will also report to you on the tax status of your earnings. If you lose any paperwork, the fund will send you copies of current or past statements.

Retirement Plans. Financial experts have long viewed mutual funds as appropriate vehicles for retirement investing; indeed, they are quite commonly used for this purpose. For retirees over the age of seventy and a half, mutual fund companies will recompute the minimum amount that needs to be taken out each year, as dictated by the IRS. Mutual funds are ideal for Keoghs, IRAs, 401(k) plans, and other employer-sponsored retirement plans. Many funds offer prototype retirement plans and standard IRA agreements. Having your own retirement plan drafted by a law firm would cost you thousands of dollars, not to mention what you would be charged for the updates that would be needed every time the laws change. Mutual funds offer these plans and required updates for free.

Accountability. There are literally dozens of sources that track and monitor mutual funds. It is easy for you to determine a fund's track record and volatility over several different time periods. Federal regulatory bodies such as the NASD (National Association of Securities Dealers) and SEC (Securities and Exchange Commission) have strict rules concerning performance figures and what appears in advertisements, brochures, and prospectuses.

Flexibility. Investment choices are almost endless: domestic stocks, foreign debt, international equities, government obligations, money market instruments, convertible securities, short- and intermediate-term bonds, real estate, gold, and natural resources. Your only limitation is the choices offered by the fund family or families you are invested in. And because you can move part or all of your money from one mutual fund to another fund within the same family, usually for only a minimal transfer fee, your portfolio can become more aggressive, conservative, or moderate with a simple phone call.

Economies of Scale. As a shareholder (investor) in a fund, you automatically get the benefit of reduced transaction charges. Since a fund is often buying or selling thousands of shares of stock at a time, it is able to conduct its transactions at dramatically reduced costs. The fees a fund pays are far lower than what you would pay even if you were buying several hundred shares of a stock from a discount broker. The same thing is true when it comes to bonds. Funds are able to add them to their portfolio without any markup. When you buy a bond through a broker, even a discounter, there is always a markup; it is hidden in the price you pay and sell the bond for. The savings for bond investors ranges anywhere from less than 1 percent all the way up to 5 percent.

Risk Reduction: Importance of Diversification

If there is one ingredient to successful investing that is universally agreed upon, it is the benefit of diversification. This concept is also backed by a great deal of research and market experience. The benefit provided by diversification is risk reduction. Risk to investors is frequently defined as volatility of return—in other words, how much an investment's return might vary. Investors prefer returns that are relatively predictable, which is to say, less volatile. On the other hand, they want returns to be high. Diversification eliminates most of the risk without reducing potential returns.

A fund's portfolio manager(s) will normally invest the fund's pool of money in 50 to 150 different securities to spread the fund's holdings over a number of investments. This diversification is an important principle in lessening the fund's overall investment risk. Such diversification is typically beyond the financial capacity of most individual investors. The table below shows the relationship between diversification and investment risk, defined as the variability of annual returns of a stock portfolio.

number of stocks	risk ratio
1	6.6
2	3.8
4	2.4
10	1.6
50	1.1
100	1.0

Note that the variability of return, or risk, associated with holding just one stock is more than six times that of a hundred-stock portfolio. Yet the *increased* potential return found in a portfolio made up of a small number of stocks is minimal.

VIII.
Reading a Mutual Fund Prospectus

The purpose of the fund's prospectus is to provide the reader with full and complete disclosure. The prospectus covers the following key points:

- The fund's investment objective: what the managers are trying to achieve.
- The investment methods it uses in trying to achieve this objective.
- The name and address of its investment advisor and a brief description of the advisor's experience.
- The level of investment risk the fund is willing to assume in pursuit of its investment objective.
- Any investments the fund will *not* make (for example, real estate, options, or commodities).
- Tax consequences of the investment for the shareholder.
- How to purchase shares of the fund, including the cost of investing.
- How to redeem shares.
- Services provided, such as IRAs, automatic investment of dividends and capital gains distributions, check writing, withdrawal plans, and any other features.
- A condensed financial statement (in tabular form, covering the last ten years, or the period the fund has been in existence, if less than ten years) called "Per Share Income and Capital Changes." The fund's performance may be calculated from the information given in this table.
- A tabular statement of any fees charged by the fund and their effect on earnings over time.

IX.
Commonly Asked Questions

Q. Are mutual funds a new kind of investment?
No. In fact, they have roots in eighteenth-century Scotland. The first U.S. mutual fund was organized in Boston in 1924. This fund, Massachusetts Investors Trust, is still in existence today. Several mutual fund companies have been in operation for over half a century.

Q. How much money do you need to invest in a mutual fund?
Literally anywhere from a few dollars to several million. Many funds have no minimum requirements for investing. A few funds are open to large institutional accounts only. The vast majority of funds require a minimum investment of between $250 and $1,000.

Q. Do mutual funds offer a fixed rate of return?
No. Mutual funds invest in securities such as stocks, bonds, and money market accounts whose yields and values fluctuate with market conditions.

Mutual funds can make money for their shareholders in three ways. First, they pay their shareholders dividends earned from the fund's investments. Second, if a security held by a fund is sold at a profit, funds pay their shareholders capital gains distributions. And third, if the value of the securities held by the fund increases, the value of each mutual fund share also increases.

In none of these cases, however, can a return be guaranteed. In fact, it is against the law for a mutual fund to make a claim as to its future performance. Ads quoting returns are based on past performance and should not be interpreted as a fixed rate yield. Past performance should not be taken as a predictor of future earnings.

Q. What are the risks of mutual fund investing?
Mutual funds are investments in financial securities with fluctuating values. The value of the securities in a fund's portfolio, for example, will rise and fall according to general economic conditions and the fortunes of the particular companies that issue those securities. Even the most conservative assets, such as U.S. government obligations, will fluctuate in value as interest rates change. These are risks that investors should be aware of when purchasing mutual fund shares.

Q. How can I evaluate a fund's long-term performance?
You can calculate a fund's performance by referring to the section in the prospectus headed "Per Share Income and Capital Changes." This section will give

you the figures needed to compute the annual rates of return earned by the fund each year for the past ten years (or for the life of the fund if less than ten years). There are also several periodicals that track the performance of funds on a regular basis. You can also telephone the fund, and they will give you performance figures.

Q. What's the difference between *yield* and *total return*?

Yield is the income per share paid to a shareholder, from the dividends and interest, over a specified period of time. Yield is expressed as a percent of the current offering price per share.

Total return is a measure of the per-share change in total value from the beginning to the end of a specified period, usually a year, including distributions paid to shareholders. This measure includes income received from dividends and interest, capital gains distributions, and any unrealized capital gains or losses. Total return looks at the whole picture: appreciation (or loss) of principal plus any dividends or income. Total return provides the best measure of overall fund performance; *do not be misled by an enticing yield.*

Q. How much does it cost to invest in a mutual fund?

A mutual fund normally contracts with its management company to provide for most of the needs of a normal business. The management company is paid a fee for these services, which usually include managing the fund's investments.

In addition, the fund may pay directly for some of its costs, such as printing, mailing, accounting, and legal services. Typically, these two annual charges average 1.5 percent. In such a fund you would be paying $10 to $15 a year on every $1,000 invested.

Some fund directors have adopted plans (with the approval of the fund's shareholders) that allow them to pay certain distribution costs (the costs of advertising, for example) directly from fund assets. These costs may range from 0.1 percent to 1.25 percent annually.

There may also be other charges involved—for example, in exchanging shares. Some funds may charge a redemption fee when a shareholder redeems his or her shares, usually within five years of purchasing them. All costs and charges assessed by the fund organization are disclosed in its prospectus.

Q. Is the management fee part of the sales charge?

No, the management fee paid by the fund to its investment advisor is for services rendered in managing the fund's portfolio. An average fee ranges from 0.5 percent to 1 percent of the fund's total assets each year. As described above, the management fee and other business expenses generally total somewhere between 1 percent and 1.5 percent. These expenses are paid from the fund's assets and are reflected in the price of the fund shares. In contrast, most sales charges are deducted from your initial investment.

Q. Is my money locked up for a certain period of time in a mutual fund?

Unlike some other types of financial accounts, mutual funds are liquid investments. That means that any shares an investor owns may be redeemed freely on any day the fund is open for business. Since a mutual fund stands ready to buy back its shares at their current net asset value, you always have a buyer for your shares at current market value.

Q. How often do I get statements from a mutual fund?
Mutual funds ordinarily send immediate confirmation statements when an investor purchases or redeems (sells) shares. Statements alerting shareholders to reinvested dividends are sent out periodically. At least semiannually, investors also receive statements on the status of the fund's investments. Tax statements, referred to as "substitute 1099s," are mailed annually. Some funds automatically send out quarterly reports.

Q. I've already purchased shares of a mutual fund. How can I tell how well my investment is doing?
Figuring out how well your fund is faring is a two-step procedure. First you need to know how many shares you *now* own. The "now" is emphasized because if you have asked the fund to plow any dividends and capital gains distributions back into the fund for you, it will do so by issuing you more shares, thereby increasing the value of your investment. Once you know how many shares you own, look up the fund's net assets value (sometimes called the sell or bid price) in the financial section of a major metropolitan daily newspaper. Next, multiply the net asset value by the number of shares you own to figure out the value of your investment as of that date. Compare today's value against your beginning value.

You will need to keep the confirmation statements you receive when you first purchase shares and as you make subsequent purchases in order to compare present value to the original purchase value. You will also need these statements for tax purposes.

Q. Do investment experts recommend mutual funds for IRAs and other qualified plans?
Financial experts view many mutual funds as compatible with the long-term objectives of saving for retirement. Indeed, fund shareholders cite this reason for investing more than any other. Many kinds of funds work best when allowed to ride out the ups and downs of market cycles over long periods of time.

Funds can also offer the owner of an IRA, Keogh, pension plan, 401(k), or 403(b) flexibility. By using the exchange privilege within a family of funds, the investor can shift investments from one kind of security to another in response to changes in personal finances or the economic outlook, or as retirement approaches.

Q. Are money market funds a good investment?
No. If I were to recommend an investment to you that lost money in seventeen of the last twenty-five calendar years (adjusted for income taxes and inflation), you would probably balk. Yet, this is the track record of CDs, money market accounts, and T-bills. Money market funds are an excellent place to park your money for the short-term—some period less than two years.

Q. Why don't more people invest in foreign (international) securities?
Ignorance. The reality is that foreign securities (stocks and bonds), when added to domestic investments, actually reduce the portfolio's level of risk. Stock and bond markets around the world rarely move up and down at the same time. This random correlation is what helps lower risk and volatility: When U.S. stocks (or bonds) are going down, securities in other parts of the world may well be moving sideways or going up.

Q. Is standard deviation the correct way to measure risk?
No. Standard deviation measures volatility (or predictability) of returns. The standard deviation for each of the mutual funds in this book is ranked under the star system next to the heading "predictability of returns." The system used in this book for measuring risk is different, punishing funds for performance that is less than that offered by T-bills, a figure commonly referred to as the "risk-free rate of return." To me this makes more sense than a system that punishes a fund for volatility by translating its high standard deviation figure as "high risk." This is what most financial writers do, whether the volatility the fund experienced was upward or downward volatility. I have yet to meet an investor who is upset that he or she did better than expected. No one minds *upward* volatility.

Q. Why not simply invest in those funds that were the best performers over the past one, three, five, or ten years?
This would be a big mistake. There is little relationship (or correlation) between the performance of one fund or fund category from one year to the next. This, by the way, is the way most investors and advisors select investments—making this one of the biggest and costliest mistakes one could make. Unfortunately, no one knows what the next best performing fund or category will be.

Q. What are you referring to when you talk about "common stocks"?
Whenever you see the words "common stocks" it refers to the Standard & Poor's 500 (S&P 500). The S&P 500 is comprised of 500 of many of the largest corporations in the United States, representing several industry groups. As of the middle of 1997, there had been 71 changes made to the S&P 500 since the beginning of 1995. The purpose of changes is to make the index more representative of the U.S. economy and the stock market. As an example, financial stocks now represent 15% of the S&P 500 capitalization, up from 8% in 1990; technology stocks represent 14%, up from 7% in 1990 (Microsoft, which was added to the index in 1994, makes up 2.3% of the index). In short, the S&P 500 is higher growth, more global, less cyclical, and more diversified than it has ever been (and therefore deserves a higher p/e ratio than in the past).

X.
How the 100 Best Funds Were Determined

With an entry field that numbers over 8,000, it is no easy task to determine the 100 best mutual funds. Magazines and newspapers report on the "best" by relying on performance figures over a specific period, usually one, three, five, or ten years. Investors often rely on these sources and invest accordingly, only to be disappointed later.

Studies from around the world bear out what investors typically experience: that there is no correlation between the performance of a stock or bond from one year to the next. The same can be said for individual money managers—and sadly, for most mutual funds.

The criteria used to determine the 100 best mutual funds are unique and far-reaching. In order for a fund to be considered for this book, it must pass several tests. First, all stock and bond funds that have had managers for less than five years were excluded; in the case of money market funds, the only remaining category, the criterion was liberalized.

This first step alone eliminated well over half the contenders. The reasoning for the cutoff is simple: a fund is often only as good as its manager. An outstanding ten-year track record may be cited in a periodical, but how relevant is this performance if the manager who oversaw the fund left a year or two ago? This criterion was liberalized in selecting money market funds because this category of funds normally requires less expertise.

Second, any fund that places in the bottom (worst) half of its *category's* risk ranking is excluded. No matter how profitable the finish line looks, the number of investors will be sparse if the fund demonstrates too much negative activity. In most cases, a little performance was gladly given up if a great deal of risk was eliminated. This reflects the book's philosophy that returns must be viewed in relation to the amount of risk that was taken. In most cases the funds described in the book possess outstanding risk management. Those few selected funds where risk control has been less than stellar have shown tremendous performance, and their risky nature has been highlighted to warn the reader.

Virtually all sources measure risk by something known as *standard deviation*. Determining an investment's standard deviation is not as difficult as you might imagine. First you calculate the asset's average annual return. Usually, the most recent three years are used, updated each quarter. Once an average annual rate of return is determined, a line is drawn on a graph, representing this return.

Next, the monthly returns are plotted on the graph. Since three years is a commonly accepted time period for such calculations, a total of thirty-six individual points are plotted—one for each month over the past three years. After all of these points are plotted, the standard deviation can be determined. Quite simply, standard deviation measures the variance of returns from the norm (the line drawn on a graph).

There is a problem in using standard deviation to determine the risk level of any investment, including a mutual fund. The shortcoming of this method is that standard deviation punishes *good* as well as bad results. An example will help expose the problem.

Suppose there were two different investments, X and Y. Investment X went up almost every month by exactly 1.5 percent but had a few months each year when it went down 1 percent. Investment Y went up only 1 percent most months, but it always went up 6 percent for each of the final months of the year. The standard deviation of Y would be substantially higher than X. It might be so high that we would avoid it because it was classified as "high risk." The fact is that we would love to own such an investment. No one ever minds *upward* volatility or surprises; it is only negative or downward volatility that is cause for alarm.

The system used for determining risk in this book is not widely used, but is certainly a fairer and more meaningful measurement. The book's method for determining risk is to see how many months over the past three years a fund underperformed what is popularly referred to as a "risk-free vehicle," something like a bank CD or U.S. Treasury bill. The more months a fund falls below this safe return, the greater the fund will be punished in its risk ranking.

Third, the fund must have performed well for the last three and five years. A one- or two-year time horizon could be attributed to luck or nonrecurring events. A ten- or fifteen-year period would certainly be better, if not for the reality that the overwhelming majority of funds are managed by a different person today than they were even six years ago.

Finally, the fund must either possess an excellent risk-adjusted return or have had superior returns with no more than average levels of risk. It is assumed that most readers are equally concerned with risk and reward. Thus, the foundation of the text is based on which mutual funds have the best *risk-adjusted returns*.

Sadly, some funds were excluded, despite their superior performance and risk control, because they were either less than five years old, had new management, or were closed to new investors.

XI.
The 100 Best Funds

This section describes the 100 very best funds. As discussed, the methodology used to narrow down the universe of funds is based on performance, risk, and management.

Every one of these 100 funds is a superlative choice. However, there must still be a means to compare and rank each of the funds within its peer group. Each one of the 100 funds is first categorized by its investment objective. The category breakdown is as follows:

category of mutual fund	number
aggressive growth	10
balanced	9
corporate bond	5
global equity	14
government bond	6
growth	13
growth & income	13
high-yield bonds	5
metals/natural resources	4
money market	6
municipal bonds	8
utilities	4
world bonds	3
total	**100 funds**

There are five areas to be ranked: (1) total return, (2) risk/volatility, (3) management, (4) tax minimization (current income in the case of bond, hybrid, and money market funds), and (5) expense control. Of these five classifications, management, risk/volatility, and total return are the most important.

The track record of a fund is only as good as its management, which is why extensive space is given to this section for each fund. The areas of concern are the length of time the manager, or team, has overseen the fund, and the management's background and investment philosophy.

The risk/volatility of the fund is the second biggest concern. Investors like to be in things that have somewhat predictable results—that aren't up 60 percent one year and down 25 percent the next. A few such highly volatile funds are included, but the risk associated with such a fund is clearly highlighted, informing the prospective investor.

Total return was the third concern. When all is said and done, people like to make lots of money with an acceptable level of risk, or at least get decent returns by taking little, if any, risk. This is also known as the *risk-adjusted return*. So, although the very safest funds within each category were preferred, this safety had to be combined with impressive returns.

The fourth category, current income, was of lesser importance. Income is important to a lot of people but often gets in the way of selecting the proper invest-ment; preservation of capital should also be considered. There is a better way to get current income than to rely on monthly dividend or interest checks. This is known as a systematic withdrawal plan (SWP). A sixty-three-year example of a SWP is shown in Appendix D. Current-income-oriented investors will truly be amazed when they see how such a system works.

In the case of equity funds, "tax minimization" was substituted for the cate-gory "current income." This was done for two reasons. First, there is no reason why a fund whose objective is capital appreciation should be punished simply because it does not throw off a high dividend. Once you are familiar with the benefits of using a systematic withdrawal plan, you will no longer care whether or not a cer-tain aggressive growth or even growth and income fund pays much in the form of dividends. Second, unless your money is sheltered in a qualified retirement plan (IRA, pension plan, etc.), income taxes are a real concern. Funds should be rewarded for minimizing shareholder tax liability. This is why every mutual fund in the book is rated, one way or another, when it comes to personal income taxes.

Tax-conscious investors want to downplay current income as much as pos-sible. For them, a high current income simply means paying more in taxes. For other categories, such as growth and income, utilities, and balanced, a healthy cur-rent income stream often translates into lower risk. And for still other categories, such as corporate bonds, government bonds, international bonds, money market, and municipal bonds, current income is, and rightfully should be, a major determi-nant for selection.

The final category, expenses, rates how effective management is in operating the fund. High expense ratios for a given category mean that the advisors are either too greedy or simply do not know or care about running an efficient operation. The actual expenses incurred by a fund are not directly seen by the client, but such costs are deducted from the portfolio's gross returns, which is important.

In addition to looking at the expense ratio of a fund, the turnover rate is studied. The turnover rate shows how often the fund buys and sells its securities. There is a real cost when such a transaction occurs. These transaction costs, also known as commissions, are borne by the fund and eat into the gross return figures. Expense ratios do not include transaction costs incurred when management decides to replace or add a security. Thus, expense ratios do not tell the whole story. By scrutinizing the turnover rate, the rankings take into account excessive trading. A fund's turnover rate may represent a larger true cost to the investor than the fund's expense ratio.

Each fund is ranked in each one of these five categories. The rating ranges from zero to five points (stars) in each category. The points can be transcribed as follows: zero points = poor, one point = fair, two points = good, three points = very good, four points = superior, and five points = excellent.

All of the rankings for each fund are based on how such a fund fared against its peer group category in the book. Thus, even though a given rating may only be fair or even poor, it is within the context of the category and its peers that have made the book—a category that only includes the very best. There is a strong likelihood that a fund in the book that is given a low score in one category would still rate as great when compared to the entire universe of funds or even compared to other funds within the same category but not included in this book.

Do not be fooled by a low rating for any fund in any of the five areas. All 100 of these funds are true winners. Keep in mind that only about one in eighty funds can appear in the book. The purpose of the ratings is to show the best of the best.

Aggressive Growth Funds

These funds focus strictly on appreciation, with no concern about generating income. Aggressive growth funds strive for maximum capital growth, frequently using such trading strategies as leveraging, purchasing restricted securities, or buying stocks of emerging growth companies. Portfolio composition is almost exclusively U.S. stocks.

Aggressive growth funds can go up in value quite rapidly during favorable market conditions. These funds will often outperform other categories of U.S. stocks during bull markets, but suffer greater percentage losses during bear markets.

Over the past fifteen years, small stocks, which are included in the aggressive growth category, have underperformed common stocks by 2.4 percent per year, as measured by the Standard & Poor's 500 Stock Index. From 1981 to 1997, small stocks averaged 14.4 percent, while common stocks averaged 16.8 percent compounded per year. A $10,000 investment in small stocks grew to $75,300 over the past fifteen years; a similar initial investment in the S&P 500 grew to $100,300.

During the past twenty years, there have been sixteen five-year periods (1976–1980, 1977–1981, etc.). The Small Stock Index, made up from the smallest 20 percent of companies listed on the NYSE, as measured by market capitalization, *outperformed* the S&P 500 in eight of those sixteen five-year periods. During these same twenty years, there have been eleven ten-year periods (1976–1985, 1977–1986, etc.). The Small Stock Index *outperformed* the S&P 500 in just four of those eleven ten-year periods.

During the past thirty years, there have been eleven twenty-year periods (1965–1984, 1966–1985, etc.). The Small Stock Index *outperformed* the S&P 500 in every twenty-year period.

Over the past fifty years, there have been forty-six five-year periods (1946–1950, 1947–1951, etc.). The Small Stock Index outperformed the S&P 500 in twenty-seven of those forty-six five-year periods. Over the past fifty years, there have been forty-one ten-year periods (1946–1955, 1947–1956, etc.). The Small Stock Index outperformed the S&P 500 in twenty-seven of those forty-one ten-year periods, the last such period being 1979–1988.

A dollar invested in small stocks for the past fifty years grew to $5,463 by the end of 1996 (versus $856 for $1 invested in the S&P 500). This translates into an average compound return of 14.4 percent per year. Over the past fifty years, the worst year for small stocks was 1973, when a loss of 31 percent was suffered. Two years later these same stocks posted a gain of almost 53 percent in one year. The best year so far has been 1967, when small stocks posted a gain of 84 percent. The best five years in a row for this category were 1975 to 1979, when the rate of return averaged 40 percent *per year*. The worst five-year period over the past half-century has been 1969 to 1973, when this group lost an average of 11 percent per year. For ten-year periods, the best has been 1975 to 1984 (30 percent per year); the worst has been 1965 to 1974 (3 percent per year).

In order to obtain the kinds of returns described above, investors would have needed quite a bit of patience and understanding. Small-company stocks have had a standard deviation (variation of return) of 24.8 percent, compared to 16.2 percent for common stocks and 10.4 percent for long-term government bonds. This means that an investor's return in small stocks over each of the past fifty years would have ranged from +39.2 percent to –10.4 percent two-thirds of the time (14.4 + 24.8 to 14.4 – 24.8).

During the past three years, aggressive growth funds have *underperformed* the S&P 500 by 8 percent per year. Over the past five years, this fund category has underperformed the S&P 500 by an average 3 percent per year. Average turnover during the last three years has been 150 percent.

The p/e ratio is 32 for the typical aggressive growth *fund*, 20 percent higher than the S&P 500. The typical stock in these portfolios is less than 15 percent the size of the average stock in the S&P 500. The average beta is 1.0, which means the group has a market-related risk that is almost identical to that of the S&P 500. There is over $90 billion in all aggressive growth funds combined. The average aggressive growth fund throws virtually no annual income stream. The typical annual expense ratio for this group is 1.7 percent.

The p/e ratio for the typical small-company fund is 28, a figure about 10 percent higher than the S&P 500. Yet the typical stock in these portfolios is only about 2 percent the size of the average stock in the S&P 500. The average beta is 0.9, which means the group's market-related risk is 10 percent less than the S&P 500. There is about $105 billion in all small-company funds combined. The average small-company growth fund throws off an income stream of close to zero annually. The typical annual expense ratio for this group is 1.6 percent.

There are 125 funds that make up the aggressive growth category. The small-company stock category, which has 475 funds, has been combined with aggressive growth. Thus, for this section, there were a total of 600 possible candidates. Total market capitalization of these two categories combined is $195 billion.

Over the past three years, aggressive growth funds (which include small-company stock funds) have had an average compound return of 21 percent per year (22 percent for small-company stock funds alone). The *annual* return has been 17 percent for the past five years (17 percent for small-company stock funds), 13 percent for the past decade (13 percent per year for small-company stock funds), and 15 percent per year for the past fifteen years (15 percent for small-company stock funds).

The standard deviation for this combined category (aggressive growth and small-company stock) has been 19 percent over the past three years. This means that these funds have been more volatile than any other category except emerging markets, metals, and natural resources funds. Aggressive growth funds are certainly not for the faint of heart.

Aggressive Growth Funds

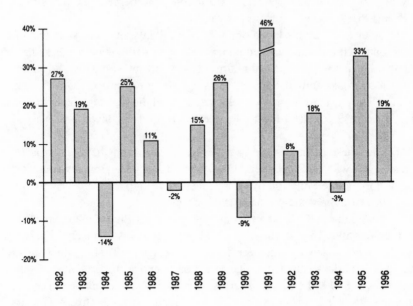

Baron Asset

Baron Asset Fund
767 Fifth Avenue, 24th Floor
New York, NY 10153
(800) 992-2766

total return	★ ★ ★ ★ ★
risk reduction	★ ★
management	★ ★
tax minimization	★ ★ ★ ★ ★
expense control	★ ★ ★ ★
symbol BARAX	18 points
up-market performance	excellent
down-market performance	fair
predictability of returns	good

Total Return

Over the past five years, Baron Asset has taken $10,000 and turned it into $29,320 ($21,130 over three years and $50,680 over the past ten years). This translates into an average annual return of 24 percent over the past five years, 28 percent over the past three years, and 18 percent for the decade. Over the past five years, this fund has outperformed 95 percent of all mutual funds; within its general category it has also done better than 95 percent of its peers. Aggressive growth funds have averaged 17 percent annually over these same five years.

Risk/Volatility

Over the past five years, Baron Asset has been safer than just 45 percent of all aggressive growth funds. Over the past decade, the fund has had one negative year, as has the S&P 500 (off 3 percent in 1990). The fund has underperformed the S&P 500 four times and the Russell 2000 twice in the last nine years.

	last 5 years		last 9 years	
worst year	7%	1994	-18%	1990
best year	35%	1995	35%	1995

In the past, Baron Asset has done better than 80 percent of its peer group in up markets but only 20 percent of its competition in down markets. Consistency, or predictability, of returns for Baron Asset can be described as good.

Management

There are seventy stocks in this $2.3 billion portfolio. The average aggressive growth fund today is $370 million in size. Close to 92 percent of the fund's holdings are in stocks. The stocks in this portfolio have an average price-earnings (p/e) ratio of 31 and a median market capitalization of $1.0 billion. The portfolio's equity holdings can be categorized as small-cap and growth-oriented issues.

Ronald Baron has managed this fund for the past ten years. There is only one other fund besides Asset within the Baron fund family. Overall, the fund family's risk-adjusted performance can be described as excellent.

Tax Minimization

During the past five years, a $10,000 initial investment grew to $26,270 after taxes, assuming a 39.6 percent income tax bracket (state and federal combined) and a capital gains rate of 28 percent. This means that investors in this fund were able to preserve 97 percent of their total returns. Compared to other equity funds, this fund's tax savings are considered to be excellent.

Expenses

Baron Asset's expense ratio is 1.4 percent; it has averaged 1.5 percent annually over the past three calendar years. The average expense ratio for the 600 funds in this category is 1.7 percent. This fund's turnover rate over the past year has been 19 percent, while its peer group average has been 108 percent.

Summary

Baron Asset has the best five-year return figures of any aggressive growth or small-company stock to appear in the book. The fund also rates number one among its peer group when it comes to tax minimization. Hopefully, this very small fund family will expand its offerings.

Profile

minimum initial investment $2,000	*IRA accounts available* . . . . yes
subsequent minimum investment $1	*IRA minimum investment* $2,000
available in all 50 states. . . . . yes	*date of inception.* . . . . June 1987
telephone exchanges. . . . . yes	*dividend/income paid* . . . . annually
number of other funds in family 1	*quality of annual reports* . . . . excellent

Fidelity Low-Priced Stock

Fidelity Group
82 Devonshire Street
Boston, MA 02109
(800) 544-8888

total return	★ ★ ★ ★ ★
risk reduction	★ ★ ★ ★
management	★ ★ ★ ★ ★
tax minimization	★ ★
expense control	★ ★ ★ ★
symbol FLPSX	20 points
up-market performance	excellent
down-market performance	excellent
predictability of returns	excellent

Total Return   ★ ★ ★ ★ ★

Over the past five years, Fidelity Low-Priced Stock has taken $10,000 and turned it into $25,940 ($18,710 over three years). This translates into an average annual return of 21 percent over the past five years and 23 percent over the past three years. Over the past five years, this fund has outperformed 95 percent of all mutual funds; within its general category it has done better than 80 percent of its peers. Aggressive growth funds have averaged 17 percent annually over these same five years.

Risk/Volatility   ★ ★ ★ ★

Over the past five years, Fidelity Low-Priced Stock has been safer than 94 percent of all aggressive growth funds. Over the past decade, the fund has had one negative year, as has the S&P 500 (off 3 percent in 1990). The fund has underperformed the S&P 500 once and the Russell 2000 once in the last seven years.

	last 5 years		last 7 years	
worst year	5%	1994	0%	1990
best year	29%	1992	46%	1991

In the past, Fidelity Low-Priced Stock has done better than 85 percent of its peer group in up markets and outperformed 95 percent of its competition in down markets. Consistency, or predictability, of returns for Fidelity Low-Priced Stock can be described as excellent.

Management   ★ ★ ★ ★ ★

There are 900 stocks in this $7.5 billion portfolio. The average aggressive growth fund today is $370 million in size. Close to 77 percent of the fund's holdings are in stocks. The stocks in this portfolio have an average price-earnings (p/e) ratio of 17 and a median market capitalization of $530 million. The portfolio's equity holdings can be categorized as small-cap and value-oriented issues.

Joel C. Tillinghast has managed this fund for the past eight years. There are 164 funds besides Low-Priced Stock within the Fidelity Group. Overall, the fund family's risk-adjusted performance can be described as good.

Tax Minimization   ★ ★

During the past five years, a $10,000 initial investment grew to $21,090 after taxes, assuming a 39.6 percent income tax bracket (state and federal combined) and a capital gains rate of 28 percent. This means that investors in this fund were able to preserve 82 percent of their total returns. Compared to other equity funds, this fund's tax savings are considered to be good.

Expenses   ★ ★ ★ ★

Fidelity Low-Priced Stock's expense ratio is 1.0 percent; it has averaged 1.1 percent annually over the past three calendar years. The average expense ratio for the 600 funds in this category is 1.7 percent. This fund's turnover rate over the past year has been 79 percent, while its peer group average has been 108 percent.

Summary

Fidelity Low-Priced Stock is the only aggressive growth or small company stock fund that has a rating of excellent in three important categories: bull market performance, bear market performance, and predictability of returns. This Fidelity offering is a fantastic choice for any equity investor.

Profile

minimum initial investment $2,500	*IRA accounts available* . . . . yes
subsequent minimum investment . . $250	*IRA minimum investment* $500
available in all 50 states. . . . . yes	*date of inception.* . . . . Dec. 1989
telephone exchanges. . . . . yes	*dividend/income paid* . . . . annually
number of other funds in family 164	*quality of annual reports* . . . . excellent

Gabelli Small Cap Growth

Gabelli Funds
One Corporate Center
Rye, NY 10580-1434
(800) 422-3554

total return	★ ★ ★
risk reduction	★ ★ ★
management	★ ★
tax minimization	★ ★ ★
expense control	★ ★ ★ ★
symbol GABSX	15 points
up-market performance	n/a
down-market performance	n/a
predictability of returns	excellent

Total Return   ★ ★ ★
Over the past five years, Gabelli Small Cap Growth has taken $10,000 and turned
it into $21,920 ($17,370 over three years). This translates into an average annual
return of 17 percent over the past five years and 20 percent over the past three
years. Over the past five years, this fund has outperformed 80 percent of all mutual
funds; within its general category it has done better than just 45 percent of its
peers. Aggressive growth funds have averaged 17 percent annually over these
same five years.

Risk/Volatility   ★ ★ ★
Over the past five years, Gabelli Small Cap Growth has been safer than 86 percent
of all aggressive growth funds. Over the past decade, the fund has had one negative year, as has the S&P 500 (off 3 percent in 1990). The fund has underperformed
the S&P 500 three times and the Russell 2000 three times in the last five years.

	last 5 years		last 7 years	
worst year	-3%	1994	-3%	1994
best year	25%	1995	25%	1995

Consistency, or predictability, of returns for Gabelli Small Cap Growth can
be described as excellent.

Management   ★ ★
There are 240 stocks in this $240 million portfolio. The average aggressive growth
fund today is $370 million in size. Close to 98 percent of the fund's holdings are
in stocks. The stocks in this portfolio have an average price-earnings (p/e) ratio of
23 and a median market capitalization of $400 million. The portfolio's equity hold-
ings can be categorized as small-cap and value-oriented issues.

Mario J. Gabelli has managed this fund for the past six years. There are nine funds besides Small Cap Growth within the Gabelli fund family. Overall, the fund family's risk-adjusted performance can be described as good.

Tax Minimization   ★ ★ ★
During the past five years, a $10,000 initial investment grew to $18,830 after taxes, assuming a 39.6 percent income tax bracket (state and federal combined) and a capital gains rate of 28 percent. This means that investors in this fund were able to preserve 88 percent of their total returns. Compared to other equity funds, this fund's tax savings are considered to be good.

Expenses   ★ ★ ★ ★
Gabelli Small Cap Growth's expense ratio is 1.6 percent; it has averaged 1.6 percent annually over the past three calendar years. The average expense ratio for the 600 funds in this category is 1.7 percent. This fund's turnover rate over the past year has been 11 percent, while its peer group average has been 108 percent.

Summary
Gabelli Small Cap Growth scores well in every important category. The fund's greatest strength is its predictability of returns—an important consideration for the stock fund investor who is nervous about the ups and downs of the market.

Profile
minimum initial investment $1,000	IRA accounts available . . . . yes
subsequent minimum investment $1	IRA minimum investment $1,000
available in all 50 states. . . . . yes	date of inception . . . . Oct. 1991
telephone exchanges. . . . . yes	dividend/income paid . . . . quarterly
number of other funds in family. 9	quality of annual reports . . . . excellent

Gradison Opportunity Value

Gradison Mutual Funds
580 Walnut Street
Cincinnati, OH 45202
(800) 869-5999

total return	★ ★
risk reduction	★ ★ ★
management	★ ★
tax minimization	★ ★ ★
expense control	★ ★ ★ ★
symbol GOGFX	14 points
up-market performance	fair
down-market performance	good
predictability of returns	excellent

Total Return   ★ ★

Over the past five years, Gradison Opportunity Value has taken $10,000 and turned it into $21,000 ($17,320 over three years and $31,760 over the past ten years). This translates into an average annual return of 16 percent over the past five years, 20 percent over the past three years, and 12 percent for the decade. Over the past five years, this fund has outperformed 75 percent of all mutual funds; within its general category it has only done better than 35 percent of its peers. Aggressive growth funds have averaged 17 percent annually over these same five years.

Risk/Volatility   ★ ★ ★
Over the past five years, Gradison Opportunity Value has been safer than 90 percent of all aggressive growth funds. Over the past decade, the fund has had three negative years, while the S&P 500 has had one (off 3 percent in 1990). The fund has underperformed the S&P 500 and the Russell 2000 six times in the last ten years.

	last 5 years		last 10 years	
worst year	-2%	1994	-13%	1990
best year	27%	1995	36%	1991

In the past, Gradison Opportunity Value has done better than 30 percent of its peer group in up markets and outperformed 50 percent of its competition in down markets. Consistency, or predictability, of returns for Gradison Opportunity Value can be described as excellent.

Management   ★ ★

There are seventy stocks in this $130 million portfolio. The average aggressive growth fund today is $370 million in size. Close to 70 percent of the fund's holdings are in stocks. The stocks in this portfolio have an average price-earnings (p/e)

ratio of 18 and a median market capitalization of $840 million. The portfolio's equity holdings can be categorized as small-cap and value-oriented issues.

William J. Leugers, Jr. and David R. Shick have managed this fund for the past thirteen years. There are six funds besides Opportunity Value within the fund family. Overall, the fund family's risk-adjusted performance can be described as good.

Tax Minimization   ★ ★ ★
During the past five years, a $10,000 initial investment grew to $19,570 after taxes, assuming a 39.6 percent income tax bracket (state and federal combined) and a capital gains rate of 28 percent. This means that investors in this fund were able to preserve 89 percent of their total returns. Compared to other equity funds, this fund's tax savings are considered to be good.

Expenses   ★ ★ ★ ★
Gradison Opportunity Value's expense ratio is 1.4 percent; it has averaged 1.4 percent annually over the past three calendar years. The average expense ratio for the 600 funds in this category is 1.7 percent. This fund's turnover rate over the past year has been 24 percent, while its peer group average has been 108 percent.

Summary
Gradison Opportunity Value is a recommended choice for the investor who wants predictable returns. The fund is also in a special category: less than two percent of its peer group qualifies to be in this book.

Profile

minimum initial investment $1,000	*IRA accounts available* . . . . yes
subsequent minimum investment . . . $50	*IRA minimum investment* $1,000
available in all 50 states. . . . . yes	*date of inception* . . . . Aug. 1983
telephone exchanges. . . . . yes	*dividend/income paid* . . . semi-annually
number of other funds in family 6	*quality of annual reports* . . . . good

Longleaf Partners Small-Cap

Longleaf Partners Funds
6075 Poplar Avenue, Suite 900
Memphis, TN 38119
(800) 445-9469

total return	★ ★ ★ ★
risk reduction	★ ★ ★ ★
management	★ ★ ★ ★
tax minimization	★ ★ ★ ★
expense control	★ ★ ★ ★
symbol LLSCX	20 points
up-market performance	fair
down-market performance	fair
predictability of returns	excellent

Total Return   ★ ★ ★ ★

Over the past five years, Longleaf Partners Small-Cap has taken $10,000 and turned it into $24,880 ($19,290 over three years). This translates into an average annual return of 20 percent over the past five years and 24 percent over the past three years. Over the past five years, this fund has outperformed 90 percent of all mutual funds; within its general category it has done better than 75 percent of its peers. Aggressive growth funds have averaged 17 percent annually over these same five years.

Risk/Volatility   ★ ★ ★ ★

Over the past five years, Longleaf Partners Small-Cap has been safer than 95 percent of all aggressive growth funds. Over the past decade, the fund has had one negative year, as has the S&P 500 (off 3 percent in 1990). The fund has underperformed the S&P 500 and the Russell 2000 four times in the last eight years.

	last 5 years		last 8 years	
worst year	4%	1994	-30%	1990
best year	31%	1996	34%	1989

In the past, Longleaf Partners Small-Cap has done better than just 20 percent of its peer group in up markets but only 25 percent of its competition in down markets. Consistency, or predictability, of returns for Longleaf Partners Small-Cap can be described as excellent.

Management   ★ ★ ★ ★

There are thirty stocks in this $530 million portfolio. The average aggressive growth fund today is $370 million in size. Close to 72 percent of the fund's holdings are in stocks. The stocks in this portfolio have an average price-earnings (p/e) ratio of 32 and a median market capitalization of $360 million. The portfolio's equity holdings can be categorized as small-cap and a blend of growth and value stocks.

Hawkins and Cates have managed this fund for the past five years. There are two funds besides Small-Cap within the Longleaf Partners fund family. Overall, the fund family's risk-adjusted performance can be described as excellent.

Tax Minimization   ★ ★ ★ ★
During the past five years, a $10,000 initial investment grew to $21,660 after taxes, assuming a 39.6 percent income tax bracket (state and federal combined) and a capital gains rate of 28 percent. This means that investors in this fund were able to preserve 93 percent of their total returns. Compared to other equity funds, this fund's tax savings are considered to be excellent.

Expenses   ★ ★ ★ ★
Longleaf Partners Small-Cap's expense ratio is 1.2 percent; it has averaged 1.3 percent annually over the past three calendar years. The average expense ratio for the 600 funds in this category is 1.7 percent. This fund's turnover rate over the past year has been 28 percent, while its peer group average has been 108 percent.

Summary
Longleaf Partners Small-Cap is the only aggressive growth or small-company fund that has a rating of very good in every single category. It is also one of only a few funds in the entire book to boast of such a fine score. Only a couple of its peers have a similar or higher overall score. The small fund family is also to be commended; Longleaf Partners has exceptional *risk-adjusted* returns across the board.

Profile
minimum initial investment $10,000	*IRA accounts available* . . . . yes
subsequent minimum investment $1	*IRA minimum investment* $10,000
available in all 50 states. . . . . yes	*date of inception* . . . . Feb. 1989
telephone exchanges. . . . . yes	*dividend/income paid* . . . . annually
number of other funds in family. 2	*quality of annual reports* . . . . good

Princor Emerging Growth A

Princor Family of Mutual Funds
P.O. Box 10423
Des Moines, IA 50306
(800) 451-5447

total return	★ ★ ★ ★
risk reduction	★ ★ ★
management	★ ★ ★
tax minimization	★ ★ ★ ★ ★
expense control	★ ★ ★ ★
symbol PEMGX	19 points
up-market performance	excellent
down-market performance	good
predictability of returns	excellent

Total Return   ★ ★ ★ ★

Over the past five years, Princor Emerging Growth A has taken $10,000 and turned it into $24,880 ($18,690 over three years). This translates into an average annual return of 20 percent over the past five years and 23 percent over the past three years. Over the past five years, this fund has outperformed 90 percent of all mutual funds; within its general category it has done better than 70 percent of its peers. Aggressive growth funds have averaged 17 percent annually over these same five years.

Risk/Volatility   ★ ★ ★

Over the past five years, Princor Emerging Growth A has been safer than 84 percent of all aggressive growth funds. Over the past decade, the fund has had one negative year, as has the S&P 500 (off 3 percent in 1990). The fund has underperformed the S&P 500 four times and the Russell 2000 three times in the last nine years.

	last 5 years		last 9 years	
worst year	3%	1994	-6%	1990
best year	34%	1995	53%	1991

In the past, Princor Emerging Growth A has done better than 85 percent of its peer group in up markets and outperformed 50 percent of its competition in down markets. Consistency, or predictability, of returns for Princor Emerging Growth A can be described as excellent.

Management   ★ ★ ★

There are ninety stocks in this $290 million portfolio. The average aggressive growth fund today is $370 million in size. Close to 83 percent of the fund's holdings are in stocks. The stocks in this portfolio have an average price-earnings (p/e) ratio of 27 and a median market capitalization of $1.3 billion. The portfolio's equity holdings can be categorized as small-cap and a blend of growth and value stocks.

Michael R. Hamilton has managed this fund for the past ten years. There are eleven funds besides Emerging Growth A within the Princor fund family. Overall, the fund family's risk-adjusted performance can be described as good.

Tax Minimization

During the past five years, a $10,000 initial investment grew to $21,940 after taxes, assuming a 39.6 percent income tax bracket (state and federal combined) and a capital gains rate of 28 percent. This means that investors in this fund were able to preserve 97 percent of their total returns. Compared to other equity funds, this fund's tax savings are considered to be excellent.

Expenses

Princor Emerging Growth A's expense ratio is 1.3 percent; it has averaged 1.5 percent annually over the past three calendar years. The average expense ratio for the 600 funds in this category is 1.7 percent. This fund's turnover rate over the past year has been 12 percent, while its peer group average has been 108 percent.

Summary

Princor Emerging Growth A is number one when it comes to tax minimization. The fund is also one of the top total point earners within its large peer group. This Princor offering does well in every category ranked. The fund is a wise choice for the bull market.

Profile

minimum initial investment $1,000	*IRA accounts available* . . . . yes
subsequent minimum investment . . . $50	*IRA minimum investment* $250
available in all 50 states . . . . no	*date of inception*. . . . . Dec. 1987
telephone exchanges. . . . . yes	*dividend/income paid* . . . semi-annually
number of other funds in family 11	*quality of annual reports* . . . . good

Royce Micro Cap

Royce Funds
1414 Avenue of the Americas
New York, NY 10019
(800) 221-4268

total return	★ ★ ★ ★
risk reduction	★ ★ ★
management	★ ★ ★
tax minimization	★ ★ ★
expense control	★ ★
symbol RYOTX	15 points
up-market performance	n/a
down-market performance	n/a
predictability of returns	excellent

Total Return   ★ ★ ★ ★

Over the past five years, Royce Micro Cap has taken $10,000 and turned it into $23,860 ($15,830 over three years). This translates into an average annual return of 19 percent over the past five years and 17 percent over the past three years. Over the past five years, this fund has outperformed 85 percent of all mutual funds; within its general category it has done better than 60 percent of its peers. Aggressive growth funds have averaged 17 percent annually over these same five years.

Risk/Volatility   ★ ★ ★

Over the past five years, Royce Micro Cap has been safer than 91 percent of all aggressive growth funds. Over the past decade, the fund has had no negative years, while the S&P 500 has had one (off 3 percent in 1990). The fund has underperformed the S&P 500 twice and the Russell 2000 twice in the last five years.

	last 5 years		last 7 years	
worst year	4%	1994	4%	1994
best year	29%	1992	29%	1992

Consistency, or predictability, of returns for Royce Micro Cap can be described as excellent.

Management   ★ ★ ★

There are 160 stocks in this $160 million portfolio. The average aggressive growth fund today is $370 million in size. Close to 98 percent of the fund's holdings are in stocks. The stocks in this portfolio have an average price-earnings (p/e) ratio of 21 and a median market capitalization of $150 million. The portfolio's equity holdings can be categorized as small-cap and value-oriented issues.

Charles M. Royce has managed this fund for the past five years. There are five funds besides Micro Cap within the Royce family. Overall, the fund family's risk-adjusted performance can be described as good.

Tax Minimization ★ ★ ★
During the past five years, a $10,000 initial investment grew to $19,300 after taxes, assuming a 39.6 percent income tax bracket (state and federal combined) and a capital gains rate of 28 percent. This means that investors in this fund were able to preserve 85 percent of their total returns. Compared to other equity funds, this fund's tax savings are considered to be good.

Expenses ★ ★
Royce Micro Cap's expense ratio is 1.8 percent; it has averaged 1.9 percent annually over the past three calendar years. The average expense ratio for the 600 funds in this category is 1.7 percent. This fund's turnover rate over the past year has been 70 percent, while its peer group average has been 108 percent.

Summary
Royce Micro Cap ranks in the top two percent of its entire peer group. This fund measures up well in virtually every category. The fund's strong suit is its predictability of returns—an uncommon trait among small-cap or aggressive growth funds.

Profile

minimum initial investment $2,000	*IRA accounts available* . . . . yes
subsequent minimum investment . . . $50	*IRA minimum investment* $500
available in all 50 states. . . . . yes	*date of inception*. . . . . Dec. 1991
telephone exchanges. . . . . yes	*dividend/income paid* . . . . annually
number of other funds in family. 5	*quality of annual reports* . . . . excellent

Royce Premier

Royce Funds
1414 Avenue of the Americas
New York, NY 10019
(800) 221-4268

total return	★ ★ ★
risk reduction	★ ★ ★ ★ ★
management	★ ★ ★ ★ ★
tax minimization	★ ★ ★ ★
expense control	★ ★ ★ ★
symbol RYPRX	21 points
up-market performance	n/a
down-market performance	n/a
predictability of returns	excellent

Total Return

Over the past five years, Royce Premier has taken $10,000 and turned it into $21,920 ($16,520 over three years). This translates into an average annual return of 17 percent over the past five years and 18 percent over the past three years. Over the past five years, this fund has outperformed 80 percent of all mutual funds; within its general category it has done better than 50 percent of its peers. Aggressive growth funds have averaged 17 percent annually over these same five years.

Risk/Volatility ★ ★ ★ ★ ★

Over the past five years, Royce Premier has been safer than 97 percent of all aggressive growth funds. Over the past decade, the fund has had no negative years, while the S&P 500 has had one (off 3 percent in 1990). The fund has underperformed the S&P 500 and the Russell 2000 twice in the last five years.

	last 5 years		last 7 years	
worst year	3%	1994	3%	1994
best year	19%	1993	19%	1993

Consistency, or predictability, of returns for Royce Premier can be described as excellent.

Management

There are fifty stocks in this $430 million portfolio. The average aggressive growth fund today is $370 million in size. Close to 85 percent of the fund's holdings are in stocks. The stocks in this portfolio have an average price-earnings (p/e) ratio of 24 and a median market capitalization of $590 million. The portfolio's equity holdings can be categorized as small-cap and value oriented issues.

Charles M. Royce has managed this fund for the past five years. There are five funds besides Premier within the Royce fund family. Overall, the fund family's risk-adjusted performance can be described as good.

Tax Minimization   ★ ★ ★ ★

During the past five years, a $10,000 initial investment grew to $19,710 after taxes, assuming a 39.6 percent income tax bracket (state and federal combined) and a capital gains rate of 28 percent. This means that investors in this fund were able to preserve 90 percent of their total returns. Compared to other equity funds, this fund's tax savings are considered to be very good.

Expenses   ★ ★ ★ ★

Royce Premier's expense ratio is 1.3 percent; it has averaged 1.3 percent annually over the past three calendar years. The average expense ratio for the 600 funds in this category is 1.7 percent. This fund's turnover rate over the past year has been 34 percent, while its peer group average has been 108 percent.

Summary

Royce Premier has a higher overall point score than any of its peers. This may well be the number one choice for the small-company or aggressive growth investor. Management and risk reduction are both superb.

Profile

minimum initial investment $2,000	*IRA accounts available* . . . . yes
subsequent minimum investment . . . $50	*IRA minimum investment* $500
available in all 50 states. . . . . yes	*date of inception.* . . . . Dec. 1991
telephone exchanges. . . . . yes	*dividend/income paid* . . . . annually
number of other funds in family 5	*quality of annual reports* . . . . excellent

T. Rowe Price Small Cap Stock

T. Rowe Price Funds
100 East Pratt Street
Baltimore, MD 21202
(800) 638-5660

total return	★ ★ ★ ★
risk reduction	★ ★ ★
management	★ ★ ★
tax minimization	★
expense control	★ ★ ★ ★ ★
symbol OTCFX	16 points
up-market performance	n/a
down-market performance	n/a
predictability of returns	very good

Total Return ★ ★ ★ ★

Over the past five years, T. Rowe Price Small Cap Stock has taken $10,000 and turned it into $24,880 ($18,810 over three years and $30,340 over the past ten years). This translates into an average annual return of 20 percent over the past five years, 23 percent over the past three years, and 12 percent for the decade. Over the past five years, this fund has outperformed 90 percent of all mutual funds; within its general category it has done better than 75 percent of its peers. Aggressive growth funds have averaged 17 percent annually over these same five years.

Risk/Volatility ★ ★ ★

Over the past five years, T. Rowe Price Small Cap Stock has been safer than 78 percent of all aggressive growth funds. Over the past decade, the fund has had two negative years, while the S&P 500 has had one (off 3 percent in 1990). The fund has underperformed the S&P 500 six times and the Russell 2000 five times in the last ten years.

	last 5 years		last 10 years	
worst year	0%	1994	-20%	1990
best year	34%	1995	39%	1991

Consistency, or predictability, of returns for T. Rowe Price Small Cap Stock can be described as very good.

Management ★ ★ ★

There are 170 stocks in this $480 million portfolio. The average aggressive growth fund today is $370 million in size. Close to 89 percent of the fund's holdings are in stocks. The stocks in this portfolio have an average price-earnings (p/e) ratio of 23 and a median market capitalization of $300 million. The portfolio's equity holdings can be categorized as small-cap and value-oriented issues.

Gregory A. McCrickard has managed this fund for the past five years. There are seventy funds besides Small Cap Stock within the T. Rowe Price fund family. Overall, the fund family's risk-adjusted performance can be described as good.

Tax Minimization   ★
During the past five years, a $10,000 initial investment grew to $18,510 after taxes, assuming a 39.6 percent income tax bracket (state and federal combined) and a capital gains rate of 28 percent. This means that investors in this fund were able to preserve 75 percent of their total returns. Compared to other equity funds, this fund's tax savings are considered to be poor.

Expenses   ★ ★ ★ ★ ★
T. Rowe Price Small Cap Stock's expense ratio is 1.1 percent; it has averaged 1.1 percent annually over the past three calendar years. The average expense ratio for the 600 funds in this category is 1.7 percent. This fund's turnover rate over the past year has been 31 percent, while its peer group average has been 108 percent.

Summary
T. Rowe Price Small Cap Stock is the most frugally run aggressive growth or small-cap fund in the book. It beats its number two competitor by a wide margin. Low expenses translate into higher returns for the fund's investors.

Profile
minimum initial investment $2,500	*IRA accounts available* . . . . yes
subsequent minimum investment . . $100	*IRA minimum investment* $1,000
available in all 50 states. . . . . yes	*date of inception.* . . . . June 1956
telephone exchanges. . . . . yes	*dividend/income paid* . . . . annually
number of other funds in family 70	*quality of annual reports* . . . . excellent

Winthrop Small Company Value A

Winthrop Funds
277 Park Avenue
New York, NY 10172-0003
(800) 225-8011

total return	★ ★ ★ ★
risk reduction	★ ★ ★ ★
management	★ ★ ★ ★
tax minimization	★ ★
expense control	★ ★ ★ ★ ★
symbol WFAGX	19 points
up-market performance	good
down-market performance	excellent
predictability of returns	excellent

Total Return ★ ★ ★ ★

Over the past five years, Winthrop Small Company Value A has taken $10,000 and turned it into $21,920 ($15,640 over three years and $32,040 over the past ten years). This translates into an average annual return of 17 percent over the past five years, 16 percent over the past three years, and 12 percent for the decade. Over the past five years, this fund has outperformed 80 percent of all mutual funds; within its general category it has done better than only 45 percent of its peers. Aggressive growth funds have averaged 17 percent annually over these same five years.

Risk/Volatility ★ ★ ★ ★

Over the past five years, Winthrop Small Company Value A has been safer than 88 percent of all aggressive growth funds. Over the past decade, the fund has had three negative years, while the S&P 500 has had one (off 3 percent in 1990). The fund has underperformed the S&P 500 six times and the Russell 2000 four times in the last ten years.

	last 5 years		last 10 years	
worst year	-1%	1994	-13%	1990
best year	22%	1993	51%	1991

In the past, Winthrop Small Company Value A has done better than 50 percent of its peer group in up markets and outperformed 80 percent of its competition in down markets. Consistency, or predictability, of returns for Winthrop Small Company Value A can be described as excellent.

Management ★ ★ ★ ★

There are ninety stocks in this $240 million portfolio. The average aggressive growth fund today is $370 million in size. Close to 99 percent of the fund's holdings are in stocks. The stocks in this portfolio have an average price-earnings (p/e) ratio of 21 and a median market capitalization of $830 million. The portfolio's equity holdings can be categorized as small-cap and value-oriented issues.

A team has managed this fund for the past five years. There are nine funds besides Small Company Value A within the Winthrop fund family. Overall, the fund family's risk-adjusted performance can be described as fair.

Tax Minimization   ★ ★
During the past five years, a $10,000 initial investment grew to $18,220 after taxes, assuming a 39.6 percent income tax bracket (state and federal combined) and a capital gains rate of 28 percent. This means that investors in this fund were able to preserve 82 percent of their total returns. Compared to other equity funds, this fund's tax savings are considered to be good.

Expenses   ★ ★ ★ ★ ★
Winthrop Small Company Value A's expense ratio is 1.5 percent; it has averaged 1.6 percent annually over the past three calendar years. The average expense ratio for the 600 funds in this category is 1.7 percent. This fund's turnover rate over the past year has been 35 percent, while its peer group average has been 108 percent.

Summary
Winthrop Small Company Value A is one of the highest total point scorers in its category. Total return, tax minimization, and management are all very good. Due to the fund's tax minimization policy, the fund is recommended more highly when it is within a qualified retirement plan.

Profile
minimum initial investment $250	*IRA accounts available* . . . . yes
subsequent minimum investment . . . $25	*IRA minimum investment* $250
available in all 50 states. . . . . yes	*date of inception* . . . . Feb. 1967
telephone exchanges. . . . . yes	*dividend/income paid* . . . . annually
number of other funds in family. 9	*quality of annual reports* . . . . good

Balanced Funds

The objective of balanced funds, also referred to as *total return funds*, is to provide both growth and income. Fund management purchases common stocks, bonds, and convertible securities. Portfolio composition is almost always exclusively U.S. securities. The weighting of stocks compared to bonds depends upon the portfolio manager's perception of the stock market, interest rates, and risk levels. It is rare for less than 30 percent of the fund's holdings to be in stocks or bonds.

Balanced funds offer neither the best nor worst of both worlds. These funds will often outperform the different categories of bond funds during bull markets, but suffer greater percentage losses during stock market declines. On the other hand, when interest rates are on the rise, balanced funds will typically decline less on a total-return basis (current yield plus or minus principal appreciation) than a bond fund. When rates are falling, balanced funds will also outperform bond funds if stocks are also doing well.

Over the past ten years, the average balanced fund had 81 percent of the return of growth funds with 43 percent less risk. Balanced funds are the perfect choice for the investor who cannot decide between stocks and bonds. This hybrid security is a middle-of-the-road approach, ideal for someone who wants a fund manager to determine the portfolio's weighting of stocks, bonds, and convertibles.

The price-earnings ratio for stocks in a typical balanced fund is 25, just slightly lower than the S&P 500's p/e ratio. The average beta is 0.6, which means that this group has only 60 percent of the market-related risk of the S&P 500. During the past three years, balanced funds have lagged the performance of the S&P 500 by over 13 percent annually. Over the past five years, this benchmark has outperformed balanced funds by an average of 7 percent per year. The figure falls to 4 percent annually for the past decade. Average turnover during the last three years has been 105 percent per annum. Balanced funds throw off an income stream of less than 3 percent annually. The typical annual expense ratio for this group is 1.5 percent.

Over 350 funds make up the balanced category; market capitalization is $140 billion. Three other categories—asset allocation (210 funds, total market capitalization of $50 billion), multi-asset global (95 funds, total market capitalization of $45 billion), and convertible (50 funds, total market capitalization of $7 billion)— have been combined with balanced. Thus, for this section, there were a total of 855 possible candidates. Total market capitalization of these four categories combined is $240 billion.

Balanced Funds

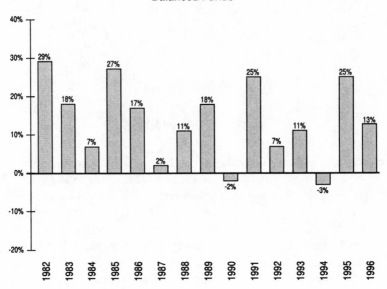

Flag Investors Value Builder A

Flag Investors Funds
135 East Baltimore Street
Baltimore, MD 21202
(800) 767-3524

total return	★ ★ ★ ★ ★
risk reduction	★ ★
management	★ ★ ★
current income	★ ★
expense control	★ ★ ★ ★
symbol FLVBX	16 points
up-market performance	n/a
down-market performance	n/a
predictability of returns	fair

Total Return   ★ ★ ★ ★ ★

Over the past five years, Flag Investors Value Builder A has taken $10,000 and turned it into $21,920 ($18,970 over three years). This translates into an average annual return of 17 percent over the past five years and 24 percent over the past three years. Over the past five years, this fund has outperformed 80 percent of all mutual funds; within its general category it has done better than 95 percent of its peers. Balanced funds have averaged 12 percent annually over these same five years.

During the past five years, a $10,000 initial investment grew to $20,740 after taxes, assuming a 39.6 percent income tax bracket (state and federal combined) and a capital gains rate of 28 percent. This means that investors in this fund were able to preserve 97 percent of their total returns. Compared to other fixed-income funds, this fund offers tax savings that are considered excellent. Compared to other equity funds, its tax savings are excellent.

Risk/Volatility   ★ ★

Over the past five years, Flag Investors Value Builder A has been safer than just 26 percent of all balanced funds. Over the past decade, the fund has had one negative year, as has the S&P 500 (off 3 percent in 1990) and the Lehman Brothers Aggregate Bond Index (off 3 percent in 1994). The fund has underperformed the S&P 500 twice in the last four years. During the same time frame, the fund outperformed the Lehman Brothers Aggregate Bond Index each year.

	last 5 years		last 4 years	
worst year	0%	1994	0%	1994
best year	33%	1995	33%	1995

Consistency, or predictability, of returns for Flag Investors Value Builder A can be described as fair.

Management   ★ ★ ★

There are sixty stocks and fifty fixed-income securities in this $420 million portfolio. The average balanced fund today is $390 million in size. Close to 60 percent of the fund's holdings are in stocks and 27 percent in bonds. The stocks in this portfolio have an average price-earnings (p/e) ratio of 24 and a median market capitalization of $10.5 billion. The average maturity of the bonds in this account is six years; the weighted coupon rate averages 8.0 percent. The portfolio's equity holdings can be categorized as large-cap and value-oriented issues. The portfolio's fixed-income holdings can be categorized as intermediate-term, medium-quality debt.

A team has managed this fund for the past five years. There are ten funds besides Value Builder A within the Flag Investors fund family. Overall, the fund family's risk-adjusted performance can be described as fair.

Current Income   ★ ★

Over the past year, Flag Investors Value Builder A had a twelve-month yield of 2.1 percent. During this same twelve-month period, the typical balanced fund had a twelve-month yield that averaged 2.6 percent.

Expenses   ★ ★ ★ ★

Flag Investors Value Builder A's expense ratio is 1.1 percent; it has averaged 1.2 percent annually over the past three calendar years. The average expense ratio for the 855 funds in this category is 1.5 percent. This fund's turnover rate over the past year has been 13 percent, while its peer group average has been 103 percent.

Summary

Flag Investors Value Builder A is number one for returns when you look at the past three and five years. There are a number of other balanced funds that are safer, but this one delivers when it comes to raw performance. The fund's tax minimization policy is truly superb—a rare commodity within the community of asset allocation, balanced, convertible, and multi-asset funds.

Profile

minimum initial investment $2,000	*IRA accounts available* . . . . yes
subsequent minimum investment . . $100	*IRA minimum investment* $2,000
available in all 50 states. . . . . yes	*date of inception.* . . . . June 1992
telephone exchanges. . . . . yes	*dividend/income paid* . . . . quarterly
number of other funds in family 10	*quality of annual reports* . . . . excellent

Founders Balanced

Founders Funds
2930 East Third Avenue
Denver, CO 80206
(800) 525-2440

total return	★ ★ ★ ★ ★
risk reduction	★ ★ ★
management	★ ★ ★ ★
current income	★ ★
expense control	★ ★
symbol FRINX	16 points
up-market performance	good
down-market performance	poor
predictability of returns	good

Total Return

Over the past five years, Founders Balanced has taken $10,000 and turned it into $21,920 ($16,960 over three years and $31,530 over the past ten years). This translates into an average annual return of 17 percent over the past five years, 19 percent over the past three years, and 12 percent for the decade. Over the past five years, this fund has outperformed 80 percent of all mutual funds; within its general category it has done better than 95 percent of its peers. Balanced funds have averaged 12 percent annually over these same five years.

During the past five years, a $10,000 initial investment grew to $19,230 after taxes, assuming a 39.6 percent income tax bracket (state and federal combined) and a capital gains rate of 28 percent. This means that investors in this fund were able to preserve 82 percent of their total returns. Compared to other fixed-income funds, this fund offers tax savings that are considered very good. Compared to other equity funds, its tax savings are also very good.

Risk/Volatility

Over the past five years, Founders Balanced has been safer than only 49 percent of all balanced funds. Over the past decade, the fund has had two negative years, while the S&P 500 has had one (off 3 percent in 1990); the Lehman Brothers Aggregate Bond Index also fell once (off 3 percent in 1994). The fund has underperformed the S&P 500 nine times and the Lehman Brothers Aggregate Bond Index three times in the last ten years.

	last 5 years		last 10 years	
worst year	-2%	1994	-5%	1990
best year	29%	1995	29%	1995

In the past, Founders Balanced has done better than 50 percent of its peer group in up markets but virtually none of its competition in down markets.

Consistency, or predictability, of returns for Founders Balanced can be described as good.

Management   ★ ★ ★ ★
There are ninety stocks and twenty fixed-income securities in this $720 million portfolio. The average balanced fund today is $390 million in size. Close to 56 percent of the fund's holdings are in stocks and 42 percent in bonds. The stocks in this portfolio have an average price-earnings (p/e) ratio of 24 and a median market capitalization of $25.3 billion. The average maturity of the bonds in this account is four years; the weighted coupon rate averages 6.0 percent. The portfolio's equity holdings can be categorized as large-cap and a blend of growth and value stocks. The portfolio's fixed-income holdings can be categorized as intermediate-term, high-quality debt.

Brian F. Kelly has managed this fund for the past nine years. There are eight funds besides Balanced within the Founders fund family. Overall, the fund family's risk-adjusted performance can be described as good.

Current Income   ★ ★
Over the past year, Founders Balanced had a twelve-month yield of 2.2 percent. During this same twelve-month period, the typical balanced fund had a twelve-month yield that averaged 2.6 percent.

Expenses   ★ ★
Founders Balanced's expense ratio is 1.1 percent; it has averaged 1.2 percent annually over the past three calendar years. The average expense ratio for the 855 funds in this category is 1.5 percent. This fund's turnover rate over the past year has been 146 percent, while its peer group average has been 103 percent.

Summary
Founders Balanced ties for number one as the best five-year performer within its broad category. It has also done extremely well over the past three years. This is no small feat when you consider this portfolio has been rated against all other asset allocation, balanced, convertible, and multi-asset funds.

Profile

minimum initial investment $1,000	*IRA accounts available* . . . . yes
subsequent minimum investment . . $100	*IRA minimum investment* $500
available in all 50 states. . . . . yes	*date of inception* . . . . Feb. 1963
telephone exchanges. . . . . yes	*dividend/income paid* . . . . quarterly
number of other funds in family 8	*quality of annual reports* . . . . good

Fremont Global

Fremont Mutual Funds
50 Beale Street, Suite 100
San Francisco, CA 94105
(800) 548-4539

total return	★ ★
risk reduction	★ ★ ★ ★
management	★ ★
current income	★ ★
expense control	★ ★ ★ ★
symbol FMAFX	14 points
up-market performance	fair
down-market performance	very good
predictability of returns	very good

Total Return   ★ ★

Over the past five years, Fremont Global has taken $10,000 and turned it into $18,420 ($15,200 over three years). This translates into an average annual return of 13 percent over the past five years and 15 percent over the past three years. Over the past five years, this fund has outperformed 60 percent of all mutual funds; within its general category it has done better than just 45 percent of its peers. Balanced funds have averaged 12 percent annually over these same five years.

During the past five years, a $10,000 initial investment grew to $16,170 after taxes, assuming a 39.6 percent income tax bracket (state and federal combined) and a capital gains rate of 28 percent. This means that investors in this fund were able to preserve 81 percent of their total returns. Compared to other fixed-income funds, this fund offers tax savings that are considered very good. Compared to other equity funds, its tax savings are very good.

Risk/Volatility   ★ ★ ★ ★

Over the past five years, Fremont Global has been safer than 72 percent of all balanced funds. Over the past decade, the fund has had two negative years, while the S&P 500 has had one (off 3 percent in 1990); the Lehman Brothers Aggregate Bond Index also fell once (off 3 percent in 1994). The fund has underperformed the S&P 500 six times and the Lehman Brothers Aggregate Bond Index three times in the last eight years.

	last 5 years		last 8 years	
worst year	-4%	1994	-4%	1994
best year	20%	1993	20%	1993

In the past, Fremont Global has done better than only 35 percent of its peer group in up markets and outperformed 60 percent of its competition in down markets. Consistency, or predictability, of returns for Fremont Global can be described as very good.

Management   ★ ★
There are 220 stocks and 50 fixed-income securities in this $650 million portfolio. The average balanced fund today is $390 million in size. Close to 66 percent of the fund's holdings are in stocks and 26 percent in bonds. The stocks in this portfolio have an average price-earnings (p/e) ratio of 23 and a median market capitalization of $16.2 billion. The portfolio's equity holdings can be categorized as large-cap and value-oriented issues. The portfolio's fixed-income holdings can be categorized as long-term, high-quality debt.

A team has managed this fund for the past seven years. There are six funds besides Global within the Fremont fund family. Overall, the fund family's risk-adjusted performance can be described as good.

Current Income   ★ ★
Over the past year, Fremont Global had a twelve-month yield of 3.4 percent. During this same twelve-month period, the typical balanced fund had a twelve-month yield that averaged 2.6 percent.

Expenses   ★ ★ ★ ★
Fremont Global's expense ratio is 0.9 percent; it has averaged 0.9 percent annually over the past three calendar years. The average expense ratio for the 855 funds in this category is 1.5 percent. This fund's turnover rate over the past year has been 71 percent, while its peer group average has been 103 percent.

Summary
Fremont Global is a solid choice for the balanced investor. The fund does a particularly good job of controlling expenses and reducing risk. This fund has also done a very good job at minimizing taxes for its investors.

Profile
minimum initial investment $2,000	*IRA accounts available* . . . . yes
subsequent minimum investment . . $200	*IRA minimum investment* $1,000
available in all 50 states. . . . . yes	*date of inception* . . . . Nov. 1988
telephone exchanges. . . . . yes	*dividend/income paid* . . . . quarterly
number of other funds in family 6	*quality of annual reports* . . . . good

Greenspring

Greenspring Fund
2330 West Joppa Road, Suite 110
Lutherville, MD 21093-4641
(800) 366-3863

total return	★ ★ ★ ★
risk reduction	★ ★ ★ ★
management	★ ★ ★ ★ ★
current income	★ ★ ★
expense control	★ ★ ★ ★
symbol GRSPX	20 points
up-market performance	poor
down-market performance	excellent
predictability of returns	very good

Total Return

Over the past five years, Greenspring has taken $10,000 and turned it into $21,920 ($16,470 over three years and $30,890 over the past ten years). This translates into an average annual return of 17 percent over the past five years, 18 percent over the past three years, and 12 percent for the decade. Over the past five years, this fund has outperformed 75 percent of all mutual funds; within its general category it has done better than 90 percent of its peers. Balanced funds have averaged 12 percent annually over these same five years.

During the past five years, a $10,000 initial investment grew to $18,850 after taxes, assuming a 39.6 percent income tax bracket (state and federal combined) and a capital gains rate of 28 percent. This means that investors in this fund were able to preserve 82 percent of their total returns. Compared to other fixed-income funds, this fund offers tax savings that are considered very good. Compared to other equity funds, its tax savings are very good.

Risk/Volatility

Over the past five years, Greenspring has been safer than 81 percent of all balanced funds. Over the past decade, the fund has had one negative year, as has the S&P 500 (off 3 percent in 1990) and the Lehman Brothers Aggregate Bond Index (off 3 percent in 1994). The fund has underperformed the S&P 500 six times and the Lehman Brothers Aggregate Bond Index twice in the last ten years.

	last 5 years		last 10 years	
worst year	3%	1994	-6%	1990
best year	23%	1996	23%	1996

In the past, Greenspring has done better than just 15 percent of its peer group in up markets but outperformed 85 percent of its competition in down markets. Consistency, or predictability, of returns for Greenspring can be described as very good.

Management   ★ ★ ★ ★ ★

There are sixty stocks and ten fixed-income securities in this $130 million port-folio. The average balanced fund today is $390 million in size. Close to 61 percent of the fund's holdings are in stocks and 19 percent in bonds. The stocks in this port-folio have an average price-earnings (p/e) ratio of 20 and a median market capital-ization of $420 million. The average maturity of the bonds in this account is four years; the weighted coupon rate averages 7.5 percent. The portfolio's equity hold-ings can be categorized as small-cap and value-oriented issues. The portfolio's fixed-income holdings can be categorized as short-term, high-quality debt.

Charles K. Carlson has managed this fund for the past ten years. There are no other funds within the Greenspring family. Overall, the fund's risk-adjusted per-formance can be described as very good.

Current Income   ★ ★ ★

Over the past year, Greenspring had a twelve-month yield of 3.4 percent. During this same twelve-month period, the typical balanced fund had a twelve-month yield that averaged 2.6 percent.

Expenses   ★ ★ ★ ★

Greenspring's expense ratio is 1.0 percent; it has averaged 1.1 percent annually over the past three calendar years. The average expense ratio for the 855 funds in this category is 1.5 percent. This fund's turnover rate over the past year has been 61 percent, while its peer group average has been 103 percent.

Summary

Greenspring is one of only two funds within its large category to have excellent management. It is also the number one total points earner. When you consider that the fund is competing against 854 other funds within its grouping, the praise is even stronger. Hopefully the management company will add other funds to this orphan family.

Profile

minimum initial investment $2,000	*IRA accounts available* . . . . yes
subsequent minimum investment . . $100	*IRA minimum investment* $1,000
available in all 50 states. . . . . yes	*date of inception* . . . . July 1983
telephone exchanges . . . . no	*dividend/income paid* . . . semi-annually
number of other funds in family. 0	*quality of annual reports* . . . . good

Income Fund of America

American Funds Group
333 South Hope Street
Los Angeles, CA 90071
(800) 421-4120

total return	★ ★ ★
risk reduction	★ ★ ★
management	★ ★ ★
current income	★ ★ ★ ★ ★
expense control	★ ★ ★ ★ ★
symbol AMECX	19 points
up-market performance	excellent
down-market performance	poor
predictability of returns	excellent

Total Return

Over the past five years, Income Fund of America has taken $10,000 and turned it into $19,250 ($16,590 over three years and $31,870 over the past ten years). This translates into an average annual return of 14 percent over the past five years, 18 percent over the past three years, and 12 percent for the decade. Over the past five years, this fund has outperformed 65 percent of all mutual funds; within its general category it has done better than 70 percent of its peers. Balanced funds have averaged 12 percent annually over these same five years.

During the past five years, a $10,000 initial investment grew to $16,750 after taxes, assuming a 39.6 percent income tax bracket (state and federal combined) and a capital gains rate of 28 percent. This means that investors in this fund were able to preserve 78 percent of their total returns. Compared to other fixed-income funds, this fund offers tax savings that are considered good. Compared to other equity funds, its tax savings are good.

Risk/Volatility

Over the past five years, Income Fund of America has been safer than 80 percent of all balanced funds. Over the past decade, the fund has had two negative years, while the S&P 500 has had one (off 3 percent in 1990); the Lehman Brothers Aggregate Bond Index also fell once (off 3 percent in 1994). The fund has underperformed the S&P 500 seven times and the Lehman Brothers Aggregate Bond Index twice in the last ten years.

	last 5 years		last 10 years	
worst year	-3%	1994	-3%	1990
best year	29%	1995	29%	1995

In the past, Income Fund of America has done better than 85 percent of its peer group in up markets but only 15 percent of its competition in down markets.

Consistency, or predictability, of returns for Income Fund of America can be described as excellent.

Management   ★ ★ ★
There are 150 stocks and 570 fixed-income securities in this $17.9 billion portfolio. The average balanced fund today is $390 million in size. Close to 62 percent of the fund's holdings are in stocks and 25 percent in bonds. The stocks in this portfolio have an average price-earnings (p/e) ratio of 19 and a median market capitalization of $13.1 billion. The average life of the bonds in this account is six years; the weighted coupon rate averages 7.5 percent. The portfolio's equity holdings can be categorized as large-cap and value-oriented issues. The portfolio's fixed-income holdings can be categorized as intermediate-term, medium-quality debt.

A management team has overseen this fund since its 1973 inception. There are twenty-four funds besides Income Fund of America within the American Funds Group. Overall, the fund family's risk-adjusted performance can be described as good.

Current Income   ★ ★ ★ ★ ★
Over the past year, Income Fund of America had a twelve-month yield of 4.9 percent. During this same twelve-month period, the typical balanced fund had a twelve-month yield that averaged 2.6 percent.

Expenses   ★ ★ ★ ★ ★
Income Fund of America's expense ratio is 0.6 percent; it has averaged 0.6 percent annually over the past three calendar years. The average expense ratio for the 855 funds in this category is 1.5 percent. This fund's turnover rate over the past year has been 38 percent, while its peer group average has been 103 percent.

Summary
Income Fund of America is just one of several offerings by the American Funds Group to make this book and all other previous editions. This member of the American Funds is one of the top total point earners among all other balanced portfolios. The fund does a good job in every area but clearly excels when it comes to current income, expense control, and low turnover (which is not reflected in any fund's expense ratio). You can never go wrong with this fund, or a large number of other funds offered by American.

Profile
minimum initial investment $1,000	IRA accounts available . . . . yes
subsequent minimum investment . . . $50	IRA minimum investment $250
available in all 50 states. . . . . yes	date of inception. . . . . Dec. 1973
telephone exchanges. . . . . yes	dividend/income paid . . . . quarterly
number of other funds in family 24	quality of annual reports . . . . excellent

Merrill Lynch Global Allocation B

Merrill Lynch Group
Box 9011
Princeton, NJ 08543-9011
(800) 637-3863

total return	★ ★ ★
risk reduction	★ ★ ★ ★ ★
management	★ ★ ★ ★
current income	★ ★ ★
expense control	★ ★
symbol MBLOX	17 points
up-market performance	good
down-market performance	very good
predictability of returns	excellent

Total Return   ★ ★ ★
Over the past five years, Merrill Lynch Global Allocation B has taken $10,000 and turned it into $18,420 ($14,910 over three years). This translates into an average annual return of 13 percent over the past five years and 14 percent over the past three years. Over the past five years, this fund has outperformed 60 percent of all mutual funds; within its general category it has also done better than 60 percent of its peers. Balanced funds have averaged 12 percent annually over these same five years.

During the past five years, a $10,000 initial investment grew to $16,550 after taxes, assuming a 39.6 percent income tax bracket (state and federal combined) and a capital gains rate of 28 percent. This means that investors in this fund were able to preserve 81 percent of their total returns. Compared to other fixed-income funds, this fund offers tax savings that are considered very good. Compared to other equity funds, its tax savings are very good.

Risk/Volatility   ★ ★ ★ ★ ★
Over the past five years, Merrill Lynch Global Allocation B has been safer than 87 percent of all balanced funds. Over the past decade, the fund has had one negative year, as has the S&P 500 (off 3 percent in 1990) and the Lehman Brothers Aggregate Bond Index (off 3 percent in 1994). The fund has underperformed the S&P 500 four times and the Lehman Brothers Aggregate Bond Index once in the last seven years.

	last 5 years		last 7 years	
worst year	-3%	1994	-3%	1994
best year	22%	1995	27%	1991

In the past, Merrill Lynch Global Allocation B has done better than 50 percent of its peer group in up markets and outperformed 75 percent of its competition in down markets. Consistency, or predictability, of returns for Merrill Lynch Global Allocation B can be described as excellent.

Management   ★ ★ ★ ★

There are 360 stocks and 180 fixed-income securities in this $9.6 billion portfolio. The average balanced fund today is $390 million in size. Close to 32 percent of the fund's holdings are in stocks and 35 percent in bonds. The stocks in this portfolio have an average price-earnings (p/e) ratio of 25 and a median market capitalization of $4.9 billion. The portfolio's equity holdings can be categorized as mid-cap and value-oriented issues.

Ison and Stattman have managed this fund for the past five years. There are 287 funds besides Global Allocation B within the Merrill Lynch fund family. Overall, the fund family's risk-adjusted performance can be described as fair.

Current Income   ★ ★ ★

Over the past year, Merrill Lynch Global Allocation B had a twelve-month yield of 4.5 percent. During this same twelve-month period, the typical balanced fund had a twelve-month yield that averaged 2.6 percent.

Expenses   ★ ★

Merrill Lynch Global Allocation B's expense ratio is 1.9 percent; it has averaged 1.9 percent annually over the past three calendar years. The average expense ratio for the 855 funds in this category is 1.5 percent. This fund's turnover rate over the past year has been 51 percent, while its peer group average has been 103 percent.

Summary

Merrill Lynch Global Allocation B is one of the very best choices for the balanced investor who wants great protection during a bear market plus overall safety. This fund excels when it comes to risk reduction. The fund also does a very good job when it comes to tax minimization—something the balanced or multi-asset investor should more carefully review.

Profile

minimum initial investment $1,000	*IRA accounts available* . . . . yes
subsequent minimum investment . . . $50	*IRA minimum investment* $100
available in all 50 states. . . . . yes	*date of inception* . . . . Feb. 1989
telephone exchanges . . . . no	*dividend/income paid* . . . . annually
number of other funds in family 287	*quality of annual reports* . . . . good

Oppenheimer Bond for Growth M

Oppenheimer Funds
P.O. Box 5270
Denver, CO 80217-5270
(800) 525-7048

total return	★ ★ ★ ★
risk reduction	★ ★ ★
management	★ ★ ★
current income	★ ★ ★ ★
expense control	★ ★ ★
symbol RCVGX	17 points
up-market performance	excellent
down-market performance	very good
predictability of returns	good

Total Return

Over the past five years, Oppenheimer Bond for Growth M has taken $10,000 and turned it into $21,920 ($15,240 over three years and $27,440 over the past ten years). This translates into an average annual return of 17 percent over the past five years, 15 percent over the past three years, and 11 percent for the decade. Over the past five years, this fund has outperformed 80 percent of all mutual funds; within its general category it has done better than 90 percent of its peers. Balanced funds have averaged 12 percent annually over these same five years.

During the past five years, a $10,000 initial investment grew to $18,940 after taxes, assuming a 39.6 percent income tax bracket (state and federal combined) and a capital gains rate of 28 percent. This means that investors in this fund were able to preserve 82 percent of their total returns. Compared to other fixed-income funds, this fund offers tax savings that are considered very good. Compared to other equity funds, its tax savings are very good.

Risk/Volatility

Over the past five years, Oppenheimer Bond for Growth M has only been safer than 36 percent of all balanced funds. Over the past decade, the fund has had three negative years, while the S&P 500 has had one (off 3 percent in 1990); the Lehman Brothers Aggregate Bond Index also fell once (off 3 percent in 1994). The fund has underperformed the S&P 500 eight times and the Lehman Brothers Aggregate Bond Index three times in the last ten years.

	last 5 years		last 10 years	
worst year	-1%	1994	-9%	1987
best year	31%	1992	31%	1992

In the past, Oppenheimer Bond for Growth M has done better than 85 percent of its peer group in up markets and outperformed 65 percent of its competition in down markets. Consistency, or predictability, of returns for Bond for Growth can be described as good.

Management
There are eight common, forty-six convertible preferred, and 126 fixed-income securities in this $790 million portfolio. The average balanced fund today is $390 million in size. Close to 95 percent of the fund's holdings are in convertibles. The convertible bonds in this portfolio have an average maturity of seven years; the weighted coupon rate averages 4.4 percent. The portfolio's fixed-income holdings can be categorized as intermediate-term, medium-quality debt.

Michael S. Rosen has managed this fund for the past eleven years. There are sixty-three funds besides Bond for Growth M within the Oppenheimer fund family. Overall, the fund family's risk-adjusted performance can be described as good.

Current Income   ★ ★ ★ ★
Over the past year, Oppenheimer Bond for Growth M had a twelve-month yield of 4.8 percent. During this same twelve-month period, the typical balanced fund had a twelve-month yield that averaged 2.6 percent.

Expenses
Oppenheimer Bond for Growth M's expense ratio is 1.5 percent; it has averaged 1.6 percent annually over the past three calendar years. The average expense ratio for the 855 funds in this category is 1.5 percent. This fund's turnover rate over the past year has been 53 percent, while its peer group average has been 103 percent.

Summary
Oppenheimer Bond for Growth M is consistent across the board. It performs well or very well in every single rated category. The fund's tax savings are also quite good. This is part of a very large fund family that has several other recommended offerings.

Profile

minimum initial investment $1,000	*IRA accounts available* . . . . yes
subsequent minimum investment . . . $25	*IRA minimum investment* $250
available in all 50 states. . . . . yes	*date of inception.* . . . . June 1986
telephone exchanges. . . . . yes	*dividend/income paid* . . . . quarterly
number of other funds in family. 63	*quality of annual reports* . . . . good

Putnam Convertible Income-Growth A

Putnam Funds
One Post Office Square
Boston, MA 02109
(800) 225-1581

total return	★ ★ ★ ★
risk reduction	★ ★ ★
management	★ ★ ★
current income	★ ★ ★
expense control	★ ★ ★ ★
symbol PCONX	17 points
up-market performance	excellent
down-market performance	poor
predictability of returns	good

Total Return ★ ★ ★ ★

Over the past five years, Putnam Convertible Income-Growth A has taken $10,000 and turned it into $21,000 ($16,410 over three years and $28,520 over the past ten years). This translates into an average annual return of 16 percent over the past five years, 18 percent over the past three years, and 11 percent for the decade. Over the past five years, this fund has outperformed 75 percent of all mutual funds; within its general category it has done better than 85 percent of its peers. Balanced funds have averaged 12 percent annually over these same five years.

During the past five years, a $10,000 initial investment grew to $17,790 after taxes, assuming a 39.6 percent income tax bracket (state and federal combined) and a capital gains rate of 28 percent. This means that investors in this fund were able to preserve 78 percent of their total returns. Compared to other fixed-income funds, this fund offers tax savings that are considered good. Compared to other equity funds, its tax savings are good.

Risk/Volatility ★ ★ ★

Over the past five years, Putnam Convertible Income-Growth A has been safer than 55 percent of all balanced funds. Over the past decade, the fund has had three negative years, while the S&P 500 has had one (off 3 percent in 1990); the Lehman Brothers Aggregate Bond Index also fell once (off 3 percent in 1994). The fund has underperformed the S&P 500 eight times and the Lehman Brothers Aggregate Bond Index twice in the last ten years.

	last 5 years		last 10 years	
worst year	-2%	1994	-10%	1990
best year	24%	1995	29%	1991

In the past, Putnam Convertible Income-Growth A has done better than 80 percent of its peer group in up markets but only 10 percent of its competition in down markets. Consistency, or predictability, of returns for Putnam Convertible Income-Growth A can be described as good.

Management   ★ ★ ★

There are 170 stocks and 130 fixed-income securities in this $1.1 billion portfolio. The average balanced fund today is $390 million in size. Close to two thirds of the fund's holdings are in convertibles; most of the balance is in stocks. The convertible bonds in the portfolio can be described as just below investment grade. The stocks in this portfolio have an average price-earnings (p/e) ratio of 22 and a median market capitalization of $16.2 billion. The portfolio's equity holdings can be categorized as large-cap and value-oriented issues.

Edward T. Shadek and Charles G. Pohl manage this fund; Pohl since October 1992, Shadek since May, 1997. There are 120 funds besides Convertible Income-Growth A within the Putnam fund family. Overall, the fund family's risk-adjusted performance can be described as good.

Current Income   ★ ★ ★

Over the past year, Putnam Convertible Income-Growth A had a twelve-month yield of 4.1 percent. During this same twelve-month period, the typical balanced fund had a twelve-month yield that averaged 2.6 percent.

Expenses   ★ ★ ★ ★

Putnam Convertible Income-Growth A's expense ratio is 1.1 percent; it has averaged 1.1 percent annually over the past three calendar years. The average expense ratio for the 855 funds in this category is 1.5 percent. This fund's turnover rate over the past year has been 61 percent, while its peer group average has been 103 percent.

Summary

Putnam Convertible Income-Growth A often gets no respect because it is a convertible securities fund; part of an unglamorous universe. Yet, this Putnam offering is one of the very best choices available for investors who can not decide between stocks and bonds (or what percentage of their holdings should be in each general category). The Putnam family of mutual funds has received a great deal of richly deserved positive publicity over the past year. Such favorable reviews are expected to continue for at least the next several years. The group is on a roll.

Profile

minimum initial investment $500	*IRA accounts available* .... yes
subsequent minimum investment ... $50	*IRA minimum investment* $250
available in all 50 states. .... yes	*date of inception*. .... June 1972
telephone exchanges. .... yes	*dividend/income paid* .... quarterly
number of other funds in family. ... 120	*quality of annual reports* .... good

SoGen International

SoGen Funds
1221 Avenue of the Americas, 8th Floor
New York, NY 10020
(800) 334-2143

total return	★ ★ ★
risk reduction	★ ★ ★ ★ ★
management	★ ★ ★ ★
current income	★ ★
expense control	★ ★ ★ ★
symbol SGENX	18 points
up-market performance	good
down-market performance	excellent
predictability of returns	excellent

Total Return   ★ ★ ★

Over the past five years, SoGen International has taken $10,000 and turned it into $19,250 ($14,590 over three years and $29,570 over the past ten years). This translates into an average annual return of 14 percent over the past five years, 13 percent over the past three years, and 11 percent for the decade. Over the past five years, this fund has outperformed 65 percent of all mutual funds; within its general category it has done better than 65 percent of its peers. Balanced funds have averaged 12 percent annually over these same five years.

During the past five years, a $10,000 initial investment grew to $17,580 after taxes, assuming a 39.6 percent income tax bracket (state and federal combined) and a capital gains rate of 28 percent. This means that investors in this fund were able to preserve 87 percent of their total returns. Compared to other fixed-income funds, this fund offers tax savings that are considered excellent. Compared to other equity funds, its tax savings are very good.

Risk/Volatility   ★ ★ ★ ★ ★

Over the past five years, SoGen International has been safer than 88 percent of all balanced funds. Over the past decade, the fund has had one negative year, as has the S&P 500 (off 3 percent in 1990) and the Lehman Brothers Aggregate Bond Index (off 3 percent in 1994). The fund has underperformed the S&P 500 five times and the Lehman Brothers Aggregate Bond Index twice in the last ten years.

	last 5 years		last 10 years	
worst year	3%	1994	-1%	1990
best year	26%	1993	26%	1993

In the past, SoGen International has done better than 55 percent of its peer group in up markets and outperformed 90 percent of its competition in down markets. Consistency, or predictability, of returns for SoGen International can be described as excellent.

Management   ★ ★ ★ ★

There are 350 stocks and 130 fixed-income securities in this $4.2 billion portfolio. The average balanced fund today is $390 million in size. Close to 58 percent of the fund's holdings are in stocks and 13 percent in bonds. The stocks in this portfolio have an average price-earnings (p/e) ratio of 25 and a median market capitalization of $1.3 billion. The portfolio's equity holdings can be categorized as small-cap and value-oriented issues.

Jean-Marie Eveillard has managed this fund for the past eighteen years; Charles de Vaulx and Elizabeth Tobin have been part of the investment management team since 1986. There are two funds besides International within the SoGen Funds fund family. Overall, the fund family's risk-adjusted performance can be described as good.

Current Income   ★ ★

Over the past year, SoGen International had a twelve-month yield of 3.7 percent. During this same twelve-month period, the typical balanced fund had a twelve-month yield that averaged 2.6 percent.

Expenses   ★ ★ ★ ★

SoGen International's expense ratio is 1.2 percent; it has averaged 1.25 percent annually over the past three calendar years. The average expense ratio for the 855 funds in this category is 1.5 percent. This fund's turnover rate over the past year has been 10 percent, while its peer group average has been 103 percent.

Summary

SoGen International is a fund that has appeared in numerous previous editions of this book. It is one of the few funds that you can buy and forget about; the longer you own the fund, the more you will like it. The fund's manager, Eveillard, never seems to like the stock market, whether it is going up, down, or sideways. Yet, the fund's long-term performance when compared to any yardstick is exceptional. The manager's defensive nature has paid off in the past and should continue to do so in the future. This is somewhat of a misunderstood portfolio since there is no universal agreement as to whether it should be categorized as a foreign, global, or multi-asset fund. But there is no disagreement when it comes to the praise this fund has enjoyed for a number of years.

Profile

minimum initial investment $1,000	*IRA accounts available* . . . . yes
subsequent minimum investment . . $100	*IRA minimum investment* $1,000
available in all 50 states. . . . . yes	*date of inception* . . . . April 1970
telephone exchanges. . . . . yes	*dividend/income paid* . . . . annually
number of other funds in family. 2	*quality of annual reports* . . . . good

Corporate Bond Funds

Traditionally, bond funds are held by investors who require high current income and low risk. Interest income is normally paid on a monthly basis. Corporate bond funds are made up primarily of bonds issued by domestic corporations; government securities often represent a moderate part of these funds. Portfolio composition is almost always exclusively U.S. issues.

Bonds are normally purchased because of their income stream; one's principal in a bond fund fluctuates. The major influence on bond prices, and therefore the value of the fund's shares, is interest rates. There is an *inverse* relationship between interest rates and bond values; whatever one does, the other does the opposite. If interest rates rise, the price per share of a bond fund will fall, and vice versa.

The amount of appreciation or loss of a corporate bond fund primarily depends upon the average maturity of the bonds in the portfolio; the cumulative amount of interest rate movement and the typical yield of the bonds in the fund's portfolio are distant secondary concerns. *Short-term* bond funds, made up of debt instruments with an average maturity of five years or less, are subject to very little interest rate risk or reward. *Medium-term* bond funds, with maturities averaging between six and ten years, are subject to one-third to one-half the risk level of long-term funds. A long-term corporate bond fund will average an 8-percent increase or decrease in share price for every cumulative 1-percent change in interest rates.

Often investors can tell what kind of corporate bond fund they are purchasing by its name. Unless the fund includes the term "short" in its title, chances are that it is a medium- or long-term bond fund. Investors would be wise to contact the fund or counsel with an investment advisor to learn more about the portfolio's average maturity; most bond funds will dramatically reduce their portfolio's average maturity during periods of interest-rate uncertainty.

The average weighted maturity for the bonds in these funds is just over eight years, the average coupon rate is 7.5 percent, and the average weighted price is $1,010 (meaning that the bonds are worth $10 more than face value, on average). A price, or value, of par ($1,000 per bond) means that the bonds in a portfolio are worth face value and are not currently being traded at a discount (a price less than $1,000 per bond) or at a premium (some figure above $1,000). The portfolio of the "average" corporate bond fund is made up of securities purchased at a $10-per-bond premium ($1,010 vs. $1,000 for bonds bought at face value). A portfolio manager purchases bonds at a premium for one of two reasons: to increase the portfolio's current income, or to decrease the fund's volatility slightly (the higher the coupon rate, the less susceptible a bond is to the effects of interest-rate changes).

During the past five and ten years, corporate bond funds have underperformed the Lehman Brothers Aggregate Bond Index by 0.5 percent per year. Over the last three years the gap widens to a little over 1 percent. Average turnover during the last three years has been 145 percent, a surprisingly high figure given the general belief that stocks are traded (turned over) much more frequently than bonds. (The typical growth fund has a turnover rate of 95 percent annually.) The average corporate bond fund throws off an annual income stream of 6 percent. The typical annual expense ratio for this group is about 1 percent.

Over the past fifteen years, *individual* corporate bonds have underperformed common stocks by over 3 percent per year. From 1982 to 1997, long-term corporate bonds averaged 13.7 percent compounded per year, compared to 16.8 percent for common stocks and 14.4 percent for small stocks. A $10,000 investment in corporate bonds grew to $68,200 over the past fifteen years; a similar initial investment in common stocks grew to $102,600 and $75,300 for small stocks.

Over the past half century, corporate bonds have only outpaced inflation on a pre-tax basis. A dollar invested in corporate bonds in 1947 grew to $19.53 by the end of 1996. This translates into an average compound return of 5.8 percent per year. During this same period, $1 inflated to $7.91; this translates into an average annual inflation rate of 4.1 percent. Over the past fifty years, the worst year for long-term corporate bonds, on a *total return* basis (yield plus or minus principal appreciation or loss), was 1969, when a loss of 8 percent was suffered. The best year so far has been 1982, when corporate bonds posted a gain of 43 percent.

Over 700 funds make up the corporate bonds category. Total market capitalization of this category is $135 billion. Over the past three and five years, corporate bond funds have had an average compound return of 7 percent per year. For the decade, *corporate bond funds* have averaged 8 percent per year and 11 percent per annum for the past fifteen years. All of these figures represent total returns. This means that bond appreciation (or depreciation) was added (or subtracted) from current yield.

The standard deviation for corporate bond funds has been 4 percent over the past three years. As you may recall, a low standard deviation means a greater predictability of returns (fewer surprises—for better or worse). If a fund, or fund category, such as corporate bonds, has an average annual return of 10 percent and a standard deviation of 4 percent, this means that returns for every two out of three years should be roughly 10 percent, + or − 4 percent (one standard deviation). If you want to increase certainty of returns, then you must look at *two* standard deviations. This means that returns, for about 95 percent of the time, would be 10 percent + or − 8 percent (or +2 percent to +18 percent). These funds have been less volatile than any equity fund and have shown similar return variances (volatility) as government bond funds.

Corporate Bond Funds

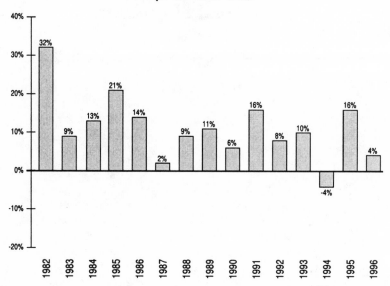

Bond Fund of America

American Funds Group
333 South Hope Street
Los Angeles, CA 90071
(800) 421-4120

total return	★ ★ ★ ★
risk reduction	★ ★ ★
management	★ ★ ★
current income	★ ★ ★ ★ ★
expense control	★ ★ ★ ★ ★
symbol ABNDX	20 points
up-market performance	excellent
down-market performance	poor
predictability of returns	good

Total Return   ★ ★ ★ ★

Over the past five years, Bond Fund of America has taken $10,000 and turned it into $15,390 ($13,140 over three years and $24,380 over the past ten years). This translates into an average annual return of 9 percent over the past five years, 10 percent over the past three years, and 9 percent for the decade. Over the past five years, this fund has outperformed 45 percent of all mutual funds; within its general category it has done better than 90 percent of its peers. Corporate bond funds have averaged 7 percent annually over these same five years.

During the past five years, a $10,000 initial investment grew to $12,940 after taxes, assuming a 39.6 percent income tax bracket (state and federal combined) and a capital gains rate of 28 percent. This means that investors in this fund were able to preserve 62 percent of their total returns. Compared to other fixed-income funds, this fund offers tax savings that are considered fair.

Risk/Volatility   ★ ★ ★

Over the past five years, Bond Fund of America has been safer than 43 percent of all corporate bond funds. Over the past decade, the fund has had one negative year, as has the Lehman Brothers Aggregate Bond Index (off 3 percent in 1994). The fund has underperformed the Lehman Brothers Aggregate Bond Index and the Lehman Brothers Corporate Bond Index five times in the last ten years.

	last 5 years		last 10 years	
worst year	-5%	1994	-5%	1994
best year	18%	1995	21%	1991

In the past, Bond Fund of America has done better than 95 percent of its peer group in up markets but virtually none of its competition in down markets. Consistency, or predictability, of returns for Bond Fund of America can be described as good.

Management   ★ ★ ★

There are 880 fixed-income securities in this $7.3 billion portfolio. The average corporate bond fund today is $170 million in size. Close to 82 percent of the fund's holdings are in bonds. The stocks in this portfolio have an average price-earnings (p/e) ratio of 17 and a median market capitalization of $12.6 billion. The average maturity of the bonds in this account is six years; the weighted coupon rate averages 8.0 percent. The portfolio's equity holdings can be categorized as large-cap and value-oriented stocks. The portfolio's fixed-income holdings can be categorized as intermediate-term, high-quality debt.

A management team has overseen this fund for the past thirteen years. There are twenty-four funds besides Bond Fund of America within the American Funds Group. Overall, the fund family's risk-adjusted performance can be described as good.

Current Income   ★ ★ ★ ★ ★

Over the past year, Bond Fund of America had a twelve-month yield of 7.3 percent. During this same twelve-month period, the typical corporate bond fund had a twelve-month yield that averaged 6.0 percent.

Expenses   ★ ★ ★ ★ ★

Bond Fund of America's expense ratio is 0.7 percent; it has averaged 0.7 percent annually over the past three calendar years. The average expense ratio for the 700 funds in this category is 1.0 percent. This fund's turnover rate over the past year has been 43 percent, while its peer group average has been 146 percent.

Summary

Bond Fund of America is the number one corporate bond fund for current income. Part of the reason this fund has such good numbers is due to very low expenses. Overall, the fund's rankings range from good to exceptional. This is another member of the American Funds Group that appears in this book as well as previous editions.

Profile

minimum initial investment $1,000	*IRA accounts available* . . . . yes
subsequent minimum investment . . . $50	*IRA minimum investment* $250
available in all 50 states. . . . . yes	*date of inception*. . . . . May 1974
telephone exchanges. . . . . yes	*dividend/income paid*. . . . . monthly
number of other funds in family 24	*quality of annual reports* . . . . excellent

FPA New Income

FPA Funds
11400 West Olympic Boulevard, Suite 1200
Los Angeles, CA 90064
(800) 982-4372

total return	★ ★ ★ ★
risk reduction	★ ★ ★ ★ ★
management	★ ★ ★ ★ ★
current income	★ ★ ★
expense control	★ ★ ★ ★ ★
symbol FPNIX	22 points
up-market performance	excellent
down-market performance	poor
predictability of returns	very good

Total Return   ★ ★ ★ ★

Over the past five years, FPA New Income has taken $10,000 and turned it into $14,690 ($12,940 over three years and $25,840 over the past ten years). This translates into an average annual return of 8 percent over the past five years, 9 percent over the past three years, and 10 percent for the decade. Over the past five years, this fund has outperformed 45 percent of all mutual funds; within its general category it has done better than 90 percent of its peers. Corporate bond funds have averaged 7 percent annually over these same five years.

During the past five years, a $10,000 initial investment grew to $13,210 after taxes, assuming a 39.6 percent income tax bracket (state and federal combined) and a capital gains rate of 28 percent. This means that investors in this fund were able to preserve 66 percent of their total returns. Compared to other fixed-income funds, this fund offers tax savings that are considered good.

Risk/Volatility   ★ ★ ★ ★ ★

Over the past five years, FPA New Income has been safer than 84 percent of all corporate bond funds. Over the past decade, the fund has had no negative years, while the Lehman Brothers Aggregate Bond Index has had one (off 3 percent in 1994). The fund has underperformed the Lehman Brothers Aggregate Bond Index three times and the Lehman Brothers Corporate Bond Index four times in the last ten years.

	last 5 years		last 10 years	
worst year	1%	1994	1%	1994
best year	14%	1995	19%	1991

In the past, FPA New Income has done better than 90 percent of its peer group in up markets but virtually none of its competition in down markets. Consistency, or predictability, of returns for FPA New Income can be described as very good.

Management   ★ ★ ★ ★ ★
There are seventy fixed-income securities in this $450 million portfolio. The average corporate bond fund today is $170 million in size. Close to 70 percent of the fund's holdings are in bonds. The portfolio's fixed-income holdings can be categorized as intermediate-term, high-quality debt.

Robert L. Rodriguez has managed this fund for the past thirteen years. There are three funds besides New Income within the FPA fund family. Overall, the fund family's risk-adjusted performance can be described as very good.

Current Income   ★ ★ ★
Over the past year, FPA New Income had a twelve-month yield of 6.1 percent. During this same twelve-month period, the typical corporate bond fund had a twelve-month yield that averaged 6.0 percent.

Expenses   ★ ★ ★ ★ ★
FPA New Income's expense ratio is 0.6 percent; it has averaged 0.7 percent annually over the past three calendar years. The average expense ratio for the 700 funds in this category is 1.0 percent. This fund's turnover rate over the past year has been 16 percent, while its peer group average has been 146 percent.

Summary
FPA New Income is the overall number one corporate bond fund. The fund is strong in every measured category. It excels in controlling expenses (none of its peers has lower operating costs), safety, and mangement. FPA is a small fund family that has other offerings that should also be considered.

Profile
minimum initial investment $1,500	*IRA accounts available* . . . . yes
subsequent minimum investment . . $100	*IRA minimum investment* $100
available in all 50 states. . . . . yes	*date of inception* . . . . April 1969
telephone exchanges. . . . . yes	*dividend/income paid* . . . . quarterly
number of other funds in family 3	*quality of annual reports* . . . . good

IDS Bond A

IDS Group
IDS Tower 10
Minneapolis, MN 55440-0010
(800) 328-8300

total return	★ ★ ★ ★ ★
risk reduction	★
management	★ ★
current income	★ ★ ★ ★
expense control	★ ★ ★ ★ ★
symbol INBNX	17 points
up-market performance	very good
down-market performance	good
predictability of returns	fair

Total Return   ★ ★ ★ ★ ★

Over the past five years, IDS Bond A has taken $10,000 and turned it into $15,390 ($13,420 over three years and $24,760 over the past ten years). This translates into an average annual return of 9 percent over the past five years, 10 percent over the past three years, and 9 percent for the decade. Over the past five years, this fund has outperformed 50 percent of all mutual funds; within its general category it has done better than 95 percent of its peers. Corporate bond funds have averaged 7 percent annually over these same five years.

During the past five years, a $10,000 initial investment grew to $13,400 after taxes, assuming a 39.6 percent income tax bracket (state and federal combined) and a capital gains rate of 28 percent. This means that investors in this fund were able to preserve 65 percent of their total returns. Compared to other fixed-income funds, this fund offers tax savings that are considered good.

Risk/Volatility   ★

Over the past five years, IDS Bond A has been safer than 21 percent of all corporate bond funds. Over the past decade, the fund has had two negative years, while the Lehman Brothers Aggregate Bond Index has had one (off 3 percent in 1994). The fund has underperformed the Lehman Brothers Aggregate Bond Index four times and the Lehman Brothers Corporate Bond Index five times in the last ten years.

	last 5 years		last 10 years	
worst year	-4%	1994	-4%	1994
best year	22%	1995	22%	1995

In the past, IDS Bond A has done better than 60 percent of its peer group in up markets and outperformed 50 percent of its competition in down markets. Consistency, or predictability, of returns for IDS Bond A can be described as fair.

Management   ★ ★

There are 310 fixed-income securities in this $2.6 billion portfolio. The average corporate bond fund today is $170 million in size. Close to 84 percent of the fund's holdings are in bonds. The average maturity of the bonds in this account is thirteen years; the weighted coupon rate averages 8.5 percent. The portfolio's fixed-income holdings can be categorized as long-term, high-quality debt.

Frederick Quirsfeld has managed this fund for the past twelve years. There are twenty-nine funds besides Bond A within the IDS Group. Overall, the fund family's risk-adjusted performance can be described as fair.

Current Income   ★ ★ ★ ★

Over the past year, IDS Bond A had a twelve-month yield of 6.9 percent. During this same twelve-month period, the typical corporate bond fund had a twelve-month yield that averaged 6.0 percent.

Expenses   ★ ★ ★ ★ ★

IDS Bond A's expense ratio is 0.8 percent; it has averaged 0.7 percent annually over the past three calendar years. The average expense ratio for the 700 funds in this category is 1.0 percent. This fund's turnover rate over the past year has been 43 percent, while its peer group average has been 146 percent.

Summary

IDS Bond A ties for number one when it comes to sheer performance. This corporate bond fund will not disappoint the total return investor or anyone interested in just current income. Part of the fund's great numbers is because management has been very disciplined about controlling costs.

Profile

minimum initial investment $2,000	*IRA accounts available* . . . . yes
subsequent minimum investment . . $100	*IRA minimum investment* $1
available in all 50 states. . . . . yes	*date of inception* . . . . Sept. 1974
telephone exchanges. . . . . yes	*dividend/income paid*. . . . . monthly
number of other funds in family 29	*quality of annual reports* . . . . good

Ivy Bond A

Ivy/Mackenzie Group of Funds
700 South Federal Highway, Suite 300
Boca Raton, FL 33432
(800) 456-5111

total return	★ ★ ★ ★ ★
risk reduction	★ ★
management	★ ★
current income	★ ★ ★
expense control	★ ★
symbol MCFIX	14 points
up-market performance	excellent
down-market performance	fair
predictability of returns	fair

Total Return   ★ ★ ★ ★ ★
Over the past five years, Ivy Bond A has taken $10,000 and turned it into $15,390 ($13,410 over three years and $26,630 over the past ten years). This translates into an average annual return of 9 percent over the past five years, 10 percent over the past three years, and 10 percent for the decade. Over the past five years, this fund has outperformed 50 percent of all mutual funds; within its general category it has done better than 95 percent of its peers. Corporate bond funds have averaged 7 percent annually over these same five years.

During the past five years, a $10,000 initial investment grew to $13,070 after taxes, assuming a 39.6 percent income tax bracket (state and federal combined) and a capital gains rate of 28 percent. This means that investors in this fund were able to preserve 62 percent of their total returns. Compared to other fixed-income funds, this fund offers tax savings that are considered fair.

Risk/Volatility   ★ ★
Over the past five years, Ivy Bond A has only been safer than 24 percent of all corporate bond funds. Over the past decade, the fund has had one negative year, as has the Lehman Brothers Aggregate Bond Index (off 3 percent in 1994). The fund has underperformed the Lehman Brothers Aggregate Bond Index four times and the Lehman Brothers Corporate Bond Index five times in the last ten years.

	last 5 years		last 10 years	
worst year	-4%	1994	-4%	1994
best year	17%	1995	17%	1995

In the past, Ivy Bond A has done better than 90 percent of its peer group in up markets but only 20 percent of its competition in down markets. Consistency, or predictability, of returns for Ivy Bond A can be described as fair.

Management   ★ ★
There are seventy fixed-income securities in this $100 million portfolio. The average corporate bond fund today is $170 million in size. Close to 100 percent of the fund's holdings are in bonds. The average maturity of the bonds in this account is twelve years; the weighted coupon rate averages 9.0 percent. The portfolio's fixed-income holdings can be categorized as intermediate-term, high-quality debt.

Leslie A. Ferris has managed this fund for the past seven years. There are sixteen funds besides Bond A within the Ivy/Mackenzie Group. Overall, the fund family's risk-adjusted performance can be described as fair.

Current Income   ★ ★ ★
Over the past year, Ivy Bond A had a twelve-month yield of 7.4 percent. During this same twelve-month period, the typical corporate bond fund had a twelve-month yield that averaged 6.0 percent.

Expenses   ★ ★
Ivy Bond A's expense ratio is 1.6 percent; it has averaged 1.5 percent annually over the past three calendar years. The average expense ratio for the 700 funds in this category is 1.0 percent. This fund's turnover rate over the past year has been 90 percent, while its peer group average has been 146 percent.

Summary
Ivy Bond A is the number one performing corporate bond fund over the past decade; it also ties for number one for the past five years. The fund's impressive track record is somewhat offset by its risk level. Still, compared to the universe of mutual funds, this one is more conservative than the great majority.

Profile
minimum initial investment $1,000	*IRA accounts available* . . . . yes
subsequent minimum investment . . $100	*IRA minimum investment* $25
available in all 50 states. . . . . yes	*date of inception* . . . . Sept. 1985
telephone exchanges. . . . . yes	*dividend/income paid.* . . . . monthly
number of other funds in family 16	*quality of annual reports.* . . . . fair

Warburg Pincus Fixed Income

Warburg Pincus Funds
466 Lexington Avenue
New York, NY 10017-3147
(800) 927-2874

total return	★ ★ ★
risk reduction	★ ★ ★ ★
management	★ ★ ★ ★
current income	★ ★ ★
expense control	★ ★ ★
symbol CUFIX	17 points
up-market performance	very good
down-market performance	poor
predictability of returns	very good

Total Return   ★ ★ ★

Over the past five years, Warburg Pincus Fixed Income has taken $10,000 and turned it into $14,690 ($12,880 over three years). This translates into an average annual return of 8 percent over the past five years and 9 percent over the past three years. Over the past five years, this fund has outperformed 45 percent of all mutual funds; within its general category it has done better than 80 percent of its peers. Corporate bond funds have averaged 7 percent annually over these same five years.

During the past five years, a $10,000 initial investment grew to $12,920 after taxes, assuming a 39.6 percent income tax bracket (state and federal combined) and a capital gains rate of 28 percent. This means that investors in this fund were able to preserve 66 percent of their total returns. Compared to other fixed-income funds, this fund offers tax savings that are considered good.

Risk/Volatility   ★ ★ ★ ★

Over the past five years, Warburg Pincus Fixed Income has been safer than 70 percent of all corporate bond funds. Over the past decade, the fund has had one negative year, as has the Lehman Brothers Aggregate Bond Index (off 3 percent in 1994). The fund has underperformed the Lehman Brothers Aggregate Bond Index four times and the Lehman Brothers Corporate Bond Index seven times in the last nine years.

	last 5 years		last 9 years	
worst year	-1%	1994	-1%	1994
best year	15%	1995	17%	1991

In the past, Warburg Pincus Fixed Income has done better than 75 percent of its peer group in up markets but virtually none of its competition in down markets. Consistency, or predictability, of returns for Warburg Pincus Fixed Income can be described as very good.

Management   ★ ★ ★ ★

There are forty fixed-income securities in this $200 million portfolio. The average corporate bond fund today is $170 million in size. Close to 88 percent of the fund's holdings are in bonds. The stocks in this portfolio have an average price-earnings (p/e) ratio of 24 and a median market capitalization of $600 million. The average maturity of the bonds in this account is five years; the weighted coupon rate averages 8.0 percent. The portfolio's equity holdings can be categorized as small-cap and value-oriented stocks. The portfolio's fixed-income holdings can be categorized as intermediate-term, high-quality debt.

Christensen and Van Daalen have managed this fund for the past five years. There are twenty-nine funds besides Fixed Income within the Warburg Pincus fund family. Overall, the fund family's risk-adjusted performance can be described as good.

Current Income   ★ ★ ★

Over the past year, Warburg Pincus Fixed Income had a twelve-month yield of 6.2 percent. During this same twelve-month period, the typical corporate bond fund had a twelve-month yield that averaged 6.0 percent.

Expenses   ★ ★ ★

Warburg Pincus Fixed Income's expense ratio is 0.8 percent; it has averaged 0.8 percent annually over the past three calendar years. The average expense ratio for the 700 funds in this category is 1.0 percent. This fund's turnover rate over the past year has been 194 percent, while its peer group average has been 146 percent.

Summary

Warburg Pincus Fixed Income is solid across the spectrum. It has not disappointed investors, no matter what the criteria. The fund has very good management. Safety is the fund's greatest strength—something almost all corporate bondholders rate as critical.

Profile

minimum initial investment $2,500
subsequent minimum investment . . $100
available in all 50 states. . . . . yes
telephone exchanges. . . . . yes
number of other funds in family 29

IRA accounts available . . . . yes
IRA minimum investment $500
date of inception . . . . Aug. 1987
dividend/income paid. . . . . monthly
quality of annual reports . . . . good

Global Equity Funds

International, also known as "foreign," funds invest only in stocks of foreign companies, while *global funds* invest in both foreign and U.S. stocks. For the purposes of this book, the universe of global equity funds shown encompasses both foreign (international) and world (global) portfolios.

The economic outlook of foreign countries is the major factor in mutual fund management's decision as to which nations and industries are to be favored. A secondary concern is the future anticipated value of the U.S. dollar relative to foreign currencies. A strong or weak dollar can detract or add to an international fund's overall performance. A strong dollar will lower a foreign portfolio's return; a weak dollar will enhance international performance. Trying to gauge the direction of any currency is as difficult as trying to figure out what the U.S. stock market will do tomorrow, next week, or the following year.

Investors who do not wish to be subjected to currency swings may wish to use a fund family that practices currency hedging for their foreign holdings. Currency hedging means that management is buying a kind of insurance policy that pays off in the event of a strong U.S. dollar. Basically, the foreign or international fund that is being hurt by the dollar is making a killing in currency futures contracts. When done properly, the gains in the futures contracts, the insurance policy, offset some, most, or all security losses attributable to a strong dollar. Some people may feel that buying currency contracts is risky business for the fund; it is not.

Like automobile insurance, currency hedging only pays off if there is an accident; that is, if the U.S. dollar increases in value against the currencies represented by the portfolio's securities. If the dollar remains level or decreases in value, so much the better; the foreign securities increase in value and the currency contracts become virtually worthless. The price of these contracts becomes a cost of doing business; as with car insurance, the protection is simply renewed. In the case of a currency contract, the contract expires and a new one is purchased, covering another period of time.

To give you a tangible idea of how important currency hedging is on a *risk-adjusted basis*, consider how foreign and U.S. stock portfolios have fared against each other over the past ten years. U.S. stocks have had a risk level of 16, compared to just over 17 for foreign equities. When currency hedging is added to the foreign portfolio, the international risk level drops to a 13, while the U.S. level remains at 16.

It is wise to consider investing abroad, since different economies experience prosperity and recession at different times. During the 1980s, foreign stocks were the number one performing investment, averaging a compound return of over 22 percent per year, compared to 18 percent for U.S. stocks and 5 percent for residential real estate. But during the past decade, U.S. stocks have outperformed foreign stocks (15.3% vs. 6.6%). Over the past fifteen years (ending 6/30/97), U.S. stocks have had an average compound annual return of 16.8 percent versus 14.6 percent for foreign stocks.

To give you a broader perspective, take a look at how U.S. securities have fared against their foreign counterparts over each of the last twenty-five years.

Why Global Stocks and Bonds Deserve a Place in Every Investor's Portfolio
(The following table shows the total return for each investment category in each of the past twenty-four years.)

Year	U.S. Stocks	U.S. Bonds	Non–U.S. Stocks	Non–U.S. Bonds
1972	+19.0	+ 7.3	+37.4	+ 4.4
1973	−14.6	+ 2.3	−14.2	+ 6.3
1974	−26.5	+ 0.2	−22.1	+ 5.3
1975	+37.2	+12.3	+37.0	+ 8.8
1976	+24.0	+15.6	+ 3.8	+10.5
1977	− 7.2	+ 3.0	+19.4	+38.9
1978	+ 6.5	+ 1.2	+34.3	+18.5
1979	+18.6	+ 2.3	+ 6.2	− 5.0
1980	+32.3	+ 3.1	+24.4	+13.7
1981	− 5.0	+ 7.3	− 1.0	− 4.6
1982	+21.5	+31.1	− 0.9	+11.9
1983	+22.6	+ 8.0	+24.6	+ 4.3
1984	+ 6.3	+15.0	+ 7.9	− 2.0
1985	+31.7	+21.3	+56.7	+37.2
1986	+18.6	+15.6	+67.9	+33.9
1987	+ 5.3	+ 2.3	+24.9	+36.1
1988	+16.6	+ 7.6	+28.6	+ 3.0
1989	+31.6	+14.2	+10.8	− 4.5
1990	− 3.1	+ 8.3	−14.9	+14.1
1991	+30.4	+16.1	+12.5	+17.9
1992	+ 7.7	+ 8.1	−12.2	+ 7.1
1993	+10.1	+18.2	+32.6	+15.1
1994	+ 1.3	− 7.8	+ 7.8	+ 6.7
1995	+37.4	+31.7	+11.2	+19.6
1996	+23.1	− 0.9	+6.1	+4.1

Number of years this category achieved the best results 8 | 4 | 8 | 5

Increasing your investment returns and reducing portfolio risk are two compelling reasons for investing worldwide. Global investing allows you to maximize your returns by investing in some of the world's best managed and most profitable companies. Japan, for example, is the world's leading producer of sophisticated electronics goods; Germany of heavy machinery; the United States of biotechnology; and Southeast Asia of commodity-manufactured goods.

World market dominance is constantly changing. Ten years ago the United States represented half of the world's stock market capital, while today it represents 42 percent of total world capitalization. Only three times in the past ten years has the U.S. stock market been among the five best performers in the world (1991, 1992, and 1995). The greatest potential for growth today lies in those countries that are industrializing, have the cheapest labor and the richest natural resources, and yet remain undervalued.

Diversification reduces investment risk: Recent studies have once again proven this most basic investment principle. A 1996 study showed that the least volatile investment portfolio over the past 25 years (1972–1996) would have been composed of 60 percent U.S. equities and 40 percent foreign equities. These results reflect the importance of balancing a portfolio between U.S. and foreign equities.

Japan, the most economically mature country in the Pacific Basin, has become the dominant force behind the development of the newly industrialized countries (NICs) of Hong Kong, Korea, Thailand, Singapore, Malaysia, and Taiwan. As demand for Japanese products has grown and costs in Japan have risen, the search for affordable production of goods has caused Japanese investment to flow into neighboring countries, fostering their development as economically independent and prosperous nations.

The NICs, with some of the cheapest labor forces and richest untapped natural resources in the world, have recently experienced an enormous influx of international investment capital and today represent the world's fastest growing source of low-cost manufacturing. The Pacific Region, which includes Japan, Hong Kong, Korea, Taiwan, Thailand, Singapore, Malaysia, and Australia, has experienced outstanding economic growth and today represents 34 percent of the world's stock market capital—nearly double what it was ten years ago.

The newly industrialized countries are favored locations for the manufacture and assembly of consumer electronics products. Displaced from high-cost countries such as the United States and Japan, electronics factories in these developing countries significantly benefit from reduced labor costs. Today, in fact, Korea is the world's third-largest manufacturer of semiconductors.

The Pacific Region yields yet another country with strong economic growth: China. Opportunities to benefit from the industrialization of China come from firms listed on the Hong Kong Stock Exchange, in such basic areas as electricity, construction materials, public transportation, and fundamental telecommunications. Indeed, these low-tech and essential industries, once growth industries in the United States, are now the foundation of a natural growth progression occurring in the NICs of Southeast Asia.

Companies such as China Light and Power (Hong Kong), Siam Cement (Thailand), and Hyundai (Korea) offer much the same profit potential today as their northern European counterparts did one hundred years ago, their U.S. counterparts forty years ago, and their Japanese counterparts as recently as twenty years ago.

Investors have long been familiar with the names of many of Europe's major producers—Nestlé, Olivetti, Shell, Bayer, Volkswagen, and Perrier, to name just a few. Europe's impressive manufacturing capacity, diverse industrial base, quality labor pools, and many leading, multinational, blue-chip corporations can make it an environment for growth, accessible to you through foreign funds.

With economic deregulation and the elimination of internal trade barriers, many European companies are, for the first time in history, investing in and competing for exposure to the whole European market. Companies currently restricted to manufacturing and distributing within their national boundaries will soon be able to locate facilities anywhere in Europe, maximizing the efficient employment of labor, capital, and raw materials.

The global stock category is made up of 880 funds: 220 "World", 450 "Foreign", 65 "European" and 145 "Pacific." Total market capitalization of this entire category is $250 billion. These funds typically throw off a dividend of less than one percent and have an expense ratio of 2.0 percent. The price-earnings (p/e) ratio is 25, versus a p/e ratio of 26 for the typical stock in the S&P 500.

Over the past three years, global equity funds have had an average compound return of 11 percent per year. The annual return for the past five years has been 13 percent, 9 percent for the past ten years, and 15 percent for the last fifteen years. The standard deviation for global equity funds has been 13 percent over the past three years. This means that global equity funds have experienced about 10 percent less volatility than growth funds.

International, or foreign, funds should be part of everyone's portfolio. They provide superior returns and reduce overall portfolio risk. As with any other fund category, this one should not be looked at in a vacuum. The real beauty of foreign funds shines through when they are combined with other categories of U.S. equities. According to a Stanford University study, one's overall risk level is cut in half when a *global portfolio* of stocks is used instead of one based on U.S. issues alone. Moreover, as already demonstrated, returns are greater when we look for opportunities worldwide, instead of just domestically.

Global Stock Funds

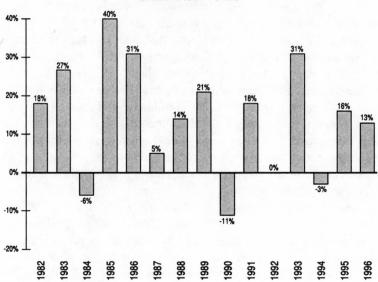

EuroPacific Growth

American Funds Group
333 South Hope Street
Los Angeles, CA 90071
(800) 421-4120

total return	★ ★ ★
risk reduction	★ ★ ★ ★
management	★ ★ ★ ★
tax minimization	★ ★ ★
expense control	★ ★ ★ ★ ★
symbol AEPGX	19 points
up-market performance	excellent
down-market performance	very good
predictability of returns	excellent

Total Return   ★ ★ ★

Over the past five years, EuroPacific Growth has taken $10,000 and turned it into
$20,110 ($15,850 over three years and $34,070 over the past ten years). This trans-
lates into an average annual return of 15 percent over the past five years, 17 percent over the past three years, and 13 percent for the decade. Over the past five
years, this fund has outperformed 70 percent of all mutual funds; within its general
category it has done better than 85 percent of its peers. Global stock funds have
averaged 13 percent annually over these same five years.

Risk/Volatility   ★ ★ ★ ★

Over the past five years, EuroPacific Growth has been safer than 92 percent of
global stock funds. Over the past decade, the fund has had one negative year, as has
the S&P 500 (off 3 percent in 1990). The fund has underperformed the S&P 500
six times and the EAFE Index three times in the last ten years.

	last 5 years		last 10 years	
worst year	1%	1994	0%	1990
best year	36%	1993	36%	1993

In the past, EuroPacific Growth has done better than 85 percent of its peer
group in up markets and outperformed 70 percent of its competition in down markets. Consistency, or predictability, of returns for EuroPacific Growth can be
described as excellent.

Management   ★ ★ ★ ★

There are 340 stocks in this $19.5 billion portfolio. The average global stock fund
today is $310 million in size. Close to 87 percent of the fund's holdings are in
stocks. The stocks in this portfolio have an average price-earnings (p/e) ratio of 26
and a median market capitalization of $11.9 billion. The portfolio's equity holdings
can be categorized as large-cap and value-oriented stocks.

A management team has overseen this fund since its inception in 1984. There are twenty-four funds besides EuroPacific Growth within the American Funds Group. Overall, the fund family's risk-adjusted performance can be described as good.

Tax Minimization   ★ ★ ★
During the past five years, a $10,000 initial investment grew to $17,650 after taxes, assuming a 39.6 percent income tax bracket (state and federal combined) and a capital gains rate of 28 percent. This means that investors in this fund were able to preserve 90 percent of their total returns. Compared to other equity funds, this fund's tax savings are considered to be very good. Over the past year, EuroPacific Growth had a twelve-month yield of 1.5 percent.

Expenses   ★ ★ ★ ★ ★
EuroPacific Growth's expense ratio is 0.9 percent; it has averaged 0.9 percent annually over the past three calendar years. The average expense ratio for the 880 funds in this category is 2.0 percent. This fund's turnover rate over the past year has been 22 percent, while its peer group average has been 72 percent.

Summary
EuroPacific Growth is yet another member of the American Funds Group that appears in this book. Unfortunately for the fund's marketing department, it is very difficult to identify members of this fund family. One of the trademarks of this group is low expenses and this is one of the fund's strongest qualities. A number of fund companies offer foreign or global portfolios; this is one of a small handful of companies that actually understands the overseas markets.

Profile

minimum initial investment $250	*IRA accounts available* . . . . yes
subsequent minimum investment . . . $50	*IRA minimum investment* $250
available in all 50 states. . . . . yes	*date of inception* . . . . April 1984
telephone exchanges. . . . . yes	*dividend/income paid* . . . semi-annually
number of other funds in family 24	*quality of annual reports* . . . . excellent

Fidelity Europe

Fidelity Group
82 Devonshire Street
Boston, MA 02109
(800) 544-8888

total return	★ ★ ★
risk reduction	★ ★ ★
management	★ ★ ★
tax minimization	★ ★ ★ ★
expense control	★ ★ ★ ★
symbol FIEUX	17 points
up-market performance	very good
down-market performance	good
predictability of returns	excellent

Total Return ★ ★ ★

Over the past five years, Fidelity Europe has taken $10,000 and turned it into $20,110 ($18,070 over three years and $26,270 over the past ten years). This translates into an average annual return of 15 percent over the past five years, 22 percent over the past three years, and 10 percent for the decade. Over the past five years, this fund has outperformed 70 percent of all mutual funds; within its general category it has done better than 85 percent of its peers. Global stock funds have averaged 13 percent annually over these same five years.

Risk/Volatility ★ ★ ★

Over the past five years, Fidelity Europe has been safer than 74 percent of global stock funds. Over the past decade, the fund has had two negative years, while the S&P 500 has had one (off 3 percent in 1990). The fund has underperformed the S&P and the EAFE Index five times in the last ten years.

	last 5 years		last 10 years	
worst year	-3%	1992	-5%	1990
best year	27%	1993	32%	1989

In the past, Fidelity Europe has done better than 70 percent of its peer group in up markets and outperformed 50 percent of its competition in down markets. Consistency, or predictability, of returns for Fidelity Europe can be described as excellent.

Management ★ ★ ★

There are 130 stocks in this $930 million portfolio. The average global stock fund today is $310 million in size. Close to 97 percent of the fund's holdings are in stocks. The stocks in this portfolio have an average price-earnings (p/e) ratio of 23 and a median market capitalization of $5.3 billion. The portfolio's equity holdings can be categorized as large-cap and value-oriented stocks.

Sally E. Walden has managed this fund for the past five years. There are 164 funds besides Europe within the Fidelity fund family. Overall, the fund family's risk-adjusted performance can be described as good.

Tax Minimization   ★ ★ ★ ★

During the past five years, a $10,000 initial investment grew to $18,790 after taxes, assuming a 39.6 percent income tax bracket (state and federal combined) and a capital gains rate of 28 percent. This means that investors in this fund were able to preserve 93 percent of their total returns. Compared to other equity funds, this fund's tax savings are considered to be excellent. Over the past year, Fidelity Europe had a twelve-month yield of 0.8 percent.

Expenses   ★ ★ ★ ★

Fidelity Europe's expense ratio is 1.3 percent; it has averaged 1.3 percent annually over the past three calendar years. The average expense ratio for the 880 funds in this category is 2.0 percent. This fund's turnover rate over the past year has been 45 percent, while its peer group average has been 72 percent.

Summary

Fidelity Europe is the only European fund to make this book. The fund has three particularly strong traits: keeping costs low, minimizing any income tax consequences, and showing quite a bit of consistency when it comes to performance.

Profile

minimum initial investment $2,500	*IRA accounts available* . . . . yes
subsequent minimum investment . . $250	*IRA minimum investment* $500
available in all 50 states. . . . . yes	*date of inception* . . . . Oct. 1986
telephone exchanges. . . . . yes	*dividend/income paid* . . . . annually
number of other funds in family 164	*quality of annual reports* . . . . excellent

Fidelity Worldwide

Fidelity Group
82 Devonshire Street
Boston, MA 02109
(800) 544-8888

total return	★ ★ ★
risk reduction	★ ★ ★ ★
management	★ ★ ★ ★
tax minimization	★ ★ ★ ★
expense control	★ ★ ★ ★
symbol FWWFX	19 points
up-market performance	very good
down-market performance	fair
predictability of returns	excellent

Total Return   ★ ★ ★
Over the past five years, Fidelity Worldwide has taken $10,000 and turned it into $20,110 ($14,560 over three years). This translates into an average annual return of 15 percent over the past five years and 13 percent over the past three years. Over the past five years, this fund has outperformed 70 percent of all mutual funds; within its general category it has done better than 80 percent of its peers. Global stock funds have averaged 13 percent annually over these same five years.

Risk/Volatility   ★ ★ ★ ★
Over the past five years, Fidelity Worldwide has been safer than 94 percent of all global stock funds. Over the past decade, the fund has had no negative years, while the S&P 500 has had one (off 3 percent in 1990). The fund has underperformed the S&P 500 four times and the EAFE Index three times in the last six years.

	last 5 years		last 6 years	
worst year	3%	1994	3%	1994
best year	37%	1993	37%	1993

In the past, Fidelity Worldwide has done better than 70 percent of its peer group in up markets but only 25 percent of its competition in down markets. Consistency, or predictability, of returns for Fidelity Worldwide can be described as excellent.

Management   ★ ★ ★ ★
There are 190 stocks in this $1.1 billion portfolio. The average global stock fund today is $310 million in size. Close to 90 percent of the fund's holdings are in stocks. The stocks in this portfolio have an average price-earnings (p/e) ratio of 22 and a median market capitalization of $2.8 billion. The portfolio's equity holdings can be categorized as mid-cap and value-oriented issues.

Penelope A. Dobkin has managed this fund for the past seven years. There are 164 funds besides Worldwide within the Fidelity fund family. Overall, the fund family's risk-adjusted performance can be described as good.

Tax Minimization

During the past five years, a $10,000 initial investment grew to $19,300 after taxes, assuming a 39.6 percent income tax bracket (state and federal combined) and a capital gains rate of 28 percent. This means that investors in this fund were able to preserve 92 percent of their total returns. Compared to other equity funds, this fund's tax savings are considered to be very good. Over the past year, Fidelity Worldwide had a twelve-month yield of 1.0 percent.

Expenses

Fidelity Worldwide's expense ratio is 1.2 percent; it has averaged 1.2 percent annually over the past three calendar years. The average expense ratio for the 880 funds in this category is 2.0 percent. This fund's turnover rate over the past year has been 49 percent, while its peer group average has been 72 percent.

Summary

Fidelity Worldwide is the only international or global equity fund that rates so highly in so many categories. The fund is not only consistent in its high ratings, it also has very predictable returns. Fidelity's performance in the foreign markets has radically improved over the past few years.

Profile

minimum initial investment $2,500	*IRA accounts available* . . . . yes
subsequent minimum investment . . $250	*IRA minimum investment* $500
available in all 50 states. . . . . yes	*date of inception.* . . . . May 1990
telephone exchanges. . . . . yes	*dividend/income paid* . . . . annually
number of other funds in family 164	*quality of annual reports* . . . . excellent

Founders Worldwide Growth

Founders Funds
2930 East Third Avenue
Denver, CO 80206
(800) 525-2440

total return	★ ★
risk reduction	★ ★ ★
management	★ ★ ★
tax minimization	★ ★ ★ ★ ★
expense control	★ ★ ★
symbol FWWGX	16 points
up-market performance	very good
down-market performance	excellent
predictability of returns	good

Total Return   ★ ★

Over the past five years, Founders Worldwide Growth has taken $10,000 and turned it into $20,110 ($15,950 over three years). This translates into an average annual return of 15 percent over the past five years and 17 percent over the past three years. Over the past five years, this fund has outperformed 70 percent of all mutual funds; within its general category it has done better than 70 percent of its peers. Global stock funds have averaged 13 percent annually over these same five years.

Risk/Volatility   ★ ★ ★

Over the past five years, Founders Worldwide Growth has been safer than 66 percent of all global stock funds. Over the past decade, the fund has had one negative year, as has the S&P 500 (off 3 percent in 1990). The fund has underperformed the S&P 500 four times and the EAFE Index twice in the last seven years.

	last 5 years		last 7 years	
worst year	-2%	1994	-2%	1994
best year	30%	1993	35%	1991

In the past, Founders Worldwide Growth has done better than 70 percent of its peer group in up markets and outperformed 95 percent of its competition in down markets. Consistency, or predictability, of returns for Founders Worldwide Growth can be described as good.

Management   ★ ★ ★

There are seventy stocks in this $350 million portfolio. The average global stock fund today is $310 million in size. Close to 90 percent of the fund's holdings are in stocks. The stocks in this portfolio have an average price-earnings (p/e) ratio of 30 and a median market capitalization of $4.4 billion. The portfolio's equity holdings can be categorized as mid-cap and value-oriented stocks.

Michael W. Gerding has managed this fund for the past seven years. There are eight funds besides Worldwide Growth within the Founders fund family. Overall, the fund family's risk-adjusted performance can be described as good.

Tax Minimization   ★ ★ ★ ★ ★

During the past five years, a $10,000 initial investment grew to $19,280 after taxes, assuming a 39.6 percent income tax bracket (state and federal combined) and a capital gains rate of 28 percent. This means that investors in this fund were able to preserve 94 percent of their total returns. Compared to other equity funds, this fund's tax savings are considered to be excellent. Over the past year, Founders Worldwide Growth had a twelve-month yield of 0.3 percent.

Expenses   ★ ★ ★

Founders Worldwide Growth's expense ratio is 1.5 percent; it has averaged 1.6 percent annually over the past three calendar years. The average expense ratio for the 880 funds in this category is 2.0 percent. This fund's turnover rate over the past year has been 72 percent, while its peer group average has been 72 percent.

Summary

Founders Worldwide Growth ties for number one as the most tax-efficient foreign or global equity fund. The fund also does a fantastic job during bear markets, yet also does quite well during bull markets.

Profile

minimum initial investment $1,000	*IRA accounts available* . . . . yes
subsequent minimum investment . . $100	*IRA minimum investment* $500
available in all 50 states. . . . . yes	*date of inception.* . . . . Dec. 1989
telephone exchanges. . . . . yes	*dividend/income paid* . . . . annually
number of other funds in family. 8	*quality of annual reports* . . . . . average

GAM International A

GAM Funds
135 East 57th Street, 25th Floor
New York, NY 10022
(800) 426-4685

total return	★ ★ ★ ★ ★
risk reduction	★ ★
management	★ ★ ★
tax minimization	★ ★
expense control	★ ★ ★
symbol GAMNX	15 points
up-market performance	excellent
down-market performance	excellent
predictability of returns	good

Total Return

Over the past five years, GAM International A has taken $10,000 and turned it into $25,940 ($16,860 over three years and $39,620 over the past ten years). This translates into an average annual return of 21 percent over the past five years, 19 percent over the past three years, and 15 percent for the decade. Over the past five years, this fund has outperformed 95 percent of all mutual funds; within its general category it has also done better than 95 percent of its peers. Global stock funds have averaged 13 percent annually over these same five years.

Risk/Volatility

Over the past five years, GAM International A has only been safer than 13 percent of all global stock funds. Over the past decade, the fund has had two negative years, while the S&P 500 has had one (off 3 percent in 1990). The fund has underperformed the S&P 500 seven times and the EAFE Index three times in the last ten years.

	last 5 years		last 10 years	
worst year	-10%	1994	-10%	1994
best year	80%	1993	80%	1993

In the past, GAM International A has done better than 95 percent of its peer group in up markets and outperformed 85 percent of its competition in down markets. Consistency, or predictability, of returns for GAM International A can be described as good.

Management

There are fifty stocks in this $1.4 billion portfolio. The average global stock fund today is $310 million in size. Close to 91 percent of the fund's holdings are in stocks. The stocks in this portfolio have an average price-earnings (p/e) ratio of 21 and a median market capitalization of $16.0 billion. The portfolio's equity holdings can be categorized as large-cap and value-oriented issues.

John R. Horseman has managed this fund for the past seven years. There are seven funds besides International A within the GAM fund family. Overall, the fund family's risk-adjusted performance can be described as good.

Tax Minimization   ★ ★
During the past five years, a $10,000 initial investment grew to $22,690 after taxes, assuming a 39.6 percent income tax bracket (state and federal combined) and a capital gains rate of 28 percent. This means that investors in this fund were able to preserve 86 percent of their total returns. Compared to other equity funds, this fund's tax savings are considered to be good. Over the past year, GAM International A had a twelve-month yield of 0.3 percent.

Expenses   ★ ★ ★
GAM International A's expense ratio is 1.7 percent; it has averaged 1.7 percent annually over the past three calendar years. The average expense ratio for the 880 funds in this category is 2.0 percent. This fund's turnover rate over the past year has been 82 percent, while its peer group average has been 72 percent.

Summary
GAM International A is becoming a recognized authority when it comes to the global markets. In a world that used to be dominated by just a couple of fund families, this small group is making quite a name for itself. Besides turning in exceptional total return figures, the fund has done a fantastic job in both bull and bear markets.

Profile
minimum initial investment $5,000	IRA accounts available . . . . yes
subsequent minimum investment . . $500	IRA minimum investment $2,000
available in all 50 states. . . . . yes	date of inception . . . . Jan. 1985
telephone exchanges. . . . . yes	dividend/income paid . . . . annually
number of other funds in family 7	quality of annual reports . . . . good

Janus Worldwide

Janus Group
100 Filmore Street, Suite 300
Denver, CO 80206-4923
(800) 525-8983

total return	★ ★ ★ ★ ★
risk reduction	★ ★ ★ ★
management	★ ★ ★ ★ ★
tax minimization	★ ★ ★ ★
expense control	★ ★ ★ ★ ★
symbol JAWWX	23 points
up-market performance	n/a
down-market performance	n/a
predictability of returns	good

Total Return   ★ ★ ★ ★ ★

Over the past five years, Janus Worldwide has taken $10,000 and turned it into $25,940 ($19,370 over three years). This translates into an average annual return of 21 percent over the past five years and 25 percent over the past three years. Over the past five years, this fund has outperformed 95 percent of all mutual funds; within its general category it has also done better than 95 percent of its peers. Global stock funds have averaged 13 percent annually over these same five years.

Risk/Volatility   ★ ★ ★ ★

Over the past five years, Janus Worldwide has been safer than 77 percent of all global stock funds. Over the past decade, the fund has had no negative years, while the S&P 500 has had one (off 3 percent in 1990). The fund has underperformed the S&P 500 once and the EAFE Index twice in the last five years.

	last 5 years		last 7 years	
worst year	4%	1994	4%	1994
best year	28%	1993	28%	1993

Consistency, or predictability, of returns for Janus Worldwide can be described as good.

Management   ★ ★ ★ ★ ★

There are 240 stocks in this $8.3 billion portfolio. The average global stock fund today is $310 million in size. Close to 96 percent of the fund's holdings are in stocks. The stocks in this portfolio have an average price-earnings (p/e) ratio of 30 and a median market capitalization of $8.3 billion. The portfolio's equity holdings can be categorized as large-cap and value-oriented issues.

Helen Young Hayes has managed this fund for the past five years. There are fifteen funds besides Worldwide within the Janus Group. Overall, the fund family's risk-adjusted performance can be described as good.

Tax Minimization ★ ★ ★ ★

During the past five years, a $10,000 initial investment grew to $24,380 after taxes, assuming a 39.6 percent income tax bracket (state and federal combined) and a capital gains rate of 28 percent. This means that investors in this fund were able to preserve 92 percent of their total returns. Compared to other equity funds, this fund's tax savings are considered to be very good.

Expenses ★ ★ ★ ★ ★

Janus Worldwide's expense ratio is 1.0 percent; it has averaged 1.1 percent annually over the past three calendar years. The average expense ratio for the 880 funds in this category is 2.0 percent. This fund's turnover rate over the past year has been 80 percent, while its peer group average has been 72 percent.

Summary

Janus Worldwide ranks as the number one global and foreign equity fund. This top point earner does very well or exceptionally in every category. It is also one of the few funds in this book to earn an almost perfect score. Several years ago, Janus was not thought of as a force to be reckoned with in the international field; things have now changed.

Profile

minimum initial investment $2,500	*IRA accounts available* . . . . yes
subsequent minimum investment . . $100	*IRA minimum investment* $500
available in all 50 states. . . . . yes	*date of inception*. . . . . May 1991
telephone exchanges. . . . . yes	*dividend/income paid* . . . . annually
number of other funds in family 15	*quality of annual reports* . . . . excellent

Managers International Equity

Managers Funds
40 Richards Avenue
Norwalk, CT 06854
(800) 835-3879

total return	★ ★ ★ ★
risk reduction	★ ★ ★ ★
management	★ ★ ★ ★
tax minimization	★ ★ ★ ★ ★
expense control	★ ★ ★ ★
symbol MGITX	21 points
up-market performance	excellent
down-market performance	fair
predictability of returns	very good

Total Return

Over the past five years, Managers International Equity has taken $10,000 and turned it into $21,000 ($15,090 over three years and $27,260 over the past ten years). This translates into an average annual return of 16 percent over the past five years, 15 percent over the past three years, and 11 percent for the decade. Over the past five years, this fund has outperformed 75 percent of all mutual funds; within its general category it has done better than 85 percent of its peers. Global stock funds have averaged 13 percent annually over these same five years.

Risk/Volatility ★ ★ ★ ★

Over the past five years, Managers International Equity has been safer than 93 percent of all global stock funds. Over the past decade, the fund has had one negative year, as has the S&P 500 (off 3 percent in 1990). The fund has underperformed the S&P 500 seven times and the EAFE Index three times in the last ten years.

	last 5 years		last 10 years	
worst year	2%	1994	-10%	1990
best year	38%	1993	38%	1993

In the past, Managers International Equity has done better than 80 percent of its peer group in up markets but only 20 percent of its competition in down markets. Consistency, or predictability, of returns for Managers International Equity can be described as very good.

Management

There are 150 stocks in this $320 million portfolio. The average global stock fund today is $310 million in size. Close to 89 percent of the fund's holdings are in stocks. The stocks in this portfolio have an average price-earnings (p/e) ratio of 26 and a median market capitalization of $11.1 billion. The portfolio's equity holdings can be categorized as large-cap and value-oriented stocks.

Holzer and Reinsberg have managed this fund for the past five years. There are eight funds besides International Equity within the Managers fund family. Overall, the fund family's risk-adjusted performance can be described as good.

Tax Minimization   ★ ★ ★ ★ ★

During the past five years, a $10,000 initial investment grew to $18,840 after taxes, assuming a 39.6 percent income tax bracket (state and federal combined) and a capital gains rate of 28 percent. This means that investors in this fund were able to preserve 94 percent of their total returns. Compared to other equity funds, this fund's tax savings are considered to be excellent. Over the past year, Managers International Equity had a twelve-month yield of 0.7 percent.

Expenses   ★ ★ ★ ★

Managers International Equity's expense ratio is 1.5 percent; it has averaged 1.5 percent annually over the past three calendar years. The average expense ratio for the 880 funds in this category is 2.0 percent. This fund's turnover rate over the past year has been 30 percent, while its peer group average has been 72 percent.

Summary

Managers International Equity is the favored choice for the investor who wants high returns with minimal tax consequences. This is simply one of the very best foreign or global stock fund offerings. The fund scores highly in every category. It is highly recommended.

Profile

minimum initial investment $2,000	*IRA accounts available* . . . . yes
subsequent minimum investment $1	*IRA minimum investment* $500
available in all 50 states. . . . . yes	*date of inception* . . . . Jan. 1986
telephone exchanges. . . . . yes	*dividend/income paid* . . . . annually
number of other funds in family 8	*quality of annual reports* . . . . good

MFS World Equity B

MFS Family of Funds
500 Boylston Street
Boston, MA 02116
(800) 637-2929

total return	★ ★ ★
risk reduction	★ ★ ★ ★
management	★ ★ ★ ★
tax minimization	★ ★
expense control	
symbol MWEBX	13 points
up-market performance	fair
down-market performance	excellent
predictability of returns	excellent

Total Return   ★ ★ ★

Over the past five years, MFS World Equity B has taken $10,000 and turned it into $20,110 ($16,080 over three years and $24,800 over the past ten years). This translates into an average annual return of 15 percent over the past five years, 17 percent over the past three years, and 10 percent for the decade. Over the past five years, this fund has outperformed 70 percent of all mutual funds; within its general category it has done better than 80 percent of its peers. Global stock funds have averaged 13 percent annually over these same five years.

Risk/Volatility   ★ ★ ★ ★

Over the past five years, MFS World Equity B has been safer than 89 percent of all global stock funds. Over the past decade, the fund has had two negative years, while the S&P 500 has had one (off 3 percent in 1990). The fund has underperformed the S&P 500 eight times and the EAFE Index four times in the last ten years.

	last 5 years		last 10 years	
worst year	-4%	1994	-5%	1990
best year	29%	1993	32%	1987

In the past, MFS World Equity B has only done better than 25 percent of its peer group in up markets but outperformed 90 percent of its competition in down markets. Consistency, or predictability, of returns for MFS World Equity B can be described as excellent.

Management   ★ ★ ★ ★

There are 110 stocks in this $230 million portfolio. The average global stock fund today is $310 million in size. Close to 92 percent of the fund's holdings are in stocks. The stocks in this portfolio have an average price-earnings (p/e) ratio of 24 and a median market capitalization of $6.6 billion. The portfolio's equity holdings can be categorized as large-cap and value-oriented issues.

David R. Mannheim has managed this fund for the past five years. There are 108 funds besides World Equity B within the MFS fund family. Overall, the fund family's risk-adjusted performance can be described as fair.

Tax Minimization   ★ ★
During the past five years, a $10,000 initial investment grew to $18,610 after taxes, assuming a 39.6 percent income tax bracket (state and federal combined) and a capital gains rate of 28 percent. This means that investors in this fund were able to preserve 86 percent of their total returns. Compared to other equity funds, this fund's tax savings are considered to be good. Over the past year, MFS World Equity B had a twelve-month yield of zero.

Expenses
MFS World Equity B's expense ratio is 2.5 percent; it has averaged 2.5 percent annually over the past three calendar years. The average expense ratio for the 880 funds in this category is 2.0 percent. This fund's turnover rate over the past year has been 83 percent, while its peer group average has been 72 percent.

Summary
MFS World Equity B is a good additional to any portfolio looking for international diversification. The fund has strong management and has been able to minimize risk. It has been safer than close to 90 percent of its peers.

Profile
minimum initial investment $1,000	*IRA accounts available* . . . . yes
subsequent minimum investment . . . $50	*IRA minimum investment* $250
available in all 50 states. . . . . yes	*date of inception.* . . . . Dec. 1986
telephone exchanges. . . . . yes	*dividend/income paid* . . . . annually
number of other funds in family 108	*quality of annual reports* . . . . excellent

New Perspective

American Funds Group
333 South Hope Street
Los Angeles, CA 90071
(800) 421-4120

total return	★ ★ ★ ★
risk reduction	★ ★ ★ ★
management	★ ★ ★ ★
tax minimization	★ ★ ★
expense control	★ ★ ★ ★ ★
symbol ANWPX	20 points
up-market performance	very good
down-market performance	very good
predictability of returns	excellent

Total Return   ★ ★ ★ ★

Over the past five years, New Perspective has taken $10,000 and turned it into $21,000 ($17,150 over three years and $33,380 over the past ten years). This translates into an average annual return of 16 percent over the past five years, 20 percent over the past three years, and 13 percent for the decade. Over the past five years, this fund has outperformed 75 percent of all mutual funds; within its general category it has done better than 90 percent of its peers. Global stock funds have averaged 13 percent annually over these same five years.

Risk/Volatility   ★ ★ ★ ★

Over the past five years, New Perspective has been safer than 95 percent of all global stock funds. Over the past decade, the fund has had one negative year, as has the S&P 500 (off 3 percent in 1990). The fund has underperformed the S&P 500 six times and the EAFE Index four times in the last ten years.

	last 5 years		last 10 years	
worst year	3%	1994	-2%	1990
best year	27%	1993	27%	1993

In the past, New Perspective has done better than 75 percent of its peer group in up markets and outperformed 60 percent of its competition in down markets. Consistency, or predictability, of returns for New Perspective can be described as excellent.

Management   ★ ★ ★ ★

There are 240 stocks in this $14.9 billion portfolio. The average global stock fund today is $310 million in size. Close to 86 percent of the fund's holdings are in stocks. The stocks in this portfolio have an average price-earnings (p/e) ratio of 26 and a median market capitalization of $14.6 billion. The portfolio's equity holdings can be categorized as large-cap and value-oriented stocks.

A management team has overseen this fund for the past fifteen years. There are twenty-four funds besides New Perspective within the American Funds Group. Overall, the fund family's risk-adjusted performance can be described as good.

Tax Minimization   ★ ★ ★

During the past five years, a $10,000 initial investment grew to $19,740 after taxes, assuming a 39.6 percent income tax bracket (state and federal combined) and a capital gains rate of 28 percent. This means that investors in this fund were able to preserve 89 percent of their total returns. Compared to other equity funds, this fund's tax savings are considered to be very good. Over the past year, New Perspective had a twelve-month yield of 1.5 percent.

Expenses   ★ ★ ★ ★ ★

New Perspective's expense ratio is 0.8 percent; it has averaged 0.8 percent annually over the past three calendar years. The average expense ratio for the 880 funds in this category is 2.0 percent. This fund's turnover rate over the past year has been 18 percent, while its peer group average has been 72 percent.

Summary

New Perspective is one of two American Funds to make the list as one of the very best international and global funds (EuroPacific Growth being the other). This fund does very well in virtually every criteria measured. Like other members of the American Funds Group, this offering earns high marks in management expertise, risk reduction, and expense control.

Profile

minimum initial investment $250	*IRA accounts available* . . . . yes
subsequent minimum investment . . . $50	*IRA minimum investment* $250
available in all 50 states. . . . . yes	*date of inception* . . . . March 1973
telephone exchanges. . . . . yes	*dividend/income paid* . . . semi-annually
number of other funds in family 24	*quality of annual reports* . . . . excellent

Oppenheimer Quest Global Value A

Oppenheimer Funds
P.O. Box 5270
Denver, CO 80217-5270
(800) 525-7048

total return	★ ★ ★ ★
risk reduction	★ ★ ★ ★ ★
management	★ ★ ★ ★ ★
tax minimization	★ ★
expense control	★ ★
symbol QVGLX	18 points
up-market performance	good
down-market performance	n/a
predictability of returns	excellent

Total Return   ★ ★ ★ ★

Over the past five years, Oppenheimer Quest Global Value A has taken $10,000 and turned it into $21,000 ($16,210 over three years). This translates into an average annual return of 16 percent over the past five years and 17 percent over the past three years. Over the past five years, this fund has outperformed 75 percent of all mutual funds; within its general category it has done better than 85 percent of its peers. Global stock funds have averaged 13 percent annually over these same five years.

Risk/Volatility   ★ ★ ★ ★ ★

Over the past five years, Oppenheimer Quest Global Value A has been safer than 98 percent of all global stock funds. Over the past decade, the fund has had no negative years, while the S&P 500 has had one (off 3 percent in 1990). The fund has under-performed the S&P 500 four times and the EAFE Index twice in the last six years.

	last 5 years		last 6 years	
worst year	2%	1992	2%	1992
best year	25%	1993	25%	1993

In the past, Oppenheimer Quest Global Value A has done better than half of its peer group in up markets. Consistency, or predictability, of returns for Oppenheimer Quest Global Value A can be described as excellent.

Management   ★ ★ ★ ★ ★

There are 120 stocks in this $250 million portfolio. The average global stock fund today is $310 million in size. Close to 89 percent of the fund's holdings are in stocks. The stocks in this portfolio have an average price-earnings (p/e) ratio of 25 and a median market capitalization of $11.3 billion. The portfolio's equity holdings can be categorized as large-cap and value-oriented issues.

Daviron and Glasebrook have managed this fund for the past five years. There are sixty-three funds besides Quest Global Value A within the Oppenheimer fund family. Overall, the fund family's risk-adjusted performance can be described as good.

Tax Minimization   ★ ★
During the past five years, a $10,000 initial investment grew to $18,770 after taxes, assuming a 39.6 percent income tax bracket (state and federal combined) and a capital gains rate of 28 percent. This means that investors in this fund were able to preserve 86 percent of their total returns. Compared to other equity funds, this fund's tax savings are considered to be good. Over the past year, Oppenheimer Quest Global Value A had a twelve-month yield of zero.

Expenses   ★ ★
Oppenheimer Quest Global Value A's expense ratio is 1.9 percent; it has averaged 1.9 percent annually over the past three calendar years. The average expense ratio for the 880 funds in this category is 2.0 percent. This fund's turnover rate over the past year has been 76 percent, while its peer group average has been 72 percent.

Summary
Oppenheimer Quest Global Value A may well be the safest foreign or international equity fund. The fund gets very high marks in the most important categories: total return, risk reduction, and management. Look for other Oppenheimer funds in this book. A very large percentage of U.S. investors are still avoiding foreign securities. This is the kind of fund that will help change their thinking.

Profile
minimum initial investment $1,000	*IRA accounts available* . . . . yes
subsequent minimum investment . . . $25	*IRA minimum investment* $250
available in all 50 states. . . . . yes	*date of inception* . . . . July 1990
telephone exchanges. . . . . yes	*dividend/income paid* . . . . annually
number of other funds in family 63	*quality of annual reports* . . . . good

Putnam Global Growth A

Putnam Funds
One Post Office Square
Boston, MA 02109
(800) 225-1581

total return	★ ★
risk reduction	★ ★ ★
management	★ ★ ★
tax minimization	★ ★ ★
expense control	★ ★ ★ ★
symbol PEQUX	15 points
up-market performance	good
down-market performance	fair
predictability of returns	very good

Total Return   ★ ★

Over the past five years, Putnam Global Growth A has taken $10,000 and turned it into $20,110 ($15,730 over three years and $25,560 over the past ten years). This translates into an average annual return of 15 percent over the past five years, 16 percent over the past three years, and 10 percent for the decade. Over the past five years, this fund has outperformed 70 percent of all mutual funds; within its general category it has also done better than 70 percent of its peers. Global stock funds have averaged 13 percent annually over these same five years.

Risk/Volatility   ★ ★ ★

Over the past five years, Putnam Global Growth A has been safer than 86 percent of all global stock funds. Over the past decade, the fund has had two negative years, while the S&P 500 has had one (off 3 percent in 1990). The fund has underperformed the S&P 500 eight times and the EAFE Index four times in the last ten years.

	last 5 years		last 10 years	
worst year	-1%	1994	-9%	1990
best year	32%	1993	32%	1993

In the past, Putnam Global Growth A has done better than 50 percent of its peer group in up markets but only 35 percent of its competition in down markets. Consistency, or predictability, of returns for Putnam Global Growth A can be described as very good.

Management   ★ ★ ★

There are 320 stocks in this $2.6 billion portfolio. The average global stock fund today is $310 million in size. Close to 97 percent of the fund's holdings are in stocks. The stocks in this portfolio have an average price-earnings (p/e) ratio of 28 and a median market capitalization of $10.0 billion. The portfolio's equity holdings can be categorized as large-cap and value-oriented stocks.

This fund is team managed. Its managers are Ami Kuan Danoff, Thomas R. Haslett, Carol C. McMullen, Kelly A. Morgan, and Robert J. Swift. There are about 290 stocks in the Global Growth portfolio. Overall, the fund family's risk-adjusted performance can be described as good.

Tax Minimization

During the past five years, a $10,000 initial investment grew to $18,560 after taxes, assuming a 39.6 percent income tax bracket (state and federal combined) and a capital gains rate of 28 percent. This means that investors in this fund were able to preserve 90 percent of their total returns. Compared to other equity funds, this fund's tax savings are considered to be very good. Over the past year, Putnam Global Growth A had a twelve-month yield of 2.1 percent.

Expenses

Putnam Global Growth A's expense ratio is 1.3 percent; it has averaged 1.3 percent annually over the past three calendar years. The average expense ratio for the 880 funds in this category is 2.0 percent. This fund's turnover rate over the past year has been 73 percent, while its peer group average has been 72 percent.

Summary

Putnam Global Growth A is a fine choice. This Putnam fund is part of an elite group: less than two percent of all global and foreign funds appear in this book. Even though this is certainly one of the better global funds, Putnam has even stronger performers in a number of other categories. The fund group now rivals the Vanguard and Fidelity giants as a well rounded family.

Profile

minimum initial investment $500	*IRA accounts available* . . . . yes
subsequent minimum investment . . . $50	*IRA minimum investment* $250
available in all 50 states. . . . . yes	*date of inception* . . . . Sept. 1967
telephone exchanges. . . . . yes	*dividend/income paid* . . . . annually
number of other funds in family 120	*quality of annual reports* . . . . good

Scudder Global

Scudder Funds
Two International Place
Boston, MA 02110
(800) 225-2470

total return	★ ★ ★
risk reduction	★ ★ ★ ★ ★
management	★ ★ ★ ★
tax minimization	★ ★ ★ ★
expense control	★ ★ ★ ★ ★
symbol SCOBX	21 points
up-market performance	good
down-market performance	very good
predictability of returns	excellent

Total Return   ★ ★ ★

Over the past five years, Scudder Global has taken $10,000 and turned it into $20,110 ($15,870 over three years and $31,340 over the past ten years). This translates into an average annual return of 15 percent over the past five years, 17 percent over the past three years, and 12 percent for the decade. Over the past five years, this fund has outperformed 70 percent of all mutual funds; within its general category it has done better than 80 percent of its peers. Global stock funds have averaged 13 percent annually over these same five years.

Risk/Volatility   ★ ★ ★ ★ ★

Over the past five years, Scudder Global has been safer than 97 percent of all global stock funds. Over the past decade, the fund has had two negative years, while the S&P 500 has had one (off 3 percent in 1990). The fund has underperformed the S&P 500 seven times and the EAFE Index four times in the last ten years.

	last 5 years		last 10 years	
worst year	-4%	1994	-6%	1990
best year	31%	1993	37%	1989

In the past, Scudder Global has done better than 55 percent of its peer group in up markets and outperformed 60 percent of its competition in down markets. Consistency, or predictability, of returns for Scudder Global can be described as excellent.

Management   ★ ★ ★ ★

There are 130 stocks in this $1.5 billion portfolio. The average global stock fund today is $310 million in size. Close to 94 percent of the fund's holdings are in stocks. The stocks in this portfolio have an average price-earnings (p/e) ratio of 27 and a median market capitalization of $10.4 billion. The portfolio's equity holdings can be categorized as large-cap and value-oriented stocks.

A team has managed this fund for the past six years. There are thirty-one funds besides Global within the Scudder fund family. Overall, the fund family's risk-adjusted performance can be described as good.

Tax Minimization
During the past five years, a $10,000 initial investment grew to $19,310 after taxes, assuming a 39.6 percent income tax bracket (state and federal combined) and a capital gains rate of 28 percent. This means that investors in this fund were able to preserve 92 percent of their total returns. Compared to other equity funds, this fund's tax savings are considered to be very good. Over the past year, Scudder Global had a twelve-month yield of 0.8 percent.

Expenses
Scudder Global's expense ratio is 1.3 percent; it has averaged 1.4 percent annually over the past three calendar years. The average expense ratio for the 880 funds in this category is 2.0 percent. This fund's turnover rate over the past year has been 29 percent, while its peer group average has been 72 percent.

Summary
Scudder Global has long enjoyed a reputation as being one of the few funds whose management truly understands foreign securities. This is one of the very top ranking global funds. This Scudder portfolio scores highly in every rated category. The fund's three strongest areas are risk reduction, consistency of returns, and controlling expenses.

Profile
minimum initial investment $2,500	*IRA accounts available* . . . . yes
subsequent minimum investment . . $100	*IRA minimum investment* $1,000
available in all 50 states. . . . . yes	*date of inception* . . . . July 1986
telephone exchanges. . . . . yes	*dividend/income paid* . . . . annually
number of other funds in family 31	*quality of annual reports* . . . . excellent

Templeton Developing Markets I

Templeton Group
700 Central Avenue
St. Petersburg, FL 33701-3628
(800) 292-9293

total return	★ ★ ★ ★
risk reduction	★ ★
management	★ ★
tax minimization	★ ★ ★ ★
expense control	★ ★ ★
symbol TEDMX	15 points
up-market performance	n/a
down-market performance	n/a
predictability of returns	fair

Total Return

Over the past five years, Templeton Developing Markets I has taken $10,000 and turned it into $21,000 ($14,940 over three years). This translates into an average annual return of 16 percent over the past five years and 14 percent over the past three years. Over the past five years, this fund has outperformed 75 percent of all mutual funds; within its general category it has done better than 90 percent of its peers. Global stock funds have averaged 13 percent annually over these same five years.

Risk/Volatility ★ ★

Over the past five years, Templeton Developing Markets I has been safer than just 21 percent of all global stock funds. Since its 1991 inception, the fund has had two negative years, while the S&P 500 has had one (off 3 percent in 1990). The fund has underperformed the S&P 500 four times and the EAFE Index twice in the last five years.

	last 5 years		last 7 years	
worst year	-10%	1992	-10%	1992
best year	75%	1993	75%	1993

Consistency, or predictability, of returns for Templeton Developing Markets I can be described as fair.

Management

There are 560 stocks in this $4.6 billion portfolio. The average global stock fund today is $310 million in size. Close to 85 percent of the fund's holdings are in stocks. The stocks in this portfolio have an average price-earnings (p/e) ratio of 20 and a median market capitalization of $2.5 billion. The portfolio's equity holdings can be categorized as mid-cap and value-oriented stocks.

J. Mark Mobius has managed this fund for the past six years. There are nineteen funds besides Developing Markets I within the Templeton fund family (119 within the Franklin Templeton Group). Overall, the fund family's risk-adjusted performance can be described as good.

Tax Minimization   ★ ★ ★ ★
During the past five years, a $10,000 initial investment grew to $18,460 after taxes, assuming a 39.6 percent income tax bracket (state and federal combined) and a capital gains rate of 28 percent. This means that investors in this fund were able to preserve 92 percent of their total returns. Compared to other equity funds, this fund's tax savings are considered to be very good. Over the past year, Templeton Developing Markets I had a twelve-month yield of 0.9 percent.

Expenses   ★ ★ ★
Templeton Developing Markets I's expense ratio is 2.0 percent; it has averaged 2.1 percent annually over the past three calendar years. The average expense ratio for the 880 funds in this category is 2.0 percent. This fund's turnover rate over the past year has been 12 percent, while its peer group average has been 72 percent.

Summary
Templeton Developing Markets I is the only recommended emerging markets fund. Templeton, now Franklin Templeton, has long been known as the best, long-term global investor, with over four decades of international expertise. Few investors realize how great this group is at risk reduction. This fund is highly recommended and is an excellent addition for virtually any portfolio seeking diversification and high returns.

Profile
minimum initial investment $100	IRA accounts available . . . . yes
subsequent minimum investment . . . $25	IRA minimum investment $100
available in all 50 states. . . . . yes	date of inception . . . . Oct. 1991
telephone exchanges. . . . . yes	dividend/income paid . . . . annually
number of other funds in family 19	quality of annual reports . . . . excellent

Templeton Growth I

Templeton Group
700 Central Avenue
St. Petersburg, FL 33701-3628
(800) 292-9293

total return	★ ★ ★ ★
risk reduction	★ ★ ★ ★
management	★ ★ ★ ★ ★
tax minimization	★
expense control	★ ★ ★ ★ ★
symbol TEPLX	19 points
up-market performance	excellent
down-market performance	poor
predictability of returns	excellent

Total Return   ★ ★ ★ ★

Over the past five years, Templeton Growth I has taken $10,000 and turned it into $21,920 ($16,810 over three years and $35,800 over the past ten years). This translates into an average annual return of 17 percent over the past five years, 19 percent over the past three years, and 14 percent for the decade. Over the past five years, this fund has outperformed 80 percent of all mutual funds; within its general category it has done better than 95 percent of its peers. Global stock funds have averaged 13 percent annually over these same five years.

Risk/Volatility   ★ ★ ★ ★

Over the past five years, Templeton Growth I has been safer than 95 percent of all global stock funds. Over the past decade, the fund has had one negative year, as has the S&P 500 (off 3 percent in 1990). The fund has underperformed the S&P 500 seven times and the EAFE Index three times in the last ten years.

	last 5 years		last 10 years	
worst year	1%	1994	-9%	1990
best year	33%	1993	33%	1993

In the past, Templeton Growth I has done better than 85 percent of its peer group in up markets but only 15 percent of its competition in down markets. Consistency, or predictability, of returns for Templeton Growth I can be described as excellent.

Management   ★ ★ ★ ★ ★

There are 240 stocks in this $10.5 billion portfolio. The average global stock fund today is $310 million in size. Close to 83 percent of the fund's holdings are in stocks. The stocks in this portfolio have an average price-earnings (p/e) ratio of 20 and a median market capitalization of $10.9 billion. The portfolio's equity holdings can be categorized as large-cap and value-oriented stocks.

Mark G. Holowesko has managed this fund for the past ten years. There are nineteen funds besides Growth I within the Templeton fund family family (119 within the Franklin Templeton Group). Overall, the fund family's risk-adjusted performance can be described as good.

Tax Minimization   ★
During the past five years, a $10,000 initial investment grew to $19,000 after taxes, assuming a 39.6 percent income tax bracket (state and federal combined) and a capital gains rate of 28 percent. This means that investors in this fund were able to preserve 81 percent of their total returns. Compared to other equity funds, this fund's tax savings are considered to be fair. Over the past year, Templeton Growth I had a twelve-month yield of 2.1 percent.

Expenses   ★ ★ ★ ★ ★
Templeton Growth I's expense ratio is 1.1 percent; it has averaged 1.1 percent annually over the past three calendar years. The average expense ratio for the 880 funds in this category is 2.0 percent. This fund's turnover rate over the past year has been 20 percent, while its peer group average has been 72 percent.

Summary
Templeton Growth I is the oldest and one of the very best global stock funds. The fund excels during bull markets but has also done a superb job in reducing risk during bear markets. The Franklin Templeton Group may well be the leader when it comes to international investing, particularly when compared to other large fund families.

Profile

minimum initial investment $100	*IRA accounts available* . . . . yes
subsequent minimum investment . . . $25	*IRA minimum investment* $100
available in all 50 states. . . . . yes	*date of inception* . . . . Nov. 1954
telephone exchanges. . . . . yes	*dividend/income paid* . . . . annually
number of other funds in family 119	*quality of annual reports* . . . . excellent

Government Bond Funds

These funds invest in direct and indirect U.S. government obligations. Government bond funds are made up of one or more of the following: T-bills, T-notes, T-bonds, GNMAs, and FNMAs. Treasury bills, notes, and bonds make up the entire marketable debt of the U.S. government. Such instruments are exempt from state income taxes.

Although GNMAs are considered an *indirect obligation* of the government, they are still backed by the full faith and credit of the United States. FNMAs are not issued by the government but are considered virtually identical in safety to GNMAs. FNMAs and GNMAs are both subject to state and local income taxes. *All* of the securities in a government bond fund are subject to federal income taxes.

The average maturity of securities found in government bond funds varies broadly, depending upon the type of fund, as well as on management's perception of risk and the future direction of interest rates. A more thorough discussion of interest rates and the volatility of bond fund prices can be found in the introductory pages of the corporate bond section.

Over the past fifteen years, government bonds have returned an average compound return of 13 percent—the same as long-term corporate bonds. During this same period, government bond funds have underperformed corporate bond funds, returning 11.3 percent, compared to 10.0 percent. A $10,000 investment in U.S. government bonds grew to $65,300 over the past fifteen years; a similar initial investment in corporate bonds grew to $68,200.

Looking at a longer time frame, government bonds have only slightly outperformed inflation. A dollar invested in governments in 1947 grew to $13.43 by the end of 1996. This translates into an average compound return of 5.3 percent per year. Adjusted for inflation, the figure falls to $1.82. Over the past fifty years, the worst year for government bonds was 1967, when a loss of 9 percent was suffered. The best year so far has been 1982, when government bonds posted a gain of 40 percent. All of these figures are based on total return (current yield plus or minus any appreciation or loss of principal).

Over the past half century, there have been forty-six five-year periods (1946–1950, 1947–1951, etc.). On a pre-tax basis, government bonds have outperformed inflation during twenty-four of the forty-six five-year periods. Over the past fifty years, there have been forty-one ten-year periods (1946–1955, 1947–1956, etc.). On a pre-tax basis, government bonds have outperformed inflation during only nineteen of the forty-one ten-year periods. Over the past half century, there have been thirty-one twenty-year periods (1946–1965, 1947–1966, etc.).

On a pre-tax basis, government bonds have outperformed inflation during only eleven of these thirty-one periods. All eleven of those twenty-year periods were the most recent in time (1967–1986, 1968–1987, 1969–1988, 1970–1989, 1971–1990, 1972–1991, 1973–1992, 1974–1993, 1975–1994, 1976-1995, and 1977–1996).

Six hundred funds make up the government bonds category. Total market capitalization of this category is $130 billion.

Over the past three and five years, government funds have had an average compound annual return of 7 and 6 percent, respectively. For the decade, these funds have averaged 8 percent a year; over the last fifteen years, 10 percent a year. The standard deviation for government bond funds has been 4 percent over the past three years. This means that these funds have been less volatile than any other category except corporate bonds and money market funds.

Government bond funds are the perfect choice for the conservative investor who wants to avoid any possibility of defaults. These securities should be avoided by even conservative investors who are in a high tax bracket or unable to shelter such an investment in a retirement plan or annuity. Such investors should first look at the advantages of municipal bond funds.

The prospective investor should always remember that government and corporate bonds are generally not a good investment once inflation and taxes are factored in. The investor who appreciates the cumulative effects of even low levels of inflation should probably avoid government and corporate bonds except as part of a retirement plan.

Government Bond Funds

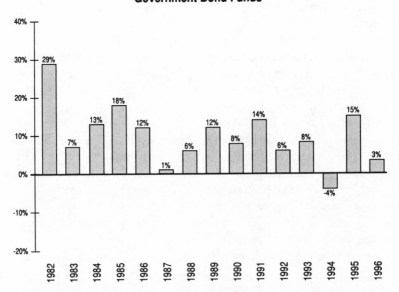

Asset Management Adjustable Rate

Asset Management Fund (AMF)
111 East Wacker Drive
Chicago, IL 60601
(800) 527-3713

total return	★ ★
risk reduction	★ ★ ★ ★ ★
management	★ ★ ★ ★ ★
current income	★ ★ ★
expense control	★ ★ ★ ★ ★
symbol ASARX	20 points
up-market performance	n/a
down-market performance	n/a
predictability of returns	excellent

Total Return   ★ ★

Over the past five years, Asset Management Adjustable Rate has taken $10,000 and turned it into $13,380 ($12,190 over three years). This translates into an average annual return of 6 percent over the past five years and 7 percent over the past three years. Over the past five years, this fund has outperformed 10 percent of all mutual funds; within its general category it has done better than 40 percent of its peers. Government bond funds have averaged 6 percent annually over these same five years.

During the past five years, a $10,000 initial investment grew to $11,720 after taxes, assuming a 39.6 percent income tax bracket (state and federal combined) and a capital gains rate of 28 percent. This means that investors in this fund were able to preserve 61 percent of their total returns. Compared to other fixed-income funds, this fund offers tax savings that are considered fair.

Risk/Volatility   ★ ★ ★ ★ ★

Over the past five years, Asset Management Adjustable Rate has been safer than 98 percent of all government bond funds. Over the past decade, the fund has had no negative years, while the Lehman Brothers Aggregate Bond Index has had one (off 3 percent in 1994). The fund has underperformed the Lehman Brothers Aggregate Bond and the Lehman Brothers Government Bond Index three times in the last five years.

	last 5 years		last 7 years	
worst year	2%	1994	2%	1994
best year	9%	1995	9%	1995

Consistency, or predictability, of returns for Asset Management Adjustable Rate can be described as excellent.

Management   ★ ★ ★ ★ ★

There are thirty fixed-income securities in this $670 million portfolio. The average government bond fund today is $211 million in size. Close to 95 percent of the fund's holdings are in bonds. The average maturity of the bonds in this account is three years; the weighted coupon rate averages 7.6 percent. The portfolio's fixed-income holdings can be categorized as short-term, high-quality debt.

Edward E. Sammons, Jr. has managed this fund for the past six years. There are three funds besides Asset Management Adjustable Rate within the Asset Management Fund (AMF) fund family. Overall, the fund family's risk-adjusted performance can be described as good.

Current Income   ★ ★ ★

Over the past year, Asset Management Adjustable Rate had a twelve-month yield of 6.6 percent. During this same twelve-month period, the typical government bond fund had a twelve-month yield that averaged 5.8 percent.

Expenses   ★ ★ ★ ★ ★

Asset Management Adjustable Rate's expense ratio is 0.5 percent; it has averaged 0.5 percent annually over the past three calendar years. The average expense ratio for the 600 funds in this category is 1.2 percent. This fund's turnover rate over the past year has been 60 percent, while its peer group average has been 171 percent.

Summary

Asset Management Adjustable Rate is the top-rated government bond fund. It is also the only government securities fund to receive the highest marks for risk reduction, management, and the control of expenses. This is not a highly visible fund, but one that is highly recommended.

Profile

minimum initial investment $10,000	*IRA accounts available* .... yes
subsequent minimum investment $1	*IRA minimum investment* $1
available in all 50 states .... no	*date of inception* .... Sept. 1991
telephone exchanges............. yes	*dividend/income paid*........ monthly
number of other funds in family...... 3	*quality of annual reports* .... good

Fidelity Spartan Limited Maturity Government

Fidelity Group
82 Devonshire Street
Boston, MA 02109
(800) 544-8888

total return	★ ★ ★
risk reduction	★ ★ ★
management	★ ★
current income	★ ★ ★ ★ ★
expense control	★ ★ ★ ★ ★
symbol FSTGX	18 points
up-market performance	good
down-market performance	very good
predictability of returns	very good

Total Return ★ ★ ★

Over the past five years, Fidelity Spartan Limited Maturity Government has taken $10,000 and turned it into $13,380 ($12,290 over three years). This translates into an average annual return of 6 percent over the past five years and 7 percent over the past three years. Over the past five years, this fund has outperformed 15 percent of all mutual funds; within its general category it has done better than 55 percent of its peers. Government bond funds have averaged 6 percent annually over these same five years.

During the past five years, a $10,000 initial investment grew to $11,650 after taxes, assuming a 39.6 percent income tax bracket (state and federal combined) and a capital gains rate of 28 percent. This means that investors in this fund were able to preserve 54 percent of their total returns. Compared to other fixed-income funds, this fund offers tax savings that are considered poor.

Risk/Volatility ★ ★ ★

Over the past five years, Fidelity Spartan Limited Maturity Government has been safer than 78 percent of all government bond funds. Over the past decade, the fund has had one negative year, as has the Lehman Brothers Aggregate Bond Index (off 3 percent in 1994). The fund has underperformed the Lehman Brothers Aggregate Bond Index and the Lehman Brothers Government Bond Index five times in the last eight years.

	last 5 years		last 8 years	
worst year	-1%	1994	-1%	1994
best year	14%	1995	14%	1995

In the past, Fidelity Spartan Limited Maturity Government has done better than 45 percent of its peer group in up markets and outperformed 75 percent of its competition in down markets. Consistency, or predictability, of returns for Fidelity Spartan Limited Maturity Government can be described as very good.

Management   ★ ★

There are 150 fixed-income securities in this $690 million portfolio. The average government bond fund today is $211 million in size. Close to 98 percent of the fund's holdings are in bonds. The average maturity of the bonds in this account is four years; the weighted coupon rate averages 8.0 percent. The portfolio's fixed-income holdings can be categorized as short-term, high-quality debt.

Curtis Hollingsworth has managed this fund for the past nine years. There are 164 funds besides Spartan Limited Maturity Government within the Fidelity fund family. Overall, the fund family's risk-adjusted performance can be described as good.

Current Income   ★ ★ ★ ★ ★

Over the past year, Fidelity Spartan Limited Maturity Government had a twelve-month yield of 6.8 percent. During this same twelve-month period, the typical government bond fund had a twelve-month yield that averaged 5.8 percent.

Expenses   ★ ★ ★ ★ ★

Fidelity Spartan Limited Maturity Government's expense ratio is 0.6 percent; it has averaged 0.6 percent annually over the past three calendar years. The average expense ratio for the 600 funds in this category is 1.2 percent. This fund's turnover rate over the past year has been 105 percent, while its peer group average has been 171 percent.

Summary

Fidelity Spartan Limited Maturity Government is the number one choice for the investor who wants to maximize current income while getting a good night's sleep. The Spartan division at Fidelity is known for keeping costs quite low; this fund is no exception. Few fund groups have learned the benefits of having bond funds with short- and intermediate-term maturities: low volatility and high risk-adjusted returns. Fidelity is one of the few companies that gets it.

Profile

minimum initial investment $10,000	*IRA accounts available* . . . . yes
subsequent minimum investment . $1,000	*IRA minimum investment* $10,000
available in all 50 states. . . . . yes	*date of inception.* . . . . May 1988
telephone exchanges. . . . . yes	*dividend/income paid.* . . . . monthly
number of other funds in family 164	*quality of annual reports* . . . . excellent

Lexington GNMA Income

Lexington Group
P.O. Box 1515
Park 80 West Plaza Two
Saddle Brook, NJ 07662
(800) 526-0056

total return	★ ★ ★ ★
risk reduction	★ ★
management	★
current income	★ ★ ★ ★ ★
expense control	★ ★ ★
symbol LEXNX	15 points
up-market performance	excellent
down-market performance	poor
predictability of returns	good

Total Return　　★ ★ ★ ★

Over the past five years, Lexington GNMA Income has taken $10,000 and turned it into $14,030 ($12,810 over three years and $22,260 over the past ten years). This translates into an average annual return of 7 percent over the past five years, 9 percent over the past three years, and 8 percent for the decade. Over the past five years, this fund has outperformed 30 percent of all mutual funds; within its general category it has done better than 80 percent of its peers. Government bond funds have averaged 6 percent annually over these same five years.

During the past five years, a $10,000 initial investment grew to $12,150 after taxes, assuming a 39.6 percent income tax bracket (state and federal combined) and a capital gains rate of 28 percent. This means that investors in this fund were able to preserve 59 percent of their total returns. Compared to other fixed-income funds, this fund offers tax savings that are considered fair.

Risk/Volatility　　★ ★

Over the past five years, Lexington GNMA Income has been safer than 58 percent of all government bond funds. Over the past decade, the fund has had one negative year, as has the Lehman Brothers Aggregate Bond Index (off 3 percent in 1994). The fund has underperformed the Lehman Brothers Aggregate Bond Index six times and the Lehman Brothers Government Bond Index five times in the last ten years.

	last 5 years		last 10 years	
worst year	-2%	1994	-2%	1994
best year	16%	1995	16%	1995

In the past, Lexington GNMA Income has done better than 90 percent of its peer group in up markets but only 15 percent of its competition in down markets.

Consistency, or predictability, of returns for Lexington GNMA Income can be described as good.

Management   ★
There are fifty fixed-income securities in this $140 million portfolio. The average government bond fund today is $211 million in size. Close to 98 percent of the fund's holdings are in bonds. The portfolio's fixed-income holdings can be categorized as long-term, high-quality debt.

Denis P. Jamison has managed this fund for the past sixteen years. There are twelve funds besides GNMA Income within the Lexington fund family. Overall, the fund family's risk-adjusted performance can be described as fair.

Current Income
Over the past year, Lexington GNMA Income had a twelve-month yield of 6.3 percent. During this same twelve-month period, the typical government bond fund had a twelve-month yield that averaged 5.8 percent.

Expenses
Lexington GNMA Income's expense ratio is 1.0 percent; it has averaged 1.0 percent annually over the past three calendar years. The average expense ratio for the 600 funds in this category is 1.2 percent. This fund's turnover rate over the past year has been 31 percent, while its peer group average has been 171 percent.

Summary
Lexington GNMA Income is the smart choice for any investor who wants high current income that is free from state and local income taxes. Part of the reason Lexington has been able to provide such high yields is due to its watchful eye on expense control. Due to the nature of this entire category, and this fund in particular, this GNMA fund is a good choice for qualified retirement plans.

Profile

minimum initial investment $1,000	IRA accounts available . . . . yes
subsequent minimum investment . . . $50	IRA minimum investment $250
available in all 50 states. . . . . yes	date of inception . . . . Oct. 1973
telephone exchanges. . . . . yes	dividend/income paid. . . . . monthly
number of other funds in family 12	quality of annual reports . . . . . average

SIT U.S. Government Securities

Sit Group
4600 Norwest Center 90 South 7th Street
Minneapolis, MN 55402-4130
(800) 332-5580

total return	★ ★ ★
risk reduction	★ ★ ★ ★
management	★ ★ ★
current income	★ ★ ★ ★
expense control	★ ★ ★ ★
symbol SNGVX	18 points
up-market performance	good
down-market performance	good
predictability of returns	very good

Total Return   ★ ★ ★

Over the past five years, SIT U.S. Government Securities has taken $10,000 and turned it into $13,380 ($12,240 over three years and $21,870 over the past ten years). This translates into an average annual return of 6 percent over the past five years, 7 percent over the past three years, and 8 percent for the decade. Over the past five years, this fund has outperformed 20 percent of all mutual funds; within its general category it has done better than 75 percent of its peers. Government bond funds have averaged 6 percent annually over these same five years.

During the past five years, a $10,000 initial investment grew to $11,960 after taxes, assuming a 39.6 percent income tax bracket (state and federal combined) and a capital gains rate of 28 percent. This means that investors in this fund were able to preserve 58 percent of their total returns. Compared to other fixed-income funds, this fund offers tax savings that are considered fair.

Risk/Volatility   ★ ★ ★ ★

Over the past five years, SIT U.S. Government Securities has been safer than 89 percent of all government bond funds. Over the past decade, the fund has had no negative years, while the Lehman Brothers Aggregate Bond Index has had one (off 3 percent in 1994). The fund has underperformed the Lehman Brothers Aggregate Bond Index six times and the Lehman Brothers Government Bond Index five times in the last nine years.

	last 5 years		last 9 years	
worst year	2%	1994	2%	1994
best year	12%	1995	13%	1991

In the past, SIT U.S. Government Securities has only done better than 40 percent of its peer group in up and down markets. Consistency, or predictability, of returns for SIT U.S. Government Securities can be described as very good.

Management   ★ ★ ★

There are 170 fixed-income securities in this $80 million portfolio. The average government bond fund today is $211 million in size. Close to 96 percent of the fund's holdings are in bonds. The average maturity of the bonds in this account is four years; the weighted coupon rate averages 7.5 percent. The portfolio's fixed-income holdings can be categorized as short-term, high-quality debt.

Brilley and Doty have managed this fund for the past six years. There are nine funds besides U.S. Government Securities within the SIT fund family. Overall, the fund family's risk-adjusted performance can be described as good.

Current Income   ★ ★ ★ ★

Over the past year, SIT U.S. Government Securities had a twelve-month yield of 6.2 percent. During this same twelve-month period, the typical government bond fund had a twelve-month yield that averaged 5.8 percent.

Expenses   ★ ★ ★ ★

SIT U.S. Government Securities's expense ratio is 0.8 percent; it has averaged 0.8 percent annually over the past three calendar years. The average expense ratio for the 600 funds in this category is 1.2 percent. This fund's turnover rate over the past year has been 85 percent, while its peer group average has been 171 percent.

Summary

SIT U.S. Government Securities does a fine job in every single rated category. The fund has been safer than close to 90 percent of its peers and over the past decade it has not had a negative year—something few funds can say.

Profile

minimum initial investment $2,000	*IRA accounts available* . . . . yes
subsequent minimum investment . . $100	*IRA minimum investment* $1
available in all 50 states. . . . . yes	*date of inception.* . . . . June 1987
telephone exchanges. . . . . yes	*dividend/income paid.* . . . . monthly
number of other funds in family. 9	*quality of annual reports* . . . . excellent

Smith Breeden Short Duration Government Series

Smith Breeden Family of Funds
100 Europa Drive, Suite 200
Chapel Hill, NC 27514
(800) 221-3138

total return	★ ★
risk reduction	★ ★ ★ ★
management	★ ★ ★ ★
current income	★ ★ ★
expense control	★ ★ ★ ★
symbol SBSHX	17 points
up-market performance	n/a
down-market performance	n/a
predictability of returns	excellent

Total Return   ★ ★

Over the past five years, Smith Breeden Short Duration Government Series has taken $10,000 and turned it into $12,760 ($12,050 over three years). This translates into an average annual return of 5 percent over the past five years and 6 percent over the past three years. Over the past five years, this fund has outperformed 10 percent of all mutual funds; within its general category it has done better than 40 percent of its peers. Government bond funds have averaged 6 percent annually over these same five years.

During the past five years, a $10,000 initial investment grew to $11,640 after taxes, assuming a 39.6 percent income tax bracket (state and federal combined) and a capital gains rate of 28 percent. This means that investors in this fund were able to preserve 58 percent of their total returns. Compared to other fixed-income funds, this fund offers tax savings that are considered fair.

Risk/Volatility   ★ ★ ★ ★

Over the past five years, Smith Breeden Short Duration Government Series has been safer than 94 percent of all government bond funds. Over the past decade, the fund has had no negative years, while the Lehman Brothers Aggregate Bond Index has had one (off 3 percent in 1994). The fund has underperformed the Lehman Brothers Aggregate Bond Index and the Lehman Brothers Government Bond Index twice in the last four years.

	last 5 years		last 4 years	
worst year	4%	1994	4%	1994
best year	6%	1996	6%	1996

Consistency, or predictability, of returns for Smith Breeden Short Duration Government Series can be described as excellent.

Management
There are thirty fixed-income securities in this $110 million portfolio. The average government bond fund today is $211 million in size. Close to 84 percent of the fund's holdings are in bonds. The average maturity of the bonds in this account is less than one year; the weighted coupon rate averages 8.0 percent. The portfolio's fixed-income holdings can be categorized as short-term, high-quality debt.

Daniel C. Dektar has managed this fund for the past five years. There are two funds besides Short Duration Government Series within the Smith Breeden fund family. Overall, the fund family's risk-adjusted performance can be described as very good.

Current Income
Over the past year, Smith Breeden Short Duration Government Series had a twelve-month yield of 5.3 percent. During this same twelve-month period, the typical government bond fund had a twelve-month yield that averaged 5.8 percent.

Expenses
Smith Breeden Short Duration Government Series's expense ratio is 0.8 percent; it has averaged 0.4 percent annually over the past three calendar years. The average expense ratio for the 600 funds in this category is 1.2 percent. This fund's turnover rate over the past year has been 556 percent, while its peer group average has been 171 percent.

Summary
Smith Breeden Short Duration Government Series is in the top one percent of all government securities funds. This small fund family has other selections that should also be seriously considered. Tax minimization has not been particular good with this government bond portfolio, but such a concern can be eliminated by making this part of the conservative portion of a qualified retirement plan.

Profile
minimum initial investment $250	*IRA accounts available* . . . . yes
subsequent minimum investment . . . $50	*IRA minimum investment* $500
available in all 50 states. . . . . yes	*date of inception* . . . . March 1992
telephone exchanges. . . . . yes	*dividend/income paid*. . . . . monthly
number of other funds in family. 2	*quality of annual reports* . . . . . average

Vanguard Fixed-Income Securities
Short-Term Federal Bond
Vanguard Group
Vanguard Financial Center
P.O. Box 2600
Valley Forge, PA 19482
(800) 662-7447

total return	★ ★ ★
risk reduction	★ ★ ★
management	★ ★
current income	★ ★ ★ ★
expense control	★ ★ ★ ★
symbol VSGBX	16 points
up-market performance	good
down-market performance	very good
predictability of returns	very good

Total Return   ★ ★ ★
Over the past five years, Vanguard Fixed-Income Securities Short-Term Federal
Bond has taken $10,000 and turned it into $13,380 ($12,150 over three years). This
translates into an average annual return of 6 percent over the past five years and 7
percent over the past three years. Over the past five years, this fund has outperformed 15 percent of all mutual funds; within its general category it has done better
than 50 percent of its peers. Government bond funds have averaged 6 percent annually over these same five years.

During the past five years, a $10,000 initial investment grew to $11,930 after
taxes, assuming a 39.6 percent income tax bracket (state and federal combined) and
a capital gains rate of 28 percent. This means that investors in this fund were able
to preserve 60 percent of their total returns. Compared to other fixed-income funds,
this fund offers tax savings that are considered fair.

Risk/Volatility   ★ ★ ★
Over the past five years, Vanguard Fixed-Income Securities Short-Term Federal
Bond has been safer than 80 percent of all government bond funds. Over the past
decade, the fund has had one negative year, as has the Lehman Brothers Aggregate
Bond Index (off 3 percent in 1994). The fund has underperformed the Lehman
Brothers Aggregate Bond Index six times and the Lehman Brothers Government
Bond Index six times in the last nine years.

	last 5 years		last 9 years	
worst year	-1%	1994	-1%	1994
best year	12%	1995	12%	1995

In the past, Vanguard Fixed-Income Securities Short-Term Federal Bond has done better than 50 percent of its peer group in up markets and outperformed 60 percent of its competition in down markets. Consistency, or predictability, of returns for Vanguard Fixed-Income Securities Short-Term Federal Bond can be described as very good.

Management ★ ★
There are seventy fixed-income securities in this $1.4 billion portfolio. The average government bond fund today is $211 million in size. Close to 98 percent of the fund's holdings are in bonds. The average maturity of the bonds in this account is two years; the weighted coupon rate averages 6.5 percent. The portfolio's fixed-income holdings can be categorized as short-term, high-quality debt.

MacKinnon and Hollyer have managed this fund for the past six years. There are sixty-four funds besides Fixed-Income Securities Short-Term Federal Bond within the Vanguard Group. Overall, the fund family's risk-adjusted performance can be described as good.

Current Income ★ ★ ★ ★
Over the past year, Vanguard Fixed-Income Securities Short-Term Federal Bond had a twelve-month yield of 6.1 percent. During this same twelve-month period, the typical government bond fund had a twelve-month yield that averaged 5.8 percent.

Expenses
Vanguard Fixed-Income Securities Short-Term Federal Bond's expense ratio is 0.3 percent; it has averaged 0.3 percent annually over the past three calendar years. The average expense ratio for the 600 funds in this category is 1.2 percent. This fund's turnover rate over the past year has been 57 percent, while its peer group average has been 171 percent.

Summary
Vanguard Fixed-Income Securities Short-Term Federal Bond is one of several Vanguard funds that has made this and previous editions of the book. By keeping expenses to a minimum, lower than any of its peers, Vanguard starts off with a tremendous advantage. This, coupled with its understanding of the benefits of a short duration, make this a wise choice for the government bond fund investor.

Profile

minimum initial investment $3,000	*IRA accounts available* . . . . yes
subsequent minimum investment . . $100	*IRA minimum investment* $1,000
available in all 50 states. . . . . yes	*date of inception.* . . . . Dec. 1987
telephone exchanges. . . . . yes	*dividend/income paid.* . . . . monthly
number of other funds in family 64	*quality of annual reports* . . . . excellent

Growth Funds

These funds generally seek capital appreciation, with current income as a distant secondary concern. Growth funds typically invest in U.S. common stocks, while avoiding speculative issues and aggressive trading techniques. The goal of most of these funds is *long-term growth*. The approaches used to attain this appreciation can vary significantly among growth funds.

Over the past fifteen years, U.S. stocks have outperformed both corporate and government bonds. From 1982 through 1996, common stocks have averaged 16.8 percent compounded per year, compared to 13.7 percent for corporate bonds and 13.3 percent for government bonds. A $10,000 investment in stocks, as measured by the S&P 500, grew to over $102,600 over the past fifteen years; a similar initial investment in corporate bonds grew to $68,200.

Looking at a longer time frame, common stocks have also fared quite well. A dollar invested in stocks in 1947 grew to $376 by the end of 1996. This translates into an average compound return of 11.9 percent per year. Over the past fifty years, the worst year for common stocks was 1974, when a loss of 26 percent was suffered. One year later, these same stocks posted a gain of 37 percent. The best year so far has been 1954, when growth stocks posted a gain of 53 percent.

Growth stocks have outperformed bonds in every single decade. If President George Washington had invested $1 in common stocks with an average return of 12 percent, his investment would be worth over $196 billion today. If George had been a bit lucky and averaged 14 percent on his stock portfolio, his portfolio would be large enough to pay our national debt three times over!

To give you an idea as to the likelihood of making money in common stocks, look at the table below. It covers more than 120 years and shows the odds of making money (a positive return) over each of several different time periods.

Standard & Poor's Composite 500 Stock Index
Various periods, 1871–1996 (dividends not included)

Length of Period	Total Number of Periods	Number of Periods in which Stock Prices			Percentage Opportunity for Profit (not including dividends)
		Rose	Declined	Unchanged	
1 year	126	80	45	1	63%
5 years	122	96	25	1	79%
10 years	117	105	12	0	90%
15 years	112	103	9	0	92%
20 years	107	104	3	0	97%
25 years	102	101	1	0	99%
30 years	97	97	0	0	100%

Eleven hundred funds make up the growth category. Total market capitalization of this category is $520 billion. The standard deviation for this group is 14 percent; beta (stock market-related risk) is 1.0, identical to that of the overall market, as measured by the S&P 500. The typical portfolio of a growth fund is divided up as follows: 91 percent S&P 500 stocks and the balance in money market instruments. Less than 6 percent of the portfolio is in foreign equities. Turnover rate is 95 percent per year. The yield on growth funds averages about 0.5 percent annually. Fund expenses for this group average 1.6 percent per year.

Over the past three years, growth funds have had an average compound return of 23 percent per year; the *annual* return for the past five years has been 17 percent. For the past decade, growth funds have averaged 13 percent annually and just over 16 percent per year for the past fifteen years.

Growth Funds

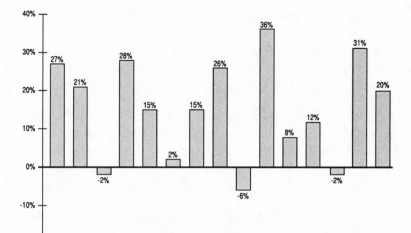

Fidelity Advisor Growth Opportunities T

Fidelity Advisor Funds
82 Devonshire Street
Boston, MA 02109
(800) 522-7297

total return	★ ★ ★
risk reduction	★ ★ ★ ★
management	★ ★ ★
tax minimization	★ ★ ★ ★
expense control	★ ★ ★
symbol FAGOX	17 points
up-market performance	excellent
down-market performance	fair
predictability of returns	very good

Total Return   ★ ★ ★

Over the past five years, Fidelity Advisor Growth Opportunities T has taken $10,000 and turned it into $24,880 ($18,550 over three years). This translates into an average annual return of 20 percent over the past five years and 23 percent over the past three years. Over the past five years, this fund has outperformed 90 percent of all mutual funds; within its general category it has done better than 80 percent of its peers. Growth funds have averaged 17 percent annually over these same five years.

Risk/Volatility   ★ ★ ★ ★

Over the past five years, Fidelity Advisor Growth Opportunities T has been safer than 81 percent of all growth funds. Over the past decade, the fund has had one negative year, as has the S&P 500 (off 3 percent in 1990). The fund has underperformed the S&P 500 three times in the last nine years.

	last 5 years		last 9 years	
worst year	3%	1994	-2%	1990
best year	33%	1995	43%	1991

In the past, Fidelity Advisor Growth Opportunities T has done better than 90 percent of its peer group in up markets but only 20 percent of its competition in down markets. Consistency, or predictability, of returns for Fidelity Advisor Growth Opportunities T can be described as very good.

Management   ★ ★ ★

There are 200 stocks in this $17.5 billion portfolio. The average growth fund today is $545 million in size. Close to 78 percent of the fund's holdings are in stocks. The stocks in this portfolio have an average price-earnings (p/e) ratio of 20 and a median market capitalization of $26.3 billion. The portfolio's equity holdings can be categorized as large-cap and value-oriented stocks.

George Vanderheiden has managed this fund for the past ten years. There are 164 funds besides Growth Opportunities T within the Fidelity fund family. Overall, the fund family's risk-adjusted performance can be described as good.

Tax Minimization   ★ ★ ★ ★
During the past five years, a $10,000 initial investment grew to $20,250 after taxes, assuming a 39.6 percent income tax bracket (state and federal combined) and a capital gains rate of 28 percent. This means that investors in this fund were able to preserve 89 percent of their total returns. Compared to other equity funds, this fund's tax savings are considered to be very good. Over the past year, Fidelity Advisor Growth Opportunities T had a twelve-month yield of 1.3 percent.

Expenses   ★ ★ ★
Fidelity Advisor Growth Opportunities T's expense ratio is 1.3 percent; it has averaged 1.5 percent annually over the past three calendar years. The average expense ratio for the 1,100 funds in this category is 1.6 percent. This fund's turnover rate over the past year has been 33 percent, while its peer group average has been 95 percent.

Summary
Fidelity Advisor Growth Opportunities T is a member of an elite division of Fidelity, the Advisor group; a couple of dozen funds that were originally designed for institutional investors. This particular stock fund performs well across the board. It does a particularly good job during bull markets.

Profile

minimum initial investment $2,500	*IRA accounts available* . . . . yes
subsequent minimum investment . . $250	*IRA minimum investment* $500
available in all 50 states. . . . . yes	*date of inception* . . . . Nov. 1987
telephone exchanges. . . . . yes	*dividend/income paid* . . . . annually
number of other funds in family. 164	*quality of annual reports* . . . . excellent

Fidelity Destiny II

Fidelity Group
82 Devonshire Street
Boston, MA 02109
(800) 752-2347

total return	★ ★ ★ ★
risk reduction	★ ★ ★ ★
management	★ ★ ★ ★
tax minimization	★
expense control	★ ★ ★ ★ ★
symbol FDETX	18 points
up-market performance	excellent
down-market performance	fair
predictability of returns	very good

Total Return   ★ ★ ★ ★

Over the past five years, Fidelity Destiny II has taken $10,000 and turned it into $27,030 ($19,170 over three years and $49,190 over the past ten years). This translates into an average annual return of 22 percent over the past five years, 24 percent over the past three years, and 17 percent for the decade. Over the past five years, this fund has outperformed 95 percent of all mutual funds; within its general category it has done better than 90 percent of its peers. Growth funds have averaged 17 percent annually over these same five years.

Risk/Volatility   ★ ★ ★ ★

Over the past five years, Fidelity Destiny II has been safer than 67 percent of all growth funds. Over the past decade, the fund has had one negative year, as has the S&P 500 (off 3 percent in 1990). The fund has underperformed the S&P 500 three times in the last ten years.

	last 5 years		last 10 years	
worst year	4%	1994	-3%	1990
best year	36%	1995	42%	1991

In the past, Fidelity Destiny II has done better than 95 percent of its peer group in up markets but only 20 percent of its competition in down markets. Consistency, or predictability, of returns for Fidelity Destiny II can be described as very good.

Management   ★ ★ ★ ★

There are 200 stocks in this $3.2 billion portfolio. The average growth fund today is $545 million in size. Close to 79 percent of the fund's holdings are in stocks. The stocks in this portfolio have an average price-earnings (p/e) ratio of 21 and a median market capitalization of $26.3 billion. The portfolio's equity holdings can be categorized as large-cap and value-oriented stocks.

George Vanderheiden has managed this fund for the past twelve years. There are 164 funds besides Destiny II within the Fidelity fund family. Overall, the fund family's risk-adjusted performance can be described as good.

Tax Minimization   ★

During the past five years, a $10,000 initial investment grew to $20,890 after taxes, assuming a 39.6 percent income tax bracket (state and federal combined) and a capital gains rate of 28 percent. This means that investors in this fund were able to preserve 81 percent of their total returns. Compared to other equity funds, this fund's tax savings are considered to be fair. Over the past year, Fidelity Destiny II had a twelve-month yield of 1.8 percent.

Expenses   ★ ★ ★ ★ ★

Fidelity Destiny II's expense ratio is 0.8 percent; it has averaged 0.8 percent annually over the past three calendar years. The average expense ratio for the 1,100 funds in this category is 1.6 percent. This fund's turnover rate over the past year has been 37 percent, while its peer group average has been 95 percent.

Summary

Fidelity Destiny II is the only contractual plan fund to appear in this book and one of the relatively few that are available anywhere. Under such a plan, investors make contributions over an extended period of time or face modest to large penalties. Such potential penalties have caused the fund's shareholders to stay the course, resulting in some very tasty returns with minimal risk. The portfolio's manager, George Vanderheiden, is considered one of the very best.

Profile

minimum initial investment $50	*IRA accounts available* . . . . yes
subsequent minimum investment . . . $50	*IRA minimum investment* . . . . n/a
available in all 50 states. . . . . yes	*date of inception.* . . . . Dec. 1985
telephone exchanges. . . . . yes	*dividend/income paid* . . . . annually
number of other funds in family 164	*quality of annual reports* . . . . excellent

Gradison Established Value

Gradison Mutual Funds
580 Walnut Street
Cincinnati, OH 45202
(800) 869-5999

total return	★ ★ ★
risk reduction	★ ★ ★ ★
management	★ ★ ★ ★ ★
tax minimization	★ ★ ★
expense control	★ ★ ★ ★
symbol GETGX	19 points
up-market performance	good
down-market performance	fair
predictability of returns	excellent

Total Return   ★ ★ ★

Over the past five years, Gradison Established Value has taken $10,000 and turned it into $23,860 ($18,080 over three years and $32,880 over the past ten years). This translates into an average annual return of 19 percent over the past five years, 22 percent over the past three years, and 13 percent for the decade. Over the past five years, this fund has outperformed 90 percent of all mutual funds; within its general category it has done better than 70 percent of its peers. Growth funds have averaged 17 percent annually over these same five years.

Risk/Volatility   ★ ★ ★ ★

Over the past five years, Gradison Established Value has been safer than 96 percent of all growth funds. Over the past decade, the fund has had one negative year, as has the S&P 500 (off 3 percent in 1990). The fund has underperformed the S&P 500 seven times in the last ten years.

	last 5 years		last 10 years	
worst year	0%	1994	-8%	1990
best year	26%	1995	26%	1995

In the past, Gradison Established Value has done better than just 45 percent of its peer group in up markets and only 35 percent of its competition in down markets. Consistency, or predictability, of returns for Gradison Established Value can be described as excellent.

Management   ★ ★ ★ ★ ★

There are fifty stocks in this $470 million portfolio. The average growth fund today is $545 million in size. Close to 72 percent of the fund's holdings are in stocks. The stocks in this portfolio have an average price-earnings (p/e) ratio of 19 and a median market capitalization of $5.9 billion. The portfolio's equity holdings can be categorized as large-cap and value-oriented issues.

William J. Leugers, Jr. and David R. Shick have managed this fund for the past fourteen years. There are six funds besides Established Value within the Gradison fund family. Overall, the fund family's risk-adjusted performance can be described as good.

Tax Minimization   ★ ★ ★
During the past five years, a $10,000 initial investment grew to $19,590 after taxes, assuming a 39.6 percent income tax bracket (state and federal combined) and a capital gains rate of 28 percent. This means that investors in this fund were able to preserve 88 percent of their total returns. Compared to other equity funds, this fund's tax savings are considered to be good. Over the past year, Gradison Established Value had a twelve-month yield of 1.3 percent.

Expenses   ★ ★ ★ ★
Gradison Established Value's expense ratio is 1.2 percent; it has averaged 1.2 percent annually over the past three calendar years. The average expense ratio for the 1,100 funds in this category is 1.6 percent. This fund's turnover rate over the past year has been 18 percent, while its peer group average has been 95 percent.

Summary
Gradison Established Value may well be the safest growth fund in the book. Management receives top marks. The fund scores well in every department. This offering is part of a small fund family that should also be reviewed for investment. Besides management, the fund's greatest attribute is its predictability of returns.

Profile

minimum initial investment $1,000	*IRA accounts available* . . . . yes
subsequent minimum investment . . . $50	*IRA minimum investment* $1,000
available in all 50 states. . . . . yes	*date of inception* . . . . Aug. 1983
telephone exchanges. . . . . yes	*dividend/income paid* . . . . quarterly
number of other funds in family. 6	*quality of annual reports* . . . . good

Guardian Park Avenue

Guardian Group
201 Park Avenue South
New York, NY 10003
(800) 221-3253

total return	★ ★ ★ ★ ★
risk reduction	★ ★ ★
management	★ ★ ★
tax minimization	★ ★ ★
expense control	★ ★ ★ ★ ★
symbol GPAFX	19 points
up-market performance	excellent
down-market performance	fair
predictability of returns	good

Total Return   ★ ★ ★ ★ ★

Over the past five years, Guardian Park Avenue has taken $10,000 and turned it into $28,150 ($20,650 over three years and $43,250 over the past ten years). This translates into an average annual return of 23 percent over the past five years, 27 percent over the past three years, and 16 percent for the decade. Over the past five years, this fund has outperformed 95 percent of all mutual funds; within its general category it has also done better than 95 percent of its peers. Growth funds have averaged 17 percent annually over these same five years.

Risk/Volatility   ★ ★ ★

Over the past five years, Guardian Park Avenue has been safer than half of all growth funds. Over the past decade, the fund has had two negative years, while the S&P 500 has had one (off 3 percent in 1990). The fund has underperformed the S&P 500 five times in the last ten years.

	last 5 years		last 10 years	
worst year	-1%	1994	-12%	1990
best year	34%	1995	35%	1991

In the past, Guardian Park Avenue has done better than 90 percent of its peer group in up markets but only 25 percent of its competition in down markets. Consistency, or predictability, of returns for Guardian Park Avenue can be described as good.

Management   ★ ★ ★

There are 300 stocks in this $1.8 billion portfolio. The average growth fund today is $545 million in size. Close to 94 percent of the fund's holdings are in stocks. The stocks in this portfolio have an average price-earnings (p/e) ratio of 23 and a median market capitalization of $23.2 billion. The portfolio's equity holdings can be categorized as large-cap and value-oriented stocks.

Charles E. Albers has managed this fund for the past twenty-five years. There are two funds besides Park Avenue within the Guardian Group fund family. Overall, the fund family's risk-adjusted performance can be described as fair.

Tax Minimization   ★ ★ ★

During the past five years, a $10,000 initial investment grew to $21,510 after taxes, assuming a 39.6 percent income tax bracket (state and federal combined) and a capital gains rate of 28 percent. This means that investors in this fund were able to preserve 87 percent of their total returns. Compared to other equity funds, this fund's tax savings are considered to be good. Over the past year, Guardian Park Avenue had a twelve-month yield of 0.9 percent.

Expenses   ★ ★ ★ ★ ★

Guardian Park Avenue's expense ratio is 0.8 percent; it has averaged 0.8 percent annually over the past three calendar years. The average expense ratio for the 1,100 funds in this category is 1.6 percent. This fund's turnover rate over the past year has been 81 percent, while its peer group average has been 95 percent.

Summary

Guardian Park Avenue is simply one of the best performers when it comes to total return, the most important criteria for equity investors. The portfolio outperforms 90 percent of its peers in bull markets. And, since the average bull market lasts about 40 months, versus 10 months for the average bear market, this is a very important characteristic. The fund also does a good job in every other area, particularly in keeping overhead costs down.

Profile

minimum initial investment $1,000
subsequent minimum investment . . $100
available in all 50 states. . . . . yes
telephone exchanges. . . . . yes
number of other funds in family 2

IRA accounts available . . . . yes
IRA minimum investment $250
date of inception. . . . . June 1972
dividend/income paid . . . semi-annually
quality of annual reports . . . . excellent

Mairs & Power Growth

Mairs & Power Funds
W-206 First National Bank Building
St. Paul, MN 55101
(800) 304-7404

total return	★ ★ ★ ★ ★
risk reduction	★ ★ ★
management	★ ★ ★
tax minimization	★ ★ ★ ★ ★
expense control	★ ★ ★ ★ ★
symbol MPGFX	21 points
up-market performance	excellent
down-market performance	good
predictability of returns	fair

Total Return   ★ ★ ★ ★ ★

Over the past five years, Mairs & Power Growth has taken $10,000 and turned it into $29,320 ($23,950 over three years and $47,620 over the past ten years). This translates into an average annual return of 24 percent over the past five years, 34 percent over the past three years, and 17 percent for the decade. Over the past five years, this fund has outperformed 95 percent of all mutual funds; within its general category it has also done better than 95 percent of its peers. Growth funds have averaged 17 percent annually over these same five years.

Risk/Volatility   ★ ★ ★

Over the past five years, Mairs & Power Growth has been safer than 38 percent of all growth funds. Over the past decade, the fund has had one negative year, as has the S&P 500 (off 3 percent in 1990). The fund has underperformed the S&P 500 three times in the last ten years.

	last 5 years		last 10 years	
worst year	6%	1994	-2%	1987
best year	48%	1995	48%	1995

In the past, Mairs & Power Growth has done better than 95 percent of its peer group in up markets and outperformed 55 percent of its competition in down markets. Consistency, or predictability, of returns for Mairs & Power Growth can be described as fair.

Management   ★ ★ ★

There are thirty-four stocks in this $280 million portfolio. The average growth fund today is $545 million in size. Close to 95 percent of the fund's holdings are in stocks. The stocks in this portfolio have an average price-earnings (p/e) ratio of 25 and a median market capitalization of $4.4 billion. The portfolio's equity holdings can be categorized as mid-cap and value-oriented stocks.

George A. Mairs, III has managed this fund for the past seventeen years. There is only one other fund besides Growth within the Mairs & Power fund family. Overall, the fund family's risk-adjusted performance can be described as very good.

Tax Minimization

During the past five years, a $10,000 initial investment grew to $24,440 after taxes, assuming a 39.6 percent income tax bracket (state and federal combined) and a capital gains rate of 28 percent. This means that investors in this fund were able to preserve 93 percent of their total returns. Compared to other equity funds, this fund's tax savings are considered to be excellent. Over the past year, Mairs & Power Growth had a twelve-month yield of 1.0 percent.

Expenses

Mairs & Power Growth's expense ratio is 0.9 percent; it has averaged 1.0 percent annually over the past three calendar years. The average expense ratio for the 1,100 funds in this category is 1.6 percent. This fund's turnover rate over the past year has been 3 percent, while its peer group average has been 95 percent.

Summary

Mairs & Power Growth is the second-best performer in its category. Great pre-tax returns coupled with an exceptional tax reduction strategy make this a highly attractive portfolio. Its total point score also makes it one of the top overall funds. This fund also has some of the lowest expenses.

Profile

minimum initial investment $2,500	*IRA accounts available* . . . . yes
subsequent minimum investment . . $100	*IRA minimum investment* $1,000
available in all 50 states . . . . no	*date of inception* . . . . Nov. 1958
telephone exchanges . . . . no	*dividend/income paid* . . . semi-annually
number of other funds in family 1	*quality of annual reports* . . . . good

MAP-Equity

Mutual Benefit Funds
520 Broad Street
Newark, NJ 07102-3111
(800) 559-5535

total return	★ ★
risk reduction	★ ★ ★ ★ ★
management	★ ★ ★ ★
tax minimization	
expense control	★ ★ ★ ★ ★
symbol MUBFX	16 points
up-market performance	good
down-market performance	very good
predictability of returns	very good

Total Return   ★ ★

Over the past five years, MAP-Equity has taken $10,000 and turned it into $23,860 ($20,190 over three years and $39,000 over the past ten years). This translates into an average annual return of 19 percent over the past five years, 26 percent over the past three years, and 15 percent for the decade. Over the past five years, this fund has outperformed 85 percent of all mutual funds; within its general category it has done better than 65 percent of its peers. Growth funds have averaged 17 percent annually over these same five years.

Risk/Volatility   ★ ★ ★ ★ ★

Over the past five years, MAP-Equity has been safer than 94 percent of all growth funds. Over the past decade, the fund has had two negative years, while the S&P 500 has had one (off 3 percent in 1990). The fund has underperformed the S&P 500 six times in the last ten years.

	last 5 years		last 10 years	
worst year	3%	1994	-5%	1990
best year	33%	1995	33%	1995

In the past, MAP-Equity has done better than 55 percent of its peer group in up markets and outperformed 65 percent of its competition in down markets. Consistency, or predictability, of returns for MAP-Equity can be described as very good.

Management   ★ ★ ★ ★

There are eighty stocks in this $80 million portfolio. The average growth fund today is $545 million in size. Close to 73 percent of the fund's holdings are in stocks. The stocks in this portfolio have an average price-earnings (p/e) ratio of 25 and a median market capitalization of $4.5 billion. The portfolio's equity holdings can be categorized as mid-cap and value-oriented stocks.

A team has managed this fund for the past fourteen years. There are no other funds besides Equity within the MAP fund family. Overall, the fund's risk-adjusted performance can be described as excellent.

Tax Minimization

During the past five years, a $10,000 initial investment grew to $17,260 after taxes, assuming a 39.6 percent income tax bracket (state and federal combined) and a capital gains rate of 28 percent. This means that investors in this fund were able to preserve 73 percent of their total returns. Compared to other equity funds, this fund's tax savings are considered to be poor. Over the past year, MAP-Equity had a twelve-month yield of 1.3 percent.

Expenses   ★ ★ ★ ★ ★

MAP-Equity's expense ratio is 0.7 percent; it has averaged 0.9 percent annually over the past three calendar years. The average expense ratio for the 1,100 funds in this category is 1.6 percent. This fund's turnover rate over the past year has been 53 percent, while its peer group average has been 95 percent.

Summary

MAP-Equity is best suited for the stock investor who wants minimal risk. Its management of taxes is not good, but that problem is easily removed if the fund is purchased inside a qualified retirement plan. For the expense-conscious investor, this is your choice—the fund has lower expenses than any other growth fund in the book. Its turnover rate is also about half its peer group average. Few investors realize the hidden costs of turnover, making this an even more attractive fund. Finally, this fund also ranks as the best during bear market periods.

Profile

minimum initial investment $250	*IRA accounts available* . . . . yes
subsequent minimum investment . . . $50	*IRA minimum investment* $1
available in all 50 states. . . . . yes	*date of inception* . . . . Jan. 1971
telephone exchanges. . . . . yes	*dividend/income paid* . . . semi-annually
number of other funds in family. 0	*quality of annual reports* . . . . good

Maxus Equity

Maxus Funds
28601 Chagrin Boulevard, Suite 500
Cleveland, OH 44122
(800) 446-2987

total return	★ ★
risk reduction	★ ★ ★ ★
management	★ ★ ★ ★
tax minimization	★
expense control	★
symbol MXSEX	12 points
up-market performance	excellent
down-market performance	fair
predictability of returns	excellent

Total Return   ★ ★

Over the past five years, Maxus Equity has taken $10,000 and turned it into $22,880 ($17,640 over three years). This translates into an average annual return of 18 percent over the past five years and 21 percent over the past three years. Over the past five years, this fund has outperformed 85 percent of all mutual funds; within its general category it has done better than 60 percent of its peers. Growth funds have averaged 17 percent annually over these same five years.

Risk/Volatility   ★ ★ ★ ★

Over the past five years, Maxus Equity has been safer than 97 percent of all growth funds. Over the past decade, the fund has had one negative year, as has the S&P 500 (off 3 percent in 1990). The fund has underperformed the S&P 500 four times in the last seven years.

	last 5 years		last 7 years	
worst year	1%	1994	-11%	1990
best year	24%	1993	36%	1991

In the past, Maxus Equity has done better than 80 percent of its peer group in up markets but only 20 percent of its competition in down markets. Consistency, or predictability, of returns for Maxus Equity can be described as excellent.

Management   ★ ★ ★ ★

There are sixty stocks in this $50 million portfolio. The average growth fund today is $545 million in size. Close to 80 percent of the fund's holdings are in stocks. The stocks in this portfolio have an average price-earnings (p/e) ratio of 19 and a median market capitalization of $720 million. The portfolio's equity holdings can be categorized as small-cap and value-oriented stocks.

Richard A. Barone has managed this fund for the past thirteen years. There are two funds besides Equity within the Maxus fund family. Overall, the fund family's risk-adjusted performance can be described as very good.

Tax Minimization   ★
During the past five years, a $10,000 initial investment grew to $17,840 after taxes, assuming a 39.6 percent income tax bracket (state and federal combined) and a capital gains rate of 28 percent. This means that investors in this fund were able to preserve 81 percent of their total returns. Compared to other equity funds, this fund's tax savings are considered to be fair. Over the past year, Maxus Equity had a twelve-month yield of 1.4 percent.

Expenses   ★
Maxus Equity's expense ratio is 1.9 percent; it has averaged 2.0 percent annually over the past three calendar years. The average expense ratio for the 1,100 funds in this category is 1.6 percent. This fund's turnover rate over the past year has been 111 percent, while its peer group average has been 95 percent.

Summary
Maxus Equity is strong when it comes to management skills and risk reduction. It also scores very highly when it comes to bull market performance and predictability of returns. This particular fund is part of a very small fund family that includes a couple of other funds that you should also seriously consider.

Profile
minimum initial investment $1,000	*IRA accounts available* . . . . yes
subsequent minimum investment . . $100	*IRA minimum investment* $1,000
available in all 50 states . . . . no	*date of inception* . . . . Oct. 1989
telephone exchanges. . . . . yes	*dividend/income paid* . . . . annually
number of other funds in family. 2	*quality of annual reports* . . . . good

Oakmark

The Oakmark Family of Funds
Two North LaSalle Street
Chicago, IL 60602-3790
(800) 625-6275

total return	★ ★ ★ ★ ★
risk reduction	★ ★ ★ ★
management	★ ★ ★ ★ ★
tax minimization	★ ★ ★ ★ ★
expense control	★ ★ ★ ★
symbol OAKMX	23 points
up-market performance	n/a
down-market performance	n/a
predictability of returns	very good

Total Return ★ ★ ★ ★ ★
Over the past five years, Oakmark has taken $10,000 and turned it into $31,760 ($19,610 over three years). This translates into an average annual return of 26 percent over the past five years and 25 percent over the past three years. Over the past five years, this fund has outperformed 95 percent of all mutual funds; within its general category it has also done better than 95 percent of its peers. Growth funds have averaged 17 percent annually over these same five years.

Risk/Volatility ★ ★ ★ ★
Over the past five years, Oakmark has been safer than 51 percent of all growth funds. Over the past decade, the fund has had no negative years, while the S&P 500 has had one (off 3 percent in 1990). The fund has underperformed the S&P 500 twice in the last five years.

	last 5 years		last 7 years	
worst year	3%	1994	3%	1994
best year	49%	1992	49%	1992

Consistency, or predictability, of returns for Oakmark can be described as very good.

Management ★ ★ ★ ★ ★
There are forty-six stocks in this $5.8 billion portfolio. The average growth fund today is $545 million in size. Close to 84 percent of the fund's holdings are in stocks. The stocks in this portfolio have an average price-earnings (p/e) ratio of 22 and a median market capitalization of $10.6 billion. The portfolio's equity holdings can be categorized as large-cap and value-oriented issues.

Robert Sanborn has managed this fund for the past six years. There are five other funds within the Oakmark Fund Family. Overall, the fund family's risk-adjusted performance can be described as very good.

Tax Minimization   ★ ★ ★ ★ ★
During the past five years, a $10,000 initial investment grew to $27,970 after taxes, assuming a 39.6 percent income tax bracket (state and federal combined) and a capital gains rate of 28 percent. This means that investors in this fund were able to preserve 93 percent of their total returns. Compared to other equity funds, this fund's tax savings are considered to be excellent. Over the past year, Oakmark had a twelve-month yield of 0.9 percent.

Expenses   ★ ★ ★ ★
Oakmark's expense ratio is 1.1 percent; it has averaged 1.2 percent annually over the past three calendar years. The average expense ratio for the 1,100 funds in this category is 1.6 percent. This fund's turnover rate over the past year has been 24 percent, while its peer group average has been 95 percent.

Summary
Oakmark is not only the best performing growth fund in the book, it is also number one all-around. With an almost perfect score (23 out of 25 possible points), this fund has a lot going for it. The fund has no weak points; it scores highly in every single area measured. Moreover, it is part of a small fund family that has other investment gems. This fund is highly recommended to all equity investors.

Profile
minimum initial investment . . . . . $1,000   *IRA accounts available* . . . . yes
subsequent minimum investment . . $100   *IRA minimum investment* $1,000
available in all 50 states. . . . . yes   *date of inception* . . . . Aug. 1991
telephone exchanges. . . . . yes   *dividend/income paid* . . . . annually
number of other funds in family. 5   *quality of annual reports* . . . . excellent

Sound Shore

Sound Shore Fund
2 Portland Square
Portland, ME 04101
(800) 551-1980

total return	★ ★ ★ ★
risk reduction	★ ★ ★ ★
management	★ ★ ★ ★
tax minimization	★
expense control	★ ★ ★
symbol SSHFX	16 points
up-market performance	excellent
down-market performance	fair
predictability of returns	very good

Total Return

Over the past five years, Sound Shore has taken $10,000 and turned it into $27,030 ($20,930 over three years and $41,520 over the past ten years). This translates into an average annual return of 22 percent over the past five years, 28 percent over the past three years, and 15 percent for the decade. Over the past five years, this fund has outperformed 95 percent of all mutual funds; within its general category it has done better than 90 percent of its peers. Growth funds have averaged 17 percent annually over these same five years.

Risk/Volatility

Over the past five years, Sound Shore has been safer than 70 percent of all growth funds. Over the past decade, the fund has had two negative years, while the S&P 500 has had one (off 3 percent in 1990). The fund has underperformed the S&P 500 five times in the last ten years.

	last 5 years		last 10 years	
worst year	0%	1994	-11%	1990
best year	33%	1996	33%	1996

In the past, Sound Shore has done better than 85 percent of its peer group in up markets but only 35 percent of its competition in down markets. Consistency, or predictability, of returns for Sound Shore can be described as very good.

Management

There are forty stocks in this $590 million portfolio. The average growth fund today is $545 million in size. Close to 86 percent of the fund's holdings are in stocks. The stocks in this portfolio have an average price-earnings (p/e) ratio of 19 and a median market capitalization of $3.0 billion. The portfolio's equity holdings can be categorized as mid-cap and value-oriented stocks.

Harry Burn, III and T. Gibbs Kane, Jr. have managed this fund for the past twelve years. There are no other funds offered by this company. Overall, the fund's risk-adjusted performance can be described as excellent.

Tax Minimization ★

During the past five years, a $10,000 initial investment grew to $20,500 after taxes, assuming a 39.6 percent income tax bracket (state and federal combined) and a capital gains rate of 28 percent. This means that investors in this fund were able to preserve 81 percent of their total returns. Compared to other equity funds, this fund's tax savings are considered to be fair. Over the past year, Sound Shore had a twelve-month yield of 0.5 percent.

Expenses ★ ★ ★

Sound Shore's expense ratio is 1.2 percent; it has averaged 1.2 percent annually over the past three calendar years. The average expense ratio for the 1,100 funds in this category is 1.6 percent. This fund's turnover rate over the past year has been 69 percent, while its peer group average has been 95 percent.

Summary

Sound Shore is a very good choice for the stock enthusiast. The fund's total return figures are quite impressive, particularly on a risk-adjusted basis. Management is also quite strong. The only thing that really hurts this fund is its after-tax returns. Therefore, the fund is more strongly recommended when it is placed inside a qualified retirement plan. This is a one-fund family; hopefully, management will decide to come out with more offerings.

Profile

minimum initial investment $10,000	*IRA accounts available* . . . . yes
subsequent minimum investment $1	*IRA minimum investment* $250
available in all 50 states. . . . . yes	*date of inception.* . . . . May 1985
telephone exchanges. . . . . yes	*dividend/income paid* . . . semi-annually
number of other funds in family. 0	*quality of annual reports* . . . . . average

Strong Schafer Value

Strong Funds
P.O. Box 2936
Milwaukee, WI 53201-2936
(800) 368-1030

total return	★ ★ ★
risk reduction	★ ★ ★
management	★ ★ ★
tax minimization	★ ★ ★ ★
expense control	★ ★ ★ ★
symbol SCHVX	17 points
up-market performance	excellent
down-market performance	fair
predictability of returns	very good

Total Return

Over the past five years, Strong Schafer Value has taken $10,000 and turned it into $25,940 ($19,060 over three years and $42,290 over the past ten years). This translates into an average annual return of 21 percent over the past five years, 24 percent over the past three years, and 16 percent for the decade. Over the past five years, this fund has outperformed 95 percent of all mutual funds; within its general category it has done better than 85 percent of its peers. Growth funds have averaged 17 percent annually over these same five years.

Risk/Volatility

Over the past five years, Strong Schafer Value has been safer than 69 percent of all growth funds. Over the past decade, the fund has had three negative years, while the S&P 500 has had one (off 3 percent in 1990). The fund has underperformed the S&P 500 five times in the last ten years.

	last 5 years		last 10 years	
worst year	-4%	1994	-10%	1990
best year	34%	1995	41%	1991

In the past, Strong Schafer Value has done better than 90 percent of its peer group in up markets but only 20 percent of its competition in down markets. Consistency, or predictability, of returns for Strong Schafer Value can be described as very good.

Management

There are forty stocks in this $970 million portfolio. The average growth fund today is $545 million in size. Close to 99 percent of the fund's holdings are in stocks. The stocks in this portfolio have an average price-earnings (p/e) ratio of 17 and a median market capitalization of $3.8 billion. The portfolio's equity holdings can be categorized as mid-cap and value-oriented stocks.

David K. Schafer has managed this fund for the past twelve years. There are twenty-five funds besides Schafer Value within the Strong fund family. Overall, the fund family's risk-adjusted performance can be described as good.

Tax Minimization ★ ★ ★ ★

During the past five years, a $10,000 initial investment grew to $21,360 after taxes, assuming a 39.6 percent income tax bracket (state and federal combined) and a capital gains rate of 28 percent. This means that investors in this fund were able to preserve 90 percent of their total returns. Compared to other equity funds, this fund's tax savings are considered to be very good. Over the past year, Strong Schafer Value had a twelve-month yield of 0.7 percent.

Expenses ★ ★ ★ ★

Strong Schafer Value's expense ratio is 1.3 percent; it has averaged 1.3 percent annually over the past three calendar years. The average expense ratio for the 1,100 funds in this category is 1.6 percent. This fund's turnover rate over the past year has been 18 percent, while its peer group average has been 95 percent.

Summary

Strong Schafer Value is a solid choice. With a field of over 1,100 contenders, this fund rates in the top 1.5 percent on a risk-adjusted return basis. Tax minimization and expense control are also quite good.

Profile

minimum initial investment $2,500	*IRA accounts available* . . . . yes
subsequent minimum investment . . . $50	*IRA minimum investment* $250
available in all 50 states. . . . . yes	*date of inception* . . . . Oct. 1985
telephone exchanges. . . . . yes	*dividend/income paid* . . . . annually
number of other funds in family 25	*quality of annual reports* . . . . . average

T. Rowe Price Spectrum Growth

T. Rowe Price Funds
100 East Pratt Street
Baltimore, MD 21202
(800) 638-5660

total return	★ ★
risk reduction	★ ★ ★ ★
management	★ ★ ★
tax minimization	★ ★
expense control	★ ★ ★ ★ ★
symbol PRSGX	16 points
up-market performance	fair
down-market performance	n/a
predictability of returns	excellent

Total Return ★ ★

Over the past five years, T. Rowe Price Spectrum Growth has taken $10,000 and turned it into $22,880 ($18,290 over three years). This translates into an average annual return of 18 percent over the past five years and 22 percent over the past three years. Over the past five years, this fund has outperformed 85 percent of all mutual funds; within its general category it has done better than 65 percent of its peers. Growth funds have averaged 17 percent annually over these same five years.

Risk/Volatility ★ ★ ★ ★

Over the past five years, T. Rowe Price Spectrum Growth has been safer than 91 percent of all growth funds. Over the past seven years, the fund has had no negative years, while the S&P 500 has had one (off 3 percent in 1990). The fund has underperformed the S&P 500 four times in the last six years.

	last 5 years		last 7 years	
worst year	1%	1994	1%	1994
best year	30%	1995	30%	1995

In the past, T. Rowe Price Spectrum Growth has done better than 25 percent of its peer group in up markets. Consistency, or predictability, of returns for T. Rowe Price Spectrum Growth can be described as excellent.

Management ★ ★ ★

The fund invests in six different T. Rowe Price domestic and foreign equity funds. Close to 90 percent of the fund's holdings are in stocks. The stocks in this portfolio have an average price-earnings (p/e) ratio of 28 and a median market capitalization of $8.7 billion. The portfolio's equity holdings can be categorized as large cap with a larger weighting towards growth as compared with value stocks.

Peter Van Dyke has overseen this "fund of funds" for the past seventeen years. There are more than seventy funds besides Spectrum Growth within the T. Rowe Price fund family. Overall, the fund family's risk-adjusted performance can be described as good.

Tax Minimization   ★ ★

During the past five years, a $10,000 initial investment grew to $18,410 after taxes, assuming a 39.6 percent income tax bracket (state and federal combined) and a capital gains rate of 28 percent. This means that investors in this fund were able to preserve 84 percent of their total returns. Compared to other equity funds, this fund's tax savings are considered to be good. Over the past year, T. Rowe Price Spectrum Growth had a twelve-month yield of 1.1 percent.

Expenses   ★ ★ ★ ★ ★

T. Rowe Price Spectrum Growth's expense ratio is 0.8 percent. The average expense ratio for the 1,100 funds in this category is 1.6 percent. This fund's turnover rate over the past year has been 27 percent, while its peer group average has been 95 percent.

Summary

T. Rowe Price Spectrum Growth is one of the most frugally run equity funds in the industry. It is also safer than over 90 percent of its peers. Risk reduction and pre-dictability of returns are also very favorable. This offering is part of a large fund family that has several other funds that investors should also flock to.

Profile

minimum initial investment $2,500	IRA accounts available . . . . yes
subsequent minimum investment . . $100	IRA minimum investment $1,000
available in all 50 states. . . . . yes	date of inception. . . . . June 1990
telephone exchanges. . . . . yes	dividend/income paid . . . . annually
number of other funds in family 70	quality of annual reports . . . . excellent

Third Avenue Value

Third Avenue Funds
767 Third Avenue, Fifth Floor
New York, NY 10017
(800) 443-1021

total return	★ ★ ★ ★
risk reduction	★ ★ ★ ★
management	★ ★ ★ ★ ★
tax minimization	★ ★ ★ ★ ★
expense control	★ ★ ★ ★
symbol TAVFX	22 points
up-market performance	very good
down-market performance	n/a
predictability of returns	excellent

Total Return   ★ ★ ★ ★

Over the past five years, Third Avenue Value has taken $10,000 and turned it into $25,940 ($19,060 over three years). This translates into an average annual return of 21 percent over the past five years and 24 percent over the past three years. Over the past five years, this fund has outperformed 95 percent of all mutual funds; within its general category it has done better than 85 percent of its peers. Growth funds have averaged 17 percent annually over these same five years.

Risk/Volatility   ★ ★ ★ ★

Over the past five years, Third Avenue Value has been safer than 82 percent of all growth funds. Over the past decade, the fund has had one negative year, as has the S&P 500 (off 3 percent in 1990). The fund has underperformed the S&P 500 three times in the last six years.

	last 5 years		last 6 years	
worst year	-1%	1994	-1%	1994
best year	32%	1995	34%	1991

In the past, Third Avenue Value has done better than 70 percent of its peer group in up markets. Consistency, or predictability, of returns for Third Avenue Value can be described as excellent.

Management   ★ ★ ★ ★ ★

There are ninety stocks in this $1.2 billion portfolio. The average growth fund today is $545 million in size. Close to 52 percent of the fund's holdings are in stocks. The stocks in this portfolio have an average price-earnings (p/e) ratio of 21 and a median market capitalization of $810 million. The portfolio's equity holdings can be categorized as small-cap and value-oriented.

Martin J. Whitman has managed this fund for the past seven years. There is one other fund offered by this company. Overall, the fund's risk-adjusted performance can be described as excellent.

Tax Minimization

During the past five years, a $10,000 initial investment grew to $22,230 after taxes, assuming a 39.6 percent income tax bracket (state and federal combined) and a capital gains rate of 28 percent. This means that investors in this fund were able to preserve 94 percent of their total returns. Compared to other equity funds, this fund's tax savings are considered to be excellent. Over the past year, Third Avenue Value had a twelve-month yield of 1.9 percent.

Expenses

Third Avenue Value's expense ratio is 1.2 percent; it has averaged 1.2 percent annually over the past three calendar years. The average expense ratio for the 1,100 funds in this category is 1.6 percent. This fund's turnover rate over the past year has been 8 percent, while its peer group average has been 95 percent.

Summary

Third Avenue Value is number one when it comes to tax minimization. The fund also ranks as the second best overall growth fund in the book. It scores very well in every single category. Not only is the fund consistent in its ratings in every department, it is also one of the most stable performers. One can only hope that the company's management will bless us with additional members to this one-fund family.

Profile

minimum initial investment $1,000	*IRA accounts available* . . . . yes
subsequent minimum investment . $1,000	*IRA minimum investment* $500
available in all 50 states. . . . . yes	*date of inception* . . . . Nov. 1990
telephone exchanges. . . . . yes	*dividend/income paid* . . . . annually
number of other funds in family. 1	*quality of annual reports* . . . . excellent

Torray

Torray Fund
6610 Rockledge Drive
Bethesda, MD 20817
(800) 443-3036

total return	★ ★ ★ ★
risk reduction	★ ★ ★
management	★ ★
tax minimization	★ ★ ★ ★ ★
expense control	★ ★ ★ ★
symbol TORYX	18 points
up-market performance	n/a
down-market performance	n/a
predictability of returns	good

Total Return

Over the past five years, Torray has taken $10,000 and turned it into $25,940 ($22,590 over three years). This translates into an average annual return of 21 percent over the past five years and 31 percent over the past three years. Over the past five years, this fund has outperformed 95 percent of all mutual funds; within its general category it has done better than 85 percent of its peers. Growth funds have averaged 17 percent annually over these same five years.

Risk/Volatility   ★ ★ ★

Over the past five years, Torray has been safer than 53 percent of all growth funds. Over the past decade, the fund has had no negative years, while the S&P 500 has had one (off 3 percent in 1990). The fund has underperformed the S&P 500 twice in the last six years.

	last 5 years		last 6 years	
worst year	2%	1994	2%	1994
best year	50%	1995	50%	1995

Consistency, or predictability, of returns for Torray can be described as good.

Management

There are forty-six stocks in this $350 million portfolio. The average growth fund today is $545 million in size. Close to 97 percent of the fund's holdings are in stocks. The stocks in this portfolio have an average price-earnings (p/e) ratio of 20 and a median market capitalization of $8.8 billion. The portfolio's equity holdings can be categorized as large-cap and value-oriented.

Robert E. Torray has managed this fund for the past seven years; Douglas Eby has been the co-manager for the last five years. There are no other funds offered by this company. Overall, the fund's risk-adjusted performance can be described as excellent.

Tax Minimization   ★ ★ ★ ★ ★

During the past five years, a $10,000 initial investment grew to $22,620 after taxes, assuming a 39.6 percent income tax bracket (state and federal combined) and a capital gains rate of 28 percent. This means that investors in this fund were able to preserve 94 percent of their total returns. Compared to other equity funds, this fund's tax savings are considered to be excellent. Over the past year, Torray had a twelve-month yield of 0.6 percent.

Expenses   ★ ★ ★ ★

Torray's expense ratio is 1.1 percent; it has averaged 1.3 percent annually over the past three calendar years. The average expense ratio for the 1,100 funds in this category is 1.6 percent. This fund's turnover rate over the past year has been 21 percent, while its peer group average has been 95 percent.

Summary

Torray ties for number one as the most tax-efficient growth fund. The fund does a good job in every area, but it is its tax minimization policy that really stands out. Lately, investors have become concerned about their after-tax returns. With this fund they will no longer be concerned.

Profile

minimum initial investment $10,000	*IRA accounts available* . . . . yes
subsequent minimum investment . $2,000	*IRA minimum investment* $10,000
available in all 50 states. . . . . yes	*date of inception.* . . . . Dec. 1990
telephone exchanges. . . . . yes	*dividend/income paid* . . . . quarterly
number of other funds in family 0	*quality of annual reports* . . . . good

Growth and Income Funds

These funds attempt to produce both capital appreciation and current income, with priority given to appreciation potential in the stocks purchased. Growth and income fund portfolios include seasoned, well established firms that pay relatively high cash dividends. The goal of these funds is to provide long-term growth without excessive volatility in share price.

Portfolio composition is almost always exclusively U.S. stocks, with an emphasis on utility, computer, energy, retail, and financial common stocks. By selecting securities that have comparatively high yields, overall risk is reduced. Dividends prop up the overall return of growth and income funds during negative market conditions.

Over the past fifty years (ending 12/31/96), common stocks have outperformed inflation, on average, 70 percent of the time over one-year periods, 82 percent of the time over five-year periods, 85 percent of the time over ten-year periods, and 100 percent of the time over any given twenty-year period of time. Over the same period, high-quality, long-term corporate bonds have outperformed inflation, on average, 62 percent of the time over one-year periods, 61 percent of the time over five-year periods, 54 percent of the time over ten-year periods, and 55 percent over any given twenty-year period of time.

As you can see by the table below, crossing a 1,000 point barrier has become easier and easier for the Dow Jones Industrial Average (DJIA). As of March 12, 1997 (the most recent changes in the composition of the Dow), the 30 stocks that comprise the DJIA were/are: Allied Signal, Alcoa, American Express, AT&T, Boeing, Caterpillar, Chevron, Coca-Cola, Walt Disney, DuPont, Eastman Kodak, Exxon, GE, GM, Goodyear, Hewlett-Packard, IBM, International Paper, Johnson & Johnson, McDonald's, Merck, 3M, J.P. Morgan, Philip Morris, Proctor & Gamble, Sears, Travelers Group, Union Carbide, United Technology, and WalMart.

Dow Milestones

Level of the Dow & Date Reached	Description
100 (1/12/06)	Not until 10 years after the DJIA is created does it hit 100.
1,000 (11/14/72)	Flirts with the 1,000 mark many times during the previous 6 yrs.
2,000 (1/8/87)	Four years of a bull market.
3,000 (4/17/91)	Rally after Gulf War.
5,000 (11/21/95)	Nine months earlier the Dow breaks 3,000.
6,000 (10/14/96)	Inflationary concerns are subdued.
7,000 (2/13/97)	The quickest 1,000 point ever for the Dow.
8,000 (7/16/97)	Market recovers after 9.8% March and April drop.

Five hundred and fifty funds make up the growth and income category. Another category, "equity-income" funds, has been combined with growth and income. Thus, for this section, there were a total of 715 possible candidates. Total market capitalization of these two categories combined is $520 billion.

Over the past three and five years, growth and income funds have had an average compound return of 23 percent per year and 17 percent during the last five years. These funds have averaged 12 percent annually over the last ten years and 16 percent annually for the past fifteen years. The standard deviation for growth and income funds has been 11 percent over the past three years (compared to 14 percent for growth funds). This means that these funds have been safer than any other category of equity funds except utility funds.

Growth & Income Funds

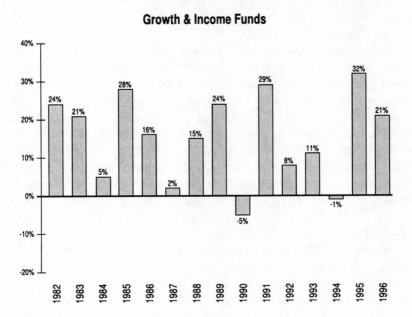

AARP Growth and Income

AARP Investment Program
42 Longwater Drive
Norwell, MA 02061-0162
(800) 322-2282

total return	★ ★ ★ ★
risk reduction	★ ★ ★ ★
management	★ ★ ★ ★
tax minimization	★ ★ ★
expense control	★ ★ ★ ★ ★
symbol AGIFX	20 points
up-market performance	excellent
down-market performance	very good
predictability of returns	very good

Total Return ★ ★ ★ ★

Over the past five years, AARP Growth and Income has taken $10,000 and turned it into $23,860 ($19,640 over three years and $37,430 over the past ten years). This translates into an average annual return of 19 percent over the past five years, 25 percent over the past three years, and 14 percent for the decade. Over the past five years, this fund has outperformed 90 percent of all mutual funds; within its general category it has done better than 85 percent of its peers. Growth and income funds have averaged 17 percent annually over these same five years.

Risk/Volatility ★ ★ ★ ★

Over the past five years, AARP Growth and Income has been safer than 62 percent of all growth & income funds. Over the past decade, the fund has had one negative year, as has the S&P 500 (off 3 percent in 1990). The fund has underperformed the S&P 500 six times in the last ten years.

	last 5 years		last 10 years	
worst year	3%	1994	-2%	1990
best year	32%	1995	32%	1995

In the past, AARP Growth and Income has done better than 80 percent of its peer group in up markets and outperformed 70 percent of its competition in down markets. Consistency, or predictability, of returns for AARP Growth and Income can be described as very good.

Management ★ ★ ★ ★

There are 140 stocks in this $5.5 billion portfolio. The average growth and income fund today is $833 million in size. Close to 93 percent of the fund's holdings are in stocks. The stocks in this portfolio have an average price-earnings (p/e) ratio of 20 and a median market capitalization of $11.4 billion. The portfolio's equity holdings can be categorized as large-cap and value-oriented.

Five co-managers, Robert T. Hoffman, 1990; Benjamin W. Thorndike, 1986; Kathleen T. Millard, 1991; Lori Ensinger, 1996; Deborah Chaplin, 1997 manages this fund. There are six funds besides Growth and Income within the AARP Investment Program. Overall, the fund family's risk-adjusted performance can be described as good.

Tax Minimization   ★ ★ ★

During the past five years, a $10,000 initial investment grew to $19,630 after taxes, assuming a 39.6 percent income tax bracket (state and federal combined) and a capital gains rate of 28 percent. This means that investors in this fund were able to preserve 88 percent of their total returns. Compared to other equity funds, this fund's tax savings are considered to be good. Over the past year, AARP Growth and Income had a twelve-month yield of 2.2 percent.

Expenses   ★ ★ ★ ★ ★

AARP Growth and Income's expense ratio is 0.7 percent; it has averaged 0.7 percent annually over the past three calendar years. The average expense ratio for the 715 funds in this category is 1.3 percent. This fund's turnover rate over the past year has been 25 percent, while its peer group average has been 66 percent.

Summary

AARP Growth and Income ties for second place as the overall best fund in its entire category. This fund does very well during bear markets and even better during up markets. The portfolio is safer than close to two thirds of its peer group. Management has done a particularly good job at keeping costs down.

Profile

minimum initial investment $500	IRA accounts available . . . . yes
subsequent minimum investment $1	IRA minimum investment $250
available in all 50 states. . . . . yes	date of inception . . . . Nov. 1984
telephone exchanges. . . . . yes	dividend/income paid . . . . quarterly
number of other funds in family. 6	quality of annual reports . . . . good

Babson Value

Babson Fund Group
Three Crown Center
2440 Pershing Road
Kansas City, MO 64108
(800) 422-2766

total return	★ ★ ★ ★ ★
risk reduction	★ ★ ★
management	★ ★ ★ ★
tax minimization	★ ★ ★ ★ ★
expense control	★ ★ ★
symbol BVALX	20 points
up-market performance	excellent
down-market performance	poor
predictability of returns	good

Total Return

Over the past five years, Babson Value has taken $10,000 and turned it into $24,880 ($18,800 over three years and $34,980 over the past ten years). This translates into an average annual return of 20 percent over the past five years, 23 percent over the past three years, and 13 percent for the decade. Over the past five years, this fund has outperformed 90 percent of all mutual funds; within its general category it has also done better than 90 percent of its peers. Growth and income funds have averaged 17 percent annually over these same five years.

Risk/Volatility

Over the past five years, Babson Value has been safer than 56 percent of all growth & income funds. Over the past decade, the fund has had one negative year, as has the S&P 500 (off 3 percent in 1990). The fund has underperformed the S&P 500 six times in the last ten years.

	last 5 years		last 10 years	
worst year	3%	1994	-11%	1990
best year	32%	1995	32%	1995

In the past, Babson Value has done better than 90 percent of its peer group in up markets but virtually none of its competition in down markets. Consistency, or predictability, of returns for Babson Value can be described as good.

Management

There are forty stocks in this $1.2 billion portfolio. The average growth and income fund today is $833 million in size. Close to 95 percent of the fund's holdings are in stocks. The stocks in this portfolio have an average price-earnings (p/e) ratio of 22 and a median market capitalization of $9.7 billion. The portfolio's equity holdings can be categorized as large-cap and value-oriented stocks.

Nick Whitridge has managed this fund for the past thirteen years. There are thirteen funds besides Value within the Babson Group. Overall, the fund family's risk-adjusted performance can be described as good.

Tax Minimization

During the past five years, a $10,000 initial investment grew to $21,620 after taxes, assuming a 39.6 percent income tax bracket (state and federal combined) and a capital gains rate of 28 percent. This means that investors in this fund were able to preserve 91 percent of their total returns. Compared to other equity funds, this fund's tax savings are considered to be very good. Over the past year, Babson Value had a twelve-month yield of 1.1 percent.

Expenses

Babson Value's expense ratio is 1.0 percent; it has averaged 1.0 percent annually over the past three calendar years. The average expense ratio for the 715 funds in this category is 1.3 percent. This fund's turnover rate over the past year has been 11 percent, while its peer group average has been 66 percent.

Summary

Babson Value is the only growth and income fund that receives the highest possible rating for both total return and tax minimization. The total point score for the fund is also quite impressive. This is not a well known defensive fund, but one that should be used by a wide range of investors. It is one of the best possible choices for anyone who wants to take a conservative approach to equities.

Profile

minimum initial investment $1,000	*IRA accounts available* . . . . yes
subsequent minimum investment . . $100	*IRA minimum investment* $250
available in all 50 states. . . . . yes	*date of inception.* . . . . Dec. 1984
telephone exchanges. . . . . yes	*dividend/income paid* . . . . quarterly
number of other funds in family 13	*quality of annual reports* . . . . good

Dodge & Cox Stock

Dodge & Cox Group
One Sansome Street, 35th Floor
San Francisco, CA 94104
(800) 621-3979

total return	★ ★ ★ ★ ★
risk reduction	★ ★
management	★ ★ ★
tax minimization	★ ★ ★ ★
expense control	★ ★ ★ ★ ★
symbol DODGX	19 points
up-market performance	excellent
down-market performance	poor
predictability of returns	fair

Total Return   ★ ★ ★ ★ ★

Over the past five years, Dodge & Cox Stock has taken $10,000 and turned it into $25,940 ($20,280 over three years and $38,630 over the past ten years). This translates into an average annual return of 21 percent over the past five years, 27 percent over the past three years, and 14 percent for the decade. Over the past five years, this fund has outperformed 95 percent of all mutual funds; within its general category it has also done better than 95 percent of its peers. Growth and income funds have averaged 17 percent annually over these same five years.

Risk/Volatility   ★ ★

Over the past five years, Dodge & Cox Stock has been safer than just 17 percent of all growth & income funds. Over the past decade, the fund has had one negative year, as has the S&P 500 (off 3 percent in 1990). The fund has underperformed the S&P 500 six times in the last ten years.

	last 5 years		last 10 years	
worst year	5%	1994	-5%	1990
best year	33%	1995	33%	1995

In the past, Dodge & Cox Stock has done better than 85 percent of its peer group in up markets but only 10 percent of its competition in down markets. Consistency, or predictability, of returns for Dodge & Cox Stock can be described as fair.

Management   ★ ★ ★

There are seventy-six stocks in this $3.3 billion portfolio. The average growth and income fund today is $833 million in size. Close to 92 percent of the fund's holdings are in stocks. The stocks in this portfolio have an average price-earnings (p/e) ratio of 20 and a median market capitalization of $10.5 billion. The portfolio's equity holdings can be categorized as large-cap and value-oriented.

A team has managed this fund for since its inception 32 years ago. There are two funds besides Stock within the Dodge & Cox fund family. Overall, the fund family's risk-adjusted performance can be described as very good.

Tax Minimization   ★ ★ ★ ★
During the past five years, a $10,000 initial investment grew to $21,060 after taxes, assuming a 39.6 percent income tax bracket (state and federal combined) and a capital gains rate of 28 percent. This means that investors in this fund were able to preserve 90 percent of their total returns. Compared to other equity funds, this fund's tax savings are considered to be very good. Over the past year, Dodge & Cox Stock had a twelve-month yield of 1.6 percent.

Expenses   ★ ★ ★ ★ ★
Dodge & Cox Stock's expense ratio is 0.6 percent; it has averaged 0.6 percent annually over the past three calendar years. The average expense ratio for the 715 funds in this category is 1.3 percent. This fund's turnover rate over the past year has been 10 percent, while its peer group average has been 66 percent.

Summary
Dodge & Cox Stock is a member of a fine family of funds. The group has distinguished itself over the years as purists. Management has stuck to its guns over the years, and its investment philosophy has certainly paid off. This, as well as other members of the Dodge & Cox group are highly recommended. This growth and income fund ranks as the number one performer when it comes to total return.

Profile

minimum initial investment $2,500	*IRA accounts available* . . . . yes
subsequent minimum investment . . $100	*IRA minimum investment* $1,000
available in all 50 states. . . . . yes	*date of inception* . . . . Jan. 1965
telephone exchanges. . . . . yes	*dividend/income paid* . . . . quarterly
number of other funds in family. 2	*quality of annual reports* . . . . good

Excelsior Income & Growth

Excelsior Funds
114 West 47th Street
New York, NY 10036-1532
(800) 446-1012

total return	★ ★ ★
risk reduction	★ ★ ★ ★
management	★ ★ ★
tax minimization	★ ★ ★ ★
expense control	★ ★ ★
symbol UMIGX	17 points
up-market performance	very good
down-market performance	poor
predictability of returns	very good

Total Return   ★ ★ ★

Over the past five years, Excelsior Income & Growth has taken $10,000 and turned it into $22,880 ($17,110 over three years and $30,450 over the past ten years). This translates into an average annual return of 18 percent over the past five years, 20 percent over the past three years, and 12 percent for the decade. Over the past five years, this fund has outperformed 85 percent of all mutual funds; within its general category it has done better than 55 percent of its peers. Growth and income funds have averaged 17 percent annually over these same five years.

Risk/Volatility   ★ ★ ★ ★

Over the past five years, Excelsior Income & Growth has been safer than 77 percent of all growth and income funds. Over the past decade, the fund has had two negative years, while the S&P 500 has had one (off 3 percent in 1990). The fund has underperformed the S&P 500 six times in the last nine years.

	last 5 years		last 9 years	
worst year	-4%	1994	-18%	1990
best year	30%	1995	30%	1995

In the past, Excelsior Income & Growth has done better than 60 percent of its peer group in up markets but only 5 percent of its competition in down markets. Consistency, or predictability, of returns for Excelsior Income & Growth can be described as very good.

Management   ★ ★ ★

There are forty stocks in this $150 million portfolio. The average growth and income fund today is $833 million in size. Close to 71 percent of the fund's holdings are in stocks. The stocks in this portfolio have an average price-earnings (p/e) ratio of 26 and a median market capitalization of $5.7 billion. The portfolio's equity holdings can be categorized as large cap and value oriented.

Richard L. Bayles has managed this fund for the past seven years. There are thirty-one funds besides Income & Growth within the Excelsior fund family. Overall, the fund family's risk-adjusted performance can be described as good.

Tax Minimization   ★ ★ ★ ★
During the past five years, a $10,000 initial investment grew to $19,710 after taxes, assuming a 39.6 percent income tax bracket (state and federal combined) and a capital gains rate of 28 percent. This means that investors in this fund were able to preserve 90 percent of their total returns. Compared to other equity funds, this fund's tax savings are considered to be very good. Over the past year, Excelsior Income & Growth had a twelve-month yield of 1.7 percent.

Expenses   ★ ★ ★
Excelsior Income & Growth's expense ratio is 1.1 percent; it has averaged 1.1 percent annually over the past three calendar years. The average expense ratio for the 715 funds in this category is 1.3 percent. This fund's turnover rate over the past year has been 22 percent, while its peer group average has been 66 percent.

Summary
Excelsior Income & Growth is not highly recommended for those with a bear market mentality. Fortunately, for the fund and the rest of us, the average bull market, which is when this fund does well, is about four times longer than the typical bear market. The fund family is not well known and neither is this fund. Despite beating out 98 percent of its peers, the fund and some of its family members may not get some of the publicity it deserves.

Profile
minimum initial investment $500
subsequent minimum investment ... $50
available in all 50 states.......... yes
telephone exchanges............. yes
number of other funds in family..... 31

IRA accounts available .... yes
IRA minimum investment $250
date of inception .... Jan. 1987
dividend/income paid .... quarterly
quality of annual reports ..... average

Fundamental Investors

American Funds Group
4 Embarcadero Center
P.O. Box 7650
San Francisco, CA 94120
(800) 421-4120

total return	★ ★ ★ ★ ★
risk reduction	★ ★ ★ ★
management	★ ★ ★ ★
tax minimization	★ ★
expense control	★ ★ ★ ★ ★
symbol ANCFX	20 points
up-market performance	excellent
down-market performance	poor
predictability of returns	good

Total Return   ★ ★ ★ ★ ★

Over the past five years, Fundamental Investors has taken $10,000 and turned it into $24,880 ($19,500 over three years and $36,970 over the past ten years). This translates into an average annual return of 20 percent over the past five years, 25 percent over the past three years, and 14 percent for the decade. Over the past five years, this fund has outperformed 90 percent of all mutual funds; within its general category it has also done better than 90 percent of its peers. Growth and income funds have averaged 17 percent annually over these same five years.

Risk/Volatility   ★ ★ ★ ★

Over the past five years, Fundamental Investors has been safer than 50 percent of all growth and income funds. Over the past decade, the fund has had one negative year, as has the S&P 500 (off 3 percent in 1990). The fund has underperformed the S&P 500 seven times in the last ten years.

	last 5 years		last 10 years	
worst year	1%	1994	-6%	1990
best year	34%	1995	34%	1995

In the past, Fundamental Investors has done better than 80 percent of its peer group in up markets but only 10 percent of its competition in down markets. Consistency, or predictability, of returns for Fundamental Investors can be described as good.

Management   ★ ★ ★ ★

There are 190 stocks in this $9.1 billion portfolio. The average growth and income fund today is $833 million in size. Close to 93 percent of the fund's holdings are in stocks. The stocks in this portfolio have an average price-earnings (p/e) ratio of

24 and a median market capitalization of $15.0 billion. The portfolio's equity holdings can be categorized as large-cap and value-oriented.

A management team has overseen this fund since its 1978 inception. There are twenty-four funds besides Fundamental Investors within the American Funds Group. Overall, the fund family's risk-adjusted performance can be described as good.

Tax Minimization ★ ★

During the past five years, a $10,000 initial investment grew to $19,090 after taxes, assuming a 39.6 percent income tax bracket (state and federal combined) and a capital gains rate of 28 percent. This means that investors in this fund were able to preserve 82 percent of their total returns. Compared to other equity funds, this fund's tax savings are considered to be good. Over the past year, Fundamental Investors had a twelve-month yield of 1.3 percent.

Expenses ★ ★ ★ ★ ★

Fundamental Investors's expense ratio is 0.7 percent; it has averaged 0.7 percent annually over the past three calendar years. The average expense ratio for the 715 funds in this category is 1.3 percent. This fund's turnover rate over the past year has been 39 percent, while its peer group average has been 66 percent.

Summary

Fundamental Investors is yet another member of the American Funds Group to appear in this and previous editions of this book. Part of the reason this fund family has done such a phenomenal job of attracting millions of investors (they do virtually no advertising) is the company's approach to management. Each fund is run under the multiple portfolio counselor system—several managers, each with lots of experience, is responsible for a segment of the portfolio. Each portion is managed by a portfolio counselor who operates autonomously and invests his or her portion as if it were an entire fund—subject to fund objectives and overall guidelines. This is a highly recommended growth and income fund.

Profile

minimum initial investment $250	IRA accounts available .... yes
subsequent minimum investment ... $50	IRA minimum investment $250
available in all 50 states.......... yes	date of inception .... Aug. 1978
telephone exchanges............. yes	dividend/income paid .... quarterly
number of other funds in family..... 24	quality of annual reports .... excellent

Homestead Value

Homestead Funds
4301 Wilson Boulevard
Arlington, VA 22203
(800) 258-3030

total return	★ ★ ★ ★
risk reduction	★ ★ ★ ★
management	★ ★ ★ ★
tax minimization	★ ★ ★ ★ ★
expense control	★ ★ ★ ★
symbol HOVLX	21 points
up-market performance	n/a
down-market performance	n/a
predictability of returns	very good

Total Return ★ ★ ★ ★

Over the past five years, Homestead Value has taken $10,000 and turned it into $23,860 ($18,650 over three years). This translates into an average annual return of 19 percent over the past five years and 23 percent over the past three years. Over the past five years, this fund has outperformed 90 percent of all mutual funds; within its general category it has done better than 75 percent of its peers. Growth and income funds have averaged 17 percent annually over these same five years.

Risk/Volatility ★ ★ ★ ★

Over the past five years, Homestead Value has been safer than 74 percent of all growth & income funds. Over the past decade, the fund has had no negative years, while the S&P 500 has had one (off 3 percent in 1990). The fund has underperformed the S&P 500 three times in the last six years.

	last 5 years		last 6 years	
worst year	3%	1994	3%	1994
best year	34%	1995	34%	1995

Consistency, or predictability, of returns for Homestead Value can be described as very good.

Management ★ ★ ★ ★

There are fifty-nine stocks in this $360 million portfolio. The average growth and income fund today is $833 million in size. Close to 89 percent of the fund's holdings are in stocks. The stocks in this portfolio have an average price-earnings (p/e) ratio of 22 and a median market capitalization of $5.3 billion. The portfolio's equity holdings can be categorized as large-cap and value-oriented.

Stuart E. Teach has managed this fund for the past seven years. There are three funds besides Value within the Homestead fund family. Overall, the fund family's risk-adjusted performance can be described as very good.

Tax Minimization   ★ ★ ★ ★ ★

During the past five years, a $10,000 initial investment grew to $20,170 after taxes, assuming a 39.6 percent income tax bracket (state and federal combined) and a capital gains rate of 28 percent. This means that investors in this fund were able to preserve 92 percent of their total returns. Compared to other equity funds, this fund's tax savings are considered to be very good. Over the past year, Homestead Value had a twelve-month yield of 1.5 percent.

Expenses   ★ ★ ★ ★

Homestead Value's expense ratio is 0.7 percent; it has averaged 0.9 percent annually over the past three calendar years. The average expense ratio for the 715 funds in this category is 1.3 percent. This fund's turnover rate over the past year has been 5 percent, while its peer group average has been 66 percent.

Summary

Homestead Value ranks overall as the best growth and income fund. This relatively unknown fund has managed to beat all the giants as well as all its other peers that make up a fund category comprised of 715 candidates. This particular fund does a very good job when it comes to performance and risk minimization. It has an extremely low turnover rate, which help keeps hidden expenses to a minimum. One of the fund's best characteristics is its tax minimization policy. This very small fund family has a couple of other members that you should check out.

Profile

minimum initial investment $500	*IRA accounts available* . . . . yes
subsequent minimum investment $1	*IRA minimum investment* . . . . n/a
available in all 50 states. . . . . yes	*date of inception* . . . . Nov. 1990
telephone exchanges. . . . . yes	*dividend/income paid* . . . semi-annually
number of other funds in family. 3	*quality of annual reports* . . . . good

Merrill Lynch Basic Value A

Merrill Lynch Group
Box 9011
Princeton, NJ 08543-9011
(800) 637-3863

total return	★ ★ ★ ★
risk reduction	★ ★ ★ ★
management	★ ★ ★
tax minimization	★ ★ ★
expense control	★ ★ ★ ★ ★
symbol MABAX	19 points
up-market performance	excellent
down-market performance	poor
predictability of returns	very good

Total Return   ★ ★ ★ ★

Over the past five years, Merrill Lynch Basic Value A has taken $10,000 and turned it into $23,860 ($18,960 over three years and $34,920 over the past ten years). This translates into an average annual return of 19 percent over the past five years, 24 percent over the past three years, and 13 percent for the decade. Over the past five years, this fund has outperformed 90 percent of all mutual funds; within its general category it has done better than 75 percent of its peers. Growth and income funds have averaged 17 percent annually over these same five years.

Risk/Volatility   ★ ★ ★ ★

Over the past five years, Merrill Lynch Basic Value A has been safer than 62 percent of all growth and income funds. Over the past decade, the fund has had one negative year, as has the S&P 500 (off 3 percent in 1990). The fund has underperformed the S&P 500 six times in the last ten years.

	last 5 years		last 10 years	
worst year	2%	1994	-13%	1990
best year	33%	1995	33%	1995

In the past, Merrill Lynch Basic Value A has done better than 80 percent of its peer group in up markets but only 5 percent of its competition in down markets. Consistency, or predictability, of returns for Merrill Lynch Basic Value A can be described as very good.

Management   ★ ★ ★

There are seventy stocks in this $4.7 billion portfolio. The average growth and income fund today is $833 million in size. Close to 85 percent of the fund's holdings are in stocks. The stocks in this portfolio have an average price-earnings (p/e) ratio of 20 and a median market capitalization of $24.8 billion. The portfolio's equity holdings can be categorized as large-cap and value-oriented.

Paul M. Hoffmann has managed this fund for the past twenty years. There are 287 funds besides Basic Value A within the Merrill Lynch fund family. Overall, the fund family's risk-adjusted performance can be described as fair.

Tax Minimization   ★ ★ ★

During the past five years, a $10,000 initial investment grew to $19,820 after taxes, assuming a 39.6 percent income tax bracket (state and federal combined) and a capital gains rate of 28 percent. This means that investors in this fund were able to preserve 87 percent of their total returns. Compared to other equity funds, this fund's tax savings are considered to be good. Over the past year, Merrill Lynch Basic Value A had a twelve-month yield of 2.1 percent.

Expenses   ★ ★ ★ ★ ★

Merrill Lynch Basic Value A's expense ratio is 0.6 percent; it has averaged 0.6 percent annually over the past three calendar years. The average expense ratio for the 715 funds in this category is 1.3 percent. This fund's turnover rate over the past year has been 14 percent, while its peer group average has been 66 percent.

Summary

Merrill Lynch Basic Value A is one of the few brokerage firm, also known as "inhouse" funds, to make this book. This excellent growth and income fund from Merrill Lynch turns in very good results coupled with low risk—quite a winning combination. Not many investors think that low expenses can be part of such a huge operation, but this fund bucks conventional wisdom in a number of ways.

Profile

minimum initial investment $1,000	*IRA accounts available* . . . . yes
subsequent minimum investment . . . $50	*IRA minimum investment* $100
available in all 50 states. . . . . yes	*date of inception* . . . . July 1977
telephone exchanges . . . . no	*dividend/income paid* . . . semi-annually
number of other funds in family 287	*quality of annual reports* . . . . good

Scudder Growth and Income

Scudder Funds
Two International Place
Boston, MA 02110
(800) 225-2470

total return	★ ★ ★ ★
risk reduction	★ ★ ★ ★
management	★ ★ ★
tax minimization	★ ★
expense control	★ ★ ★ ★
symbol SCDGX	17 points
up-market performance	very good
down-market performance	excellent
predictability of returns	very good

Total Return

Over the past five years, Scudder Growth and Income has taken $10,000 and turned it into $23,860 ($19,580 over three years and $38,600 over the past ten years). This translates into an average annual return of 19 percent over the past five years, 25 percent over the past three years, and 14 percent for the decade. Over the past five years, this fund has outperformed 90 percent of all mutual funds; within its general category it has done better than 80 percent of its peers. Growth and income funds have averaged 17 percent annually over these same five years.

Risk/Volatility

Over the past five years, Scudder Growth and Income has been safer than 54 percent of all growth and income funds. Over the past decade, the fund has had one negative year, as has the S&P 500 (off 3 percent in 1990). The fund has underperformed the S&P 500 six times in the last ten years.

	last 5 years		last 10 years	
worst year	3%	1994	-2%	1990
best year	31%	1995	31%	1995

In the past, Scudder Growth and Income has done better than 70 percent of its peer group in up markets and outperformed 90 percent of its competition in down markets. Consistency, or predictability, of returns for Scudder Growth and Income can be described as very good.

Management

There are 140 stocks in this $5.3 billion portfolio. The average growth and income fund today is $833 million in size. Close to 93 percent of the fund's holdings are in stocks. The stocks in this portfolio have an average price-earnings (p/e) ratio of 21 and a median market capitalization of $12.8 billion. The portfolio's equity holdings can be categorized as large-cap and value-oriented.

A team has managed this fund for the past five years. There are thirty-one funds besides Growth and Income within the Scudder fund family. Overall, the fund family's risk-adjusted performance can be described as good.

Tax Minimization   ★ ★
During the past five years, a $10,000 initial investment grew to $19,100 after taxes, assuming a 39.6 percent income tax bracket (state and federal combined) and a capital gains rate of 28 percent. This means that investors in this fund were able to preserve 84 percent of their total returns. Compared to other equity funds, this fund's tax savings are considered to be good. Over the past year, Scudder Growth and Income had a twelve-month yield of 2.1 percent.

Expenses   ★ ★ ★ ★
Scudder Growth and Income's expense ratio is 0.8 percent; it has averaged 0.8 percent annually over the past three calendar years. The average expense ratio for the 715 funds in this category is 1.3 percent. This fund's turnover rate over the past year has been 27 percent, while its peer group average has been 66 percent.

Summary
Scudder Growth and Income is the only fund in its category to receive a rating of excellent for bear market performance. It also has an exceptional ten-year track record. The fund has managed to do a very good job when it comes to total return and risk reduction. Look for other Scudder funds in this book.

Profile
minimum initial investment $2,500	*IRA accounts available* . . . . yes
subsequent minimum investment . . $100	*IRA minimum investment* $1,000
available in all 50 states. . . . . yes	*date of inception*. . . . . Dec. 1984
telephone exchanges. . . . . yes	*dividend/income paid* . . . . quarterly
number of other funds in family. 31	*quality of annual reports* . . . . excellent

T. Rowe Price Equity-Income

T. Rowe Price Funds
100 East Pratt Street
Baltimore, MD 21202
(800) 638-5660

total return	★ ★ ★
risk reduction	★ ★ ★ ★ ★
management	★ ★ ★ ★ ★
tax minimization	★ ★
expense control	★ ★ ★ ★
symbol PRFDX	19 points
up-market performance	excellent
down-market performance	fair
predictability of returns	excellent

Total Return   ★ ★ ★

Over the past five years, T. Rowe Price Equity-Income has taken $10,000 and turned it into $23,860 ($19,420 over three years and $38,330 over the past ten years). This translates into an average annual return of 19 percent over the past five years, 25 percent over the past three years, and 14 percent for the decade. Over the past five years, this fund has outperformed 85 percent of all mutual funds; within its general category it has done better than 70 percent of its peers. Growth and income funds have averaged 17 percent annually over these same five years.

Risk/Volatility   ★ ★ ★ ★ ★

Over the past five years, T. Rowe Price Equity-Income has been safer than 94 percent of all growth and income funds. Over the past decade, the fund has had one negative year, as has the S&P 500 (off 3 percent in 1990). The fund has underperformed the S&P 500 six times in the last ten years.

	last 5 years		last 10 years	
worst year	5%	1994	-7%	1990
best year	33%	1995	33%	1995

In the past, T. Rowe Price Equity-Income has done better than 85 percent of its peer group in up markets but only 25 percent of its competition in down markets. Consistency, or predictability, of returns for T. Rowe Price Equity-Income can be described as excellent.

Management   ★ ★ ★ ★ ★

There are 140 stocks in this $10.0 billion portfolio. The average growth and income fund today is $833 million in size. Close to 86 percent of the fund's holdings are in stocks. The stocks in this portfolio have an average price-earnings (p/e) ratio of 23 and a median market capitalization of $11.7 billion. The portfolio's equity holdings can be categorized as large-cap and value-oriented.

Brian C. Rogers has managed this fund for the past twelve years. There are seventy funds besides Equity-Income within the T. Rowe Price fund family. Overall, the fund family's risk-adjusted performance can be described as good.

Tax Minimization   ★ ★

During the past five years, a $10,000 initial investment grew to $19,390 after taxes, assuming a 39.6 percent income tax bracket (state and federal combined) and a capital gains rate of 28 percent. This means that investors in this fund were able to preserve 84 percent of their total returns. Compared to other equity funds, this fund's tax savings are considered to be good. Over the past year, T. Rowe Price Equity-Income had a twelve-month yield of 3.2 percent.

Expenses   ★ ★ ★ ★

T. Rowe Price Equity-Income's expense ratio is 0.8 percent; it has averaged 0.8 percent annually over the past three calendar years. The average expense ratio for the 715 funds in this category is 1.3 percent. This fund's turnover rate over the past year has been 25 percent, while its peer group average has been 66 percent.

Summary

T. Rowe Price Equity-Income is one of the few funds whose management is considered to be superior. The fund scores well in every important area, but it really shines when it comes to risk reduction. It is safer than about 95 percent of its peers.

Profile

minimum initial investment $2,500	*IRA accounts available* . . . . yes
subsequent minimum investment . . $100	*IRA minimum investment* $1,000
available in all 50 states. . . . . yes	*date of inception* . . . . Oct. 1985
telephone exchanges. . . . . yes	*dividend/income paid* . . . . quarterly
number of other funds in family 70	*quality of annual reports* . . . . excellent

T. Rowe Price Growth & Income

T. Rowe Price Funds
100 East Pratt Street
Baltimore, MD 21202
(800) 638-5660

total return	★ ★ ★
risk reduction	★ ★ ★ ★
management	★ ★ ★ ★
tax minimization	★ ★ ★
expense control	★ ★ ★ ★
symbol PRGIX	18 points
up-market performance	excellent
down-market performance	poor
predictability of returns	excellent

Total Return   ★ ★ ★

Over the past five years, T. Rowe Price Growth & Income has taken $10,000 and turned it into $22,880 ($19,110 over three years and $34,340 over the past ten years). This translates into an average annual return of 18 percent over the past five years, 24 percent over the past three years, and 13 percent for the decade. Over the past five years, this fund has outperformed 85 percent of all mutual funds; within its general category it has done better than 65 percent of its peers. Growth and income funds have averaged 17 percent annually over these same five years.

Risk/Volatility   ★ ★ ★ ★

Over the past five years, T. Rowe Price Growth & Income has been safer than 80 percent of all growth and income funds. Over the past decade, the fund has had three negative years, while the S&P 500 has had one (off 3 percent in 1990). The fund has underperformed the S&P 500 five times in the last ten years.

	last 5 years		last 10 years	
worst year	0%	1994	-11%	1990
best year	31%	1995	32%	1991

In the past, T. Rowe Price Growth & Income has done better than 85 percent of its peer group in up markets but only 5 percent of its competition in down markets. Consistency, or predictability, of returns for T. Rowe Price Growth & Income can be described as excellent.

Management   ★ ★ ★ ★

There are 110 stocks in this $3.1 billion portfolio. The average growth and income fund today is $833 million in size. Close to 83 percent of the fund's holdings are in stocks. The stocks in this portfolio have an average price-earnings (p/e) ratio of 27 and a median market capitalization of $11.5 billion. The portfolio's equity holdings can be categorized as large-cap and value-oriented.

Stephen W. Boesel has managed this fund for the past ten years. There are seventy funds besides Growth & Income within the T. Rowe Price fund family. Overall, the fund family's risk-adjusted performance can be described as good.

Tax Minimization   ★ ★ ★

During the past five years, a $10,000 initial investment grew to $19,200 after taxes, assuming a 39.6 percent income tax bracket (state and federal combined) and a capital gains rate of 28 percent. This means that investors in this fund were able to preserve 86 percent of their total returns. Compared to other equity funds, this fund's tax savings are considered to be good. Over the past year, T. Rowe Price Growth & Income had a twelve-month yield of 2.5 percent.

Expenses   ★ ★ ★ ★

T. Rowe Price Growth & Income's expense ratio is 0.8 percent; it has averaged 0.8 percent annually over the past three calendar years. The average expense ratio for the 715 funds in this category is 1.3 percent. This fund's turnover rate over the past year has been 17 percent, while its peer group average has been 66 percent.

Summary

T. Rowe Price Growth & Income is just one of several members of the T. Rowe Price family to appear in this book. Unlike some of its "sister" funds, this particular offering is best suited for investors who are positive on the overall stock market. A somewhat more conservative fund, T. Rowe Price Equity-Income, also makes the list as one of the top funds under the growth and income category.

Profile

minimum initial investment $2,500	*IRA accounts available* . . . . yes
subsequent minimum investment . . $100	*IRA minimum investment* $1,000
available in all 50 states. . . . . yes	*date of inception.* . . . . Dec. 1982
telephone exchanges. . . . . yes	*dividend/income paid* . . . . quarterly
number of other funds in family 70	*quality of annual reports* . . . . excellent

Van Kampen American Capital Equity-Income A

Van Kampen American Capital Funds
One Parkview Plaza
Oakbrook Terrace, IL 60181
(800) 421-5666

total return	★ ★
risk reduction	★ ★ ★ ★
management	★ ★ ★ ★
tax minimization	★ ★
expense control	★ ★ ★
symbol ACEIX	15 points
up-market performance	good
down-market performance	good
predictability of returns	excellent

Total Return   ★ ★

Over the past five years, Van Kampen American Capital Equity-Income A has taken $10,000 and turned it into $21,920 ($17,910 over three years and $30,620 over the past ten years). This translates into an average annual return of 17 percent over the past five years, 21 percent over the past three years, and 12 percent for the decade. Over the past five years, this fund has outperformed 80 percent of all mutual funds; within its general category it has done better than 40 percent of its peers. Growth and income funds have averaged 17 percent annually over these same five years.

Risk/Volatility   ★ ★ ★ ★

Over the past five years, Van Kampen American Capital Equity-Income A has been safer than 88 percent of all growth and income funds. Over the past decade, the fund has had two negative years, while the S&P 500 has had one (off 3 percent in 1990). The fund has underperformed the S&P 500 eight times in the last ten years.

	last 5 years		last 10 years	
worst year	-2%	1994	-5%	1990
best year	33%	1995	33%	1995

In the past, Van Kampen American Capital Equity-Income A has done better than 50 percent of its peer group in up markets and 45 percent of its competition in down markets. Consistency, or predictability, of returns for Van Kampen American Capital Equity-Income A can be described as excellent.

Management   ★ ★ ★ ★

There are 130 stocks in this $550 million portfolio. The average growth and income fund today is $833 million in size. Close to 71 percent of the fund's holdings are in stocks. The stocks in this portfolio have an average price-earnings (p/e) ratio of 24 and a median market capitalization of $10.6 billion. The average maturity of the bonds in this account is nine years; the weighted coupon rate averages 5.5 percent. The portfolio's equity holdings can be categorized as large-cap and value-oriented.

Gilligan and Stanley have managed this fund for the past five years. There are 100 funds besides Equity-Income A within the Van Kampen American Capital fund family. Overall, the fund family's risk-adjusted performance can be described as fair.

Tax Minimization   ★ ★

During the past five years, a $10,000 initial investment grew to $19,420 after taxes, assuming a 39.6 percent income tax bracket (state and federal combined) and a capital gains rate of 28 percent. This means that investors in this fund were able to preserve 84 percent of their total returns. Compared to other equity funds, this fund's tax savings are considered to be good. Over the past year, Van Kampen American Capital Equity-Income A had a twelve-month yield of 1.9 percent.

Expenses   ★ ★ ★

Van Kampen American Capital Equity-Income A's expense ratio is 1.0 percent; it has averaged 1.0 percent annually over the past three calendar years. The average expense ratio for the 715 funds in this category is 1.3 percent. This fund's turnover rate over the past year has been 92 percent, while its peer group average has been 66 percent.

Summary

Van Kampen American Capital Equity-Income A is a good choice for the conservative investor who wants stock market exposure. This steady performer has very strong management. The fund has been able to keep its investors safe and secure. Other funds have stronger total return figures, but few are as adept at risk minimization.

Profile

minimum initial investment $500	IRA accounts available . . . . yes
subsequent minimum investment . . . $25	IRA minimum investment $500
available in all 50 states. . . . . yes	date of inception . . . . Aug. 1960
telephone exchanges. . . . . yes	dividend/income paid . . . . quarterly
number of other funds in family 100	quality of annual reports . . . . good

Victory Diversified Stock A

Victory Group
P.O. Box 9741
Providence, RI 02940-9741
(800) 539-3863

total return	★ ★ ★ ★ ★
risk reduction	★ ★
management	★ ★ ★
tax minimization	★
expense control	★ ★ ★
symbol SRVEX	14 points
up-market performance	good
down-market performance	very good
predictability of returns	fair

Total Return

Over the past five years, Victory Diversified Stock A has taken $10,000 and turned it into $24,880 ($20,620 over three years). This translates into an average annual return of 20 percent over the past five years and 27 percent over the past three years. Over the past five years, this fund has outperformed 90 percent of all mutual funds; within its general category it has also done better than 90 percent of its peers. Growth and income funds have averaged 17 percent annually over these same five years.

Risk/Volatility   ★ ★

Over the past five years, Victory Diversified Stock A has been safer than 34 percent of all growth and income funds. Over the past decade, the fund has had no negative years, while the S&P 500 has had one (off 3 percent in 1990). The fund has underperformed the S&P 500 twice in the last seven years.

	last 5 years		last 7 years	
worst year	4%	1994	1%	1990
best year	35%	1995	35%	1995

In the past, Victory Diversified Stock A has done better than 55 percent of its peer group in up markets and outperformed 75 percent of its competition in down markets. Consistency, or predictability, of returns for Victory Diversified Stock A can be described as fair.

Management

There are eighty stocks in this $710 million portfolio. The average growth and income fund today is $833 million in size. Close to 94 percent of the fund's holdings are in stocks. The stocks in this portfolio have an average price-earnings (p/e) ratio of 23 and a median market capitalization of $20.4 billion. The portfolio's equity holdings can be categorized as large-cap and value-oriented.

Lawrence G. Babin has managed this fund for the past eight years. There are twenty-five funds besides Diversified Stock A within the Victory Group. Overall, the fund family's risk-adjusted performance can be described as good.

Tax Minimization   ★
During the past five years, a $10,000 initial investment grew to $18,740 after taxes, assuming a 39.6 percent income tax bracket (state and federal combined) and a capital gains rate of 28 percent. This means that investors in this fund were able to preserve 79 percent of their total returns. Compared to other equity funds, this fund's tax savings are considered to be poor. Over the past year, Victory Diversified Stock A had a twelve-month yield of 1.0 percent.

Expenses   ★ ★ ★
Victory Diversified Stock A's expense ratio is 1.1 percent; it has averaged 1.0 percent annually over the past three calendar years. The average expense ratio for the 715 funds in this category is 1.3 percent. This fund's turnover rate over the past year has been 94 percent, while its peer group average has been 66 percent.

Summary
Victory Diversified Stock A scores big when it comes to performance. This is not a well known fund or fund family, but one that certainly deserves strong consideration. The fund has done a good job of keeping the faith during bear markets.

Profile
minimum initial investment $500	*IRA accounts available* . . . . yes
subsequent minimum investment . . . $25	*IRA minimum investment* $250
available in all 50 states . . . . no	*date of inception* . . . . Oct. 1989
telephone exchanges. . . . . yes	*dividend/income paid* . . . . quarterly
number of other funds in family 25	*quality of annual reports* . . . . good

Washington Mutual Investors

American Funds Group
1101 Vermont Avenue, North West
Washington, DC 20005
(800) 421-4120

total return	★ ★ ★ ★
risk reduction	★ ★ ★
management	★ ★ ★
tax minimization	★ ★ ★
expense control	★ ★ ★ ★ ★
symbol AWSHX	18 points
up-market performance	very good
down-market performance	fair
predictability of returns	good

Total Return   ★ ★ ★ ★
Over the past five years, Washington Mutual Investors has taken $10,000 and turned it into $23,860 ($20,650 over three years and $37,730 over the past ten years). This translates into an average annual return of 19 percent over the past five years, 27 percent over the past three years, and 14 percent for the decade. Over the past five years, this fund has outperformed 90 percent of all mutual funds; within its general category it has done better than 85 percent of its peers. Growth and income funds have averaged 17 percent annually over these same five years.

Risk/Volatility   ★ ★ ★
Over the past five years, Washington Mutual Investors has been safer than half of all growth and income funds. Over the past decade, the fund has had one negative year, as has the S&P 500 (off 3 percent in 1990). The fund has underperformed the S&P 500 six times in the last ten years.

	last 5 years		last 10 years	
worst year	0%	1994	-4%	1990
best year	41%	1995	41%	1995

In the past, Washington Mutual Investors has done better than 75 percent of its peer group in up markets but only 35 percent of its competition in down markets. Consistency, or predictability, of returns for Washington Mutual Investors can be described as good.

Management   ★ ★ ★
There are 140 stocks in this $32.0 billion portfolio. The average growth and income fund today is $833 million in size. Close to 96 percent of the fund's holdings are in stocks. The stocks in this portfolio have an average price-earnings (p/e) ratio of 21 and a median market capitalization of $18.9 billion. The portfolio's equity holdings can be categorized as large-cap and value-oriented.

A management team has overseen this fund since 1958, when the multiple portfolio counselor system was put in place. There are twenty-four funds besides Washington Mutual Investors within the American Funds Group. Overall, the fund family's risk-adjusted performance can be described as good.

Tax Minimization   ★ ★ ★
During the past five years, a $10,000 initial investment grew to $20,320 after taxes, assuming a 39.6 percent income tax bracket (state and federal combined) and a capital gains rate of 28 percent. This means that investors in this fund were able to preserve 87 percent of their total returns. Compared to other equity funds, this fund's tax savings are considered to be good. Over the past year, Washington Mutual Investors had a twelve-month yield of 2.1 percent.

Expenses   ★ ★ ★ ★ ★
Washington Mutual Investors's expense ratio is 0.6 percent; it has averaged 0.7 percent annually over the past three calendar years. The average expense ratio for the 715 funds in this category is 1.3 percent. This fund's turnover rate over the past year has been 23 percent, while its peer group average has been 66 percent.

Summary
Washington Mutual Investors is one of a couple of American funds to appear in this category. In fact, there are a number of members of this fund family featured throughout this and previous editions of the book. Washington Mutual as well as the other couple of dozen funds offered by the parent company have a winning formula: a number of "star" managers overseeing specific industry groups within each fund. Bonuses to these managers and the analysts that support these seasoned teams is based on long-term results, not year-by-year gyrations. This fund is highly recommended.

Profile
minimum initial investment $250	*IRA accounts available* . . . . yes
subsequent minimum investment . . . $50	*IRA minimum investment* $250
available in all 50 states. . . . . yes	*date of inception* . . . . July 1952
telephone exchanges. . . . . yes	*dividend/income paid* . . . . quarterly
number of other funds in family 24	*quality of annual reports* . . . . excellent

High-Yield Funds

Sometimes referred to as "junk bond" funds, high-yield funds invest in corporate bonds rated lower than BBB or BAA. The world of bonds is divided into two general categories: "investment grade" and "high-yield." Investment grade, sometimes referred to as "bank quality," means that the bond issue has been rated AAA, AA, A, or BAA (or BBB if the rating service is Standard and Poor's instead of Moody's). Certain institutions and fiduciaries are forbidden to invest their clients' monies in anything less than investment grade. Everything less than bank quality is considered junk.

Yet the world of bonds is not black and white. There are several categories of high-yield bonds. Junk bond funds contain issues that range from BB to C; a rating less than single-C means that the bond is in default, and payment of interest and/or principal is in arrears. High-yield bond funds perform best during good economic times. Such issues should be avoided by traditional investors during recessionary periods, since the underlying corporations may have difficulty making interest and principal payments when business slows down. However, these bonds, like common stocks, can perform very well during the second half of a recession.

Although junk bonds may exhibit greater volatility than their investment-grade peers, they are safer when it comes to *interest rate risk*. Since junk issues have higher-yielding coupons and often shorter maturities than quality corporate bond funds, they fluctuate less in value when interest rates change. Thus, during expansionary periods in the economy when interest rates are rising, high-yield funds will generally drop less in value than high-quality corporate or government bond funds. Conversely, when interest rates are falling, government and corporate bonds will appreciate more in value than junk funds. High-yield bonds resemble equities at least as much as they do traditional bonds when it comes to economic cycles and certain important technical factors. Studies show that only 19 percent of the average junk fund's total return is explained by the up or down movement of the Lehman Brothers Government/Corporate Bond Index. To give an idea of how low this number is, 94 percent of a typical *high-quality* corporate bond fund's performance is explainable by movement in the same index. Indeed, even international bond funds have a higher correlation coefficient than junk, with 25 percent of their performance explained by the Lehman index.

The table below covers the five-year period ending 3/31/97 and compares the total return of three well known bond indexes: First Boston High Yield Index (bonds rated BBB or lower), the Lehman Aggregate Bond Index (securities from the Lehman Government/Corporate, Mortgage-Backed Securities, and Asset-Backed

Indexes), and the Lehman Government Bond Index (all publicly traded domestic debt of the U.S. Government).

index	1 year	3 years	5 years	10 years
high-yield	11.7%	10.3%	11.2%	11.0%
aggregate	4.9%	6.9%	7.2%	8.2%
government	4.3%	6.3%	7.1%	7.9%

The high end of the junk bond market, those debentures rated BA and BB, have been able to withstand the general beating the junk bond market incurred during the late 1980s and early 1990s. Moderate and conservative investors who want high-yield bonds as part of their portfolio should focus on funds that have a high percentage of their assets in higher-rated bonds, BB or better.

According to Salomon Brothers, the people who are responsible for the Lehman Brothers corporate and government bond indices used in this book, junk bond defaults averaged only 0.8 percent from 1980 to 1984. This rate almost tripled from 1985 to 1989 as defaults averaged 2.2 percent per year. Then, in 1990, defaults surged to 4.6 percent. Analysis based on historical data did not predict this huge increase in defaults. Bear in mind that BB-rated junk bonds can be expected to perform closer to high-quality bonds than will lower-rated junk. During 1990, for example, BB-rated bonds declined only slightly in price and actually delivered positive returns, whereas bonds rated CCC declined over 30 percent. During the mid-1990s, the default risk for the entire category had fallen to about 1.5 percent per year (well under 1 percent in the case of high-yield bond funds).

Over the past three and five years, high-yield corporate bond funds have had an average compound total return of 11 percent. The *annual* return for the past ten years has been 10 percent, and 12 percent for the last fifteen years (all figures as of 6/30/97). The standard deviation for high-yield bond funds has been 4 percent over the past three years. This means that these funds have been less volatile than any equity fund and similar in return variances to other types of bond funds. One hundred seventy-fifty funds make up the high-yield category. Total market capitalization of this category is $75 billion.

The majority of investors believe that the track record of high-yield bonds has been mixed, particularly in recent years. There was a crash in this market in 1990, but the overall track record has been quite good. These bond funds were up 13.4 percent in 1987, the year of the stock market crash. As the junk bond scare started in 1989, the fund category was still able to show a 12.8 percent return for the calendar year. The following year the group showed a negative return of just under one half percent.

Then, in 1991, high-yield bond funds suffered an almost unprecedented loss, ending the year with a 9.7 percent loss. The loss was caused by regulatory agencies putting pressure on the insurance industry, formerly the largest owner of this investment category. This, together with the demise of Drexel Burnham, the largest issuer of junk bonds, caused high-yield bonds to suffer their biggest loss in recent memory. And yet the very next year, 1992, high-yield bond funds did better than ever before, up over 36 percent. The following two years were also quite good—

up 17.2 percent in 1993 and up 18.6 percent in 1994. The following year, 1995, these funds fell 3.6 percent, followed by a gain of 13.6 percent in 1996.

For stock investors, high-yield bonds can potentially smooth out performance during down markets while providing long-term volatility reduction. Because these debt instruments have historically delivered returns approaching that of the stock market, equity (stock) investors may find them a useful way to obtain diversification. Over the past ten years ending 12/31/96, a pure stock portfolio (the S&P 500) had an average annualized return of 15.3 percent and 14.3 percent volatility (using standard deviation). During the same period, a combined portfolio of 70 percent stocks and 30 percent high-yield bonds (First Boston High Yield Index) returned an average of 14.2 percent a year with 11.5 percent volatility.

A second study shows that from January 1991 to December 1996 the Merrill Lynch High-Yield Master index had only 4.8 percent volatility. For the same period the S&P 500 had a volatility of 10.2 percent. Part of the beauty of high-yield bonds is that only about 50 percent of their movement (return) is correlated (related to) fluctuations in the stock market.

High-Yield Funds

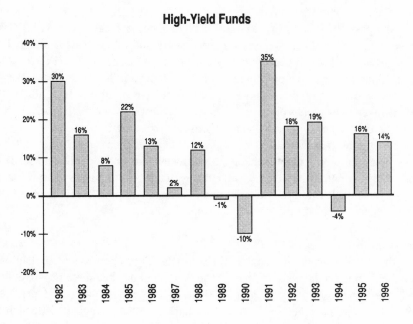

Franklin AGE High Income I

Franklin Group of Funds
777 Mariners Island Boulevard
San Mateo, CA 94403-7777
(800) 342-5236

total return	★ ★ ★
risk reduction	★ ★ ★
management	★ ★ ★
current income	★ ★ ★ ★
expense control	★ ★ ★ ★ ★
symbol AGEFX	18 points
up-market performance	excellent
down-market performance	poor
predictability of returns	good

Total Return   ★ ★ ★

Over the past five years, Franklin AGE High Income I has taken $10,000 and turned it into $17,620 ($14,570 over three years and $26,270 over the past ten years). This translates into an average annual return of 12 percent over the past five years, 13 percent over the past three years, and 10 percent for the decade. Over the past five years, this fund has outperformed 55 percent of all mutual funds; within its general category it has done better than 75 percent of its peers. High-yield bond funds have averaged 11 percent annually over these same five years.

During the past five years, a $10,000 initial investment grew to $14,220 after taxes, assuming a 39.6 percent income tax bracket (state and federal combined) and a capital gains rate of 28 percent. This means that investors in this fund were able to preserve 65 percent of their total returns. Compared to other fixed-income funds, this fund offers tax savings that are considered good.

Risk/Volatility   ★ ★ ★

Over the past five years, Franklin AGE High Income I has been safer than half of all high-yield bond funds. Over the past decade, the fund has had three negative years, while the Lehman Brothers Aggregate Bond Index has had one (off 3 percent in 1994). The fund has underperformed the Lehman Brothers Aggregate Bond Index three times and the First Boston High-Yield Bond Index six times in the last ten years.

	last 5 years		last 10 years	
worst year	-2%	1994	-14%	1990
best year	19%	1995	48%	1991

In the past, Franklin AGE High Income I has done better than 85 percent of its peer group in up markets but virtually none of its competition in down markets. Consistency, or predictability, of returns for Franklin AGE High Income I can be described as good.

Management   ★ ★ ★

There are 170 fixed-income securities in this $2.7 billion portfolio. The average high-yield bond fund today is $500 million in size. Close to 83 percent of the fund's holdings are in bonds. The average maturity of the bonds in this account is eight years; the weighted coupon rate averages 10.0 percent. The portfolio's fixed-income holdings can be categorized as intermediate-term, high-quality debt.

Molumphy and Wiskemann have managed this fund for the past sixteen years. There are 119 funds besides AGE High Income I within the Franklin Templeton Group. Overall, the fund family's risk-adjusted performance can be described as good.

Current Income   ★ ★ ★ ★

Over the past year, Franklin AGE High Income I had a twelve-month yield of 9.0 percent. During this same twelve-month period, the typical high-yield bond fund had a twelve-month yield that averaged 8.5 percent.

Expenses   ★ ★ ★ ★ ★

Franklin AGE High Income I's expense ratio is 0.7 percent; it has averaged 0.7 percent annually over the past three calendar years. The average expense ratio for the 175 funds in this category is 1.4 percent. This fund's turnover rate over the past year has been 20 percent, while its peer group average has been 104 percent.

Summary

Franklin AGE High Income I is a smart choice for anyone interested in receiving a high yield with little risk and a high after-tax total return. The Franklin Templeton Group, which now includes the Mutual Series overseen by Michael Price, has long been known as the leader of government securities and municipal bond funds. There are still a lot of people out there that do not realize that this high-yield corporate bond offering is even better—despite its comparatively low profile.

Profile

minimum initial investment $100	*IRA accounts available* . . . . yes
subsequent minimum investment . . . $25	*IRA minimum investment* $1
available in all 50 states. . . . . yes	*date of inception.* . . . . Dec. 1969
telephone exchanges. . . . . yes	*dividend/income paid.* . . . . monthly
number of other funds in family 119	*quality of annual reports* . . . . good

MainStay High-Yield Corporate Bond B

MainStay Funds
260 Cherry Hill Road
Parsippany, NJ 07054
(800) 624-6782

total return	★ ★ ★ ★ ★
risk reduction	★ ★ ★ ★ ★
management	★ ★ ★ ★ ★
current income	★ ★ ★
expense control	★ ★
symbol MKHCX	20 points
up-market performance	excellent
down-market performance	good
predictability of returns	excellent

Total Return   ★ ★ ★ ★ ★

Over the past five years, MainStay High-Yield Corporate Bond B has taken $10,000 and turned it into $19,250 ($14,730 over three years and $29,170 over the past ten years). This translates into an average annual return of 14 percent over the past five years, 14 percent over the past three years, and 11 percent for the decade. Over the past five years, this fund has outperformed 65 percent of all mutual funds; within its general category it has done better than 95 percent of its peers. High-yield bond funds have averaged 11 percent annually over these same five years.

During the past five years, a $10,000 initial investment grew to $15,560 after taxes, assuming a 39.6 percent income tax bracket (state and federal combined) and a capital gains rate of 28 percent. This means that investors in this fund were able to preserve 68 percent of their total returns. Compared to other fixed-income funds, this fund offers tax savings that are considered good.

Risk/Volatility   ★ ★ ★ ★ ★

Over the past five years, MainStay High-Yield Corporate Bond B has been safer than 90 percent of all high-yield bond funds. Over the past decade, the fund has had two negative years, while the Lehman Brothers Aggregate Bond Index has had one (off 3 percent in 1994). The fund has underperformed the Lehman Brothers Aggregate Bond Index three times and the First Boston High-Yield Bond Index four times in the last ten years.

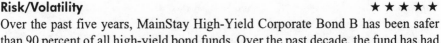

	last 5 years		last 10 years	
worst year	2%	1994	-8%	1990
best year	22%	1993	32%	1991

In the past, MainStay High-Yield Corporate Bond B has done better than 90 percent of its peer group in up markets and outperformed 55 percent of its competition in down markets. Consistency, or predictability, of returns for MainStay High-Yield Corporate Bond B can be described as excellent.

Management   ★ ★ ★ ★ ★

There are 130 fixed-income securities in this $2.9 billion portfolio. The average high-yield bond fund today is $500 million in size. Close to 71 percent of the fund's holdings are in bonds. The average maturity of the bonds in this account is five years; the weighted coupon rate averages 8.5 percent. The portfolio's fixed-income holdings can be categorized as short-term, high-quality debt.

A team has managed this fund for the past seven years. There are eighteen funds besides High-Yield Corporate Bond B within the MainStay fund family. Overall, the fund family's risk-adjusted performance can be described as good.

Current Income   ★ ★ ★

Over the past year, MainStay High-Yield Corporate Bond B had a twelve-month yield of 7.8 percent. During this same twelve-month period, the typical high-yield bond fund had a twelve-month yield that averaged 8.5 percent.

Expenses   ★ ★

MainStay High-Yield Corporate Bond B's expense ratio is 1.6 percent; it has averaged 1.6 percent annually over the past three calendar years. The average expense ratio for the 175 funds in this category is 1.4 percent. This fund's turnover rate over the past year has been 118 percent, while its peer group average has been 104 percent.

Summary

MainStay High-Yield Corporate Bond B is one of the few funds in the entire book to receive the highest possible rating when it comes to total return, risk reduction, and management. The fund's performance is even more amazing when you consider the fact that it is safer than 90 percent of its peer group.

Profile

minimum initial investment $500	*IRA accounts available* . . . . yes
subsequent minimum investment . . . $50	*IRA minimum investment* $500
available in all 50 states. . . . . yes	*date of inception.* . . . . May 1986
telephone exchanges. . . . . yes	*dividend/income paid.* . . . . monthly
number of other funds in family 18	*quality of annual reports* . . . . excellent

Northeast Investors

Northeast Investors Group
50 Congress Street
Boston, MA 02109
(800) 225-6704

total return	★ ★ ★ ★ ★
risk reduction	★ ★ ★
management	★ ★ ★ ★
current income	★ ★ ★ ★
expense control	★ ★ ★ ★ ★
symbol NTHEX	21 points
up-market performance	excellent
down-market performance	fair
predictability of returns	fair

Total Return ★ ★ ★ ★ ★

Over the past five years, Northeast Investors has taken $10,000 and turned it into $20,110 ($14,960 over three years and $28,290 over the past ten years). This translates into an average annual return of 15 percent over the past five years, 14 percent over the past three years, and 11 percent for the decade. Over the past five years, this fund has outperformed 70 percent of all mutual funds; within its general category it has done better than 95 percent of its peers. High-yield bond funds have averaged 11 percent annually over these same five years.

During the past five years, a $10,000 initial investment grew to $16,380 after taxes, assuming a 39.6 percent income tax bracket (state and federal combined) and a capital gains rate of 28 percent. This means that investors in this fund were able to preserve 71 percent of their total returns. Compared to other fixed-income funds, this fund offers tax savings that are considered very good.

Risk/Volatility ★ ★ ★

Over the past five years, Northeast Investors has been safer than only 10 percent of all high-yield bond funds. Over the past decade, the fund has had one negative year, as has the Lehman Brothers Aggregate Bond Index (off 3 percent in 1994). The fund has underperformed the Lehman Brothers Aggregate Bond Index and the First Boston High-Yield Bond Index four times in the last ten years.

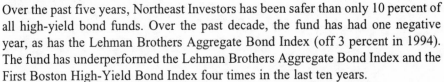

	last 5 years		last 10 years	
worst year	2%	1994	-9%	1990
best year	24%	1993	26%	1991

In the past, Northeast Investors has done better than 90 percent of its peer group in up markets but only 25 percent of its competition in down markets. Consistency, or predictability, of returns for Northeast Investors can be described as fair.

Management   ★ ★ ★ ★

There are 110 fixed-income securities in this $1.7 billion portfolio. The average high-yield bond fund today is $500 million in size. Close to 63 percent of the fund's holdings are in bonds. The average maturity of the bonds in this account is six years; the weighted coupon rate averages 10.0 percent. The portfolio's fixed-income holdings can be categorized as intermediate-term, high-quality debt.

Monrad and Monrad have managed this fund for the past twenty-one years. There is only one other fund besides Investors within the Northeast Investors fund family. Overall, the fund family's risk-adjusted performance can be described as very good.

Current Income   ★ ★ ★ ★

Over the past year, Northeast Investors had a twelve-month yield of 8.7 percent. During this same twelve-month period, the typical high-yield bond fund had a twelve-month yield that averaged 8.5 percent.

Expenses   ★ ★ ★ ★ ★

Northeast Investors's expense ratio is 0.7 percent; it has averaged 0.9 percent annually over the past three calendar years. The average expense ratio for the 175 funds in this category is 1.4 percent. This fund's turnover rate over the past year has been 32 percent, while its peer group average has been 104 percent.

Summary

Northeast Investors is the number one, overall high-yield bond fund. It is also the clear winner for sheer performance, beating out all of its peers in the book for the past five years. The fund has enjoyed some of the best tax minimization in its category. This very small fund family needs to add other portfolios so that investors can take greater advantage of the management's expertise.

Profile

minimum initial investment $1,000	*IRA accounts available* . . . . yes
subsequent minimum investment $1	*IRA minimum investment* $1,000
available in all 50 states. . . . . yes	*date of inception* . . . . Aug. 1950
telephone exchanges. . . . . yes	*dividend/income paid* . . . . quarterly
number of other funds in family 1	*quality of annual reports* . . . . . average

Oppenheimer Champion Income A

Oppenheimer Funds
P.O. Box 5270
Denver, CO 80217-5270
(800) 525-7048

total return	★ ★ ★
risk reduction	★ ★ ★ ★
management	★ ★ ★ ★
current income	★ ★ ★
expense control	★ ★ ★
symbol OPCHX	17 points
up-market performance	good
down-market performance	excellent
predictability of returns	excellent

Total Return   ★ ★ ★

Over the past five years, Oppenheimer Champion Income A has taken $10,000 and turned it into $17,620 ($13,690 over three years). This translates into an average annual return of 12 percent over the past five years and 11 percent over the past three years. Over the past five years, this fund has outperformed 55 percent of all mutual funds; within its general category it has done better than 70 percent of its peers. High-yield bond funds have averaged 11 percent annually over these same five years.

During the past five years, a $10,000 initial investment grew to $14,260 after taxes, assuming a 39.6 percent income tax bracket (state and federal combined) and a capital gains rate of 28 percent. This means that investors in this fund were able to preserve 65 percent of their total returns. Compared to other fixed-income funds, this fund offers tax savings that are considered good.

Risk/Volatility   ★ ★ ★ ★

Over the past five years, Oppenheimer Champion Income A has been safer than 83 percent of all high-yield bond funds. Over the past decade, the fund has had one negative year, as has the Lehman Brothers Aggregate Bond Index (off 3 percent in 1994). The fund has underperformed the Lehman Brothers Aggregate Bond Index three times and the First Boston High-Yield Bond Index twice in the last nine years.

	last 5 years		last 9 years	
worst year	0%	1994	0%	1994
best year	21%	1993	31%	1991

In the past, Oppenheimer Champion Income A has done better than half of its peer group in up markets and outperformed 90 percent of its competition in down markets. Consistency, or predictability, of returns for Oppenheimer Champion Income A can be described as excellent.

Management   ★ ★ ★ ★

There are 270 fixed-income securities in this $450 million portfolio. The average high-yield bond fund today is $500 million in size. Close to 93 percent of the fund's holdings are in bonds. The average maturity of the bonds in this account is eight years; the weighted coupon rate averages 8.5 percent. The portfolio's fixed-income holdings can be categorized as intermediate-term, high-quality debt.

Ralph W. Stellmacher has managed this fund for the past ten years. There are sixty-three funds besides Champion Income A within the Oppenheimer fund family. Overall, the fund family's risk-adjusted performance can be described as good.

Current Income   ★ ★ ★

Over the past year, Oppenheimer Champion Income A had a twelve-month yield of 8.8 percent. During this same twelve-month period, the typical high-yield bond fund had a twelve-month yield that averaged 8.5 percent.

Expenses   ★ ★ ★

Oppenheimer Champion Income A's expense ratio is 1.2 percent; it has averaged 1.2 percent annually over the past three calendar years. The average expense ratio for the 175 funds in this category is 1.4 percent. This fund's turnover rate over the past year has been 95 percent, while its peer group average has been 104 percent.

Summary

Oppenheimer Champion Income A is the only high-yield bond fund that has performed exceptionally during bad markets. Fund management is quite strong and so is the overall safety of the portfolio. This fund has appeared in previous editions of the book and my recommendation continues.

Profile

minimum initial investment $1,000	*IRA accounts available* . . . . yes
subsequent minimum investment . . . $25	*IRA minimum investment* $250
available in all 50 states. . . . . yes	*date of inception* . . . . Nov. 1987
telephone exchanges. . . . . yes	*dividend/income paid.* . . . . monthly
number of other funds in family 63	*quality of annual reports* . . . . good

Seligman High-Yield Bond A

Seligman Group
100 Park Avenue
New York, NY 10017
(800) 221-2783

total return	★ ★ ★ ★
risk reduction	★ ★ ★
management	★ ★ ★ ★
current income	★ ★ ★ ★ ★
expense control	★ ★ ★
symbol SHYBX	19 points
up-market performance	very good
down-market performance	good
predictability of returns	fair

Total Return   ★ ★ ★ ★

Over the past five years, Seligman High-Yield Bond A has taken $10,000 and
turned it into $18,420 ($14,830 over three years and $29,890 over the past ten
years). This translates into an average annual return of 13 percent over the past five
years, 14 percent over the past three years, and 12 percent for the decade. Over the
past five years, this fund has outperformed 60 percent of all mutual funds; within
its general category it has done better than 90 percent of its peers. High-yield bond
funds have averaged 11 percent annually over these same five years.

During the past five years, a $10,000 initial investment grew to $15,180 after
taxes, assuming a 39.6 percent income tax bracket (state and federal combined) and
a capital gains rate of 28 percent. This means that investors in this fund were able
to preserve 68 percent of their total returns. Compared to other fixed-income funds,
this fund offers tax savings that are considered good.

Risk/Volatility   ★ ★ ★

Over the past five years, Seligman High-Yield Bond A has been safer than 23 percent of all high-yield bond funds. Over the past decade, the fund has had one negative year, as has the Lehman Brothers Aggregate Bond Index (off 3 percent in
1994). The fund has underperformed the Lehman Brothers Aggregate Bond Index
twice and the First Boston High-Yield Bond Index four times in the last ten years.

	last 5 years		last 10 years	
worst year	1%	1994	-7%	1990
best year	21%	1995	31%	1991

In the past, Seligman High-Yield Bond A has done better than 75 percent of
its peer group in up markets and outperformed 55 percent of its competition in
down markets. Consistency, or predictability, of returns for Seligman High-Yield
Bond A can be described as fair.

Management   ★ ★ ★ ★

There are ninety fixed-income securities in this $530 million portfolio. The average high-yield bond fund today is $500 million in size. Close to 95 percent of the fund's holdings are in bonds. The average maturity of the bonds in this account is eight years; the weighted coupon rate averages 11.0 percent. The portfolio's fixed-income holdings can be categorized as intermediate-term, high-quality debt.

Daniel J. Charleston has managed this fund for the past eight years. There are seventy-two funds besides High-Yield Bond A within the Seligman fund family. Overall, the fund family's risk-adjusted performance can be described as fair.

Current Income   ★ ★ ★ ★ ★

Over the past year, Seligman High-Yield Bond A had a twelve-month yield of 9.5 percent. During this same twelve-month period, the typical high-yield bond fund had a twelve-month yield that averaged 8.5 percent.

Expenses   ★ ★ ★

Seligman High-Yield Bond A's expense ratio is 1.2 percent; it has averaged 1.1 percent annually over the past three calendar years. The average expense ratio for the 175 funds in this category is 1.4 percent. This fund's turnover rate over the past year has been 119 percent, while its peer group average has been 104 percent.

Summary

Seligman High-Yield Bond A is certainly the number one choice for anyone interested in the highest possible current income. Total return figures are also quite high. The Seligman family began their financial career in the debt market during the Civil War. It is obvious that the extensive experience continues to pay off.

Profile

minimum initial investment $1,000	*IRA accounts available* . . . . yes
subsequent minimum investment . . $100	*IRA minimum investment* $1,000
available in all 50 states. . . . . yes	*date of inception* . . . . March 1985
telephone exchanges. . . . . yes	*dividend/income paid.* . . . . monthly
number of other funds in family 72	*quality of annual reports* . . . . good

Metals and Natural Resources Funds

These funds purchase metals in one or more of the following forms: bullion, South African gold stocks, and non–South African mining stocks. The United States, Canada, and Australia are the three major *stock-issuing producers* of metals outside of South Africa. Metals funds, also referred to as gold funds, often own minor positions in other precious metals stocks, such as silver and platinum.

The proportion and type of metal held by a fund can have a great impact on its performance and volatility. Outright ownership of gold bullion is almost always less volatile than owning stock in a gold mining company. Thus, much greater gains or losses occur in metals funds that purchase only gold stocks, compared to funds that hold high levels of bullion, coins, and stock. Silver, incidentally, has nearly twice the volatility of gold, yet has not enjoyed any greater returns over the long term.

Gold, or metals, funds can do well during periods of political uncertainty and inflationary concerns. Over the past several hundred years, gold and silver have served as hedges against inflation. Most readers will be surprised to learn that, historically, both metals have outperformed inflation by less than one percent annually.

Metals funds are the riskiest category of mutual funds described in this book, with a standard deviation of 27—about 25 percent higher than the standard deviation of aggressive growth funds. And yet, although this is certainly a high-risk investment when viewed on its own, ownership of a metals fund can actually reduce a portfolio's overall risk level and often enhance its total return. Why? Because gold usually has a negative correlation to other investments. When the other investments go down in value, gold will often go up. Thus, a portfolio made up strictly of government bonds will actually exhibit more risk and less return than one made up of 90 percent government and 10 percent metals funds.

There are forty-five metals funds; total market capitalization is less than $5 billion. Turnover has averaged 90 percent. The p/e ratio for metals funds is 37, while dividend yield is a little over one half percent. Over the past three years, these funds have averaged -5 percent per year, 4 percent for the last five years, -2 percent for the past decade, and 4 percent for the last fifteen years.

Natural resources funds invest in the stocks of companies that deal in the ownership, production, transmission, transportation, refinement, and/or storage of oil, natural gas, and timber. These funds also invest in companies that either own or are involved in real estate.

There are fifty natural resources funds; total market capitalization is just under $7 billion. This group has had a standard deviation of 17 percent over the past three years. Beta, or market-related risk, has been 0.7 percent, but do not let this low number fool you. As you can see by the standard deviation, few equity categories are riskier. Turnover has averaged 95 percent. The p/e ratio for natural resources funds is 26; dividend yield is one half percent. Over the past three years, these funds have averaged 17 percent—15 percent for the past five years, 7 percent for the last ten years, and 13 percent for the past fifteen years.

Metals and natural resources funds should be avoided by anyone who cannot tolerate wide price swings in any single part of his portfolio. These funds are designed as an integral part of a diversified portfolio, for investors who look at the overall return of their holdings.

Precious Metals Funds

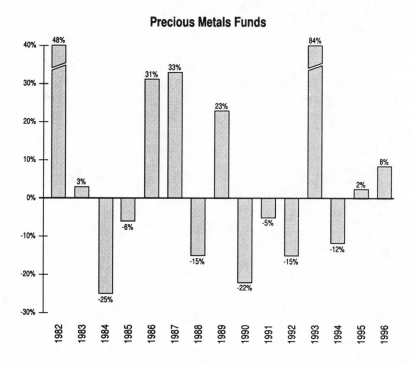

Natural Resources Funds

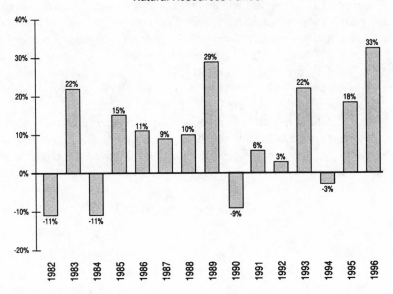

Midas

Midas Fund
11 Hanover Square
New York, NY 10005
(800) 400-6432

total return	★ ★ ★ ★ ★
risk reduction	★ ★
management	★ ★ ★
tax minimization	★ ★ ★ ★
expense control	★ ★ ★
symbol EMGSX	17 points
up-market performance	excellent
down-market performance	fair
predictability of returns	poor

Total Return   ★ ★ ★ ★ ★

Over the past five years, Midas has taken $10,000 and turned it into $18,420 ($10,670 over three years and $13,610 over the past ten years). This translates into an average annual return of 13 percent over the past five years, 2 percent over the past three years, and 3 percent for the decade. Over the past five years, this fund has outperformed 60 percent of all mutual funds; within its general category it has done better than 70 percent of its peers. Metals/natural resources funds have averaged 9 percent annually over these same five years.

Risk/Volatility   ★ ★

Over the past five years, Midas has been safer than half of all metals/natural resources funds. Over the past decade, the fund has had five negative years, while the S&P 500 has had one (off 3 percent in 1990). The fund has underperformed the S&P 500 eight times in the last ten years.

	last 5 years		last 10 years	
worst year	-17%	1994	-19%	1988
best year	99%	1993	99%	1993

In the past, Midas has done better than 95 percent of its peer group in up markets but only 35 percent of its competition in down markets. Consistency, or predictability, of returns for Midas can be described as poor.

Management   ★ ★ ★

There are 110 stocks in this $150 million portfolio. The average metals/natural resources fund today is $129 million in size. Close to 100 percent of the fund's holdings are in stocks. The stocks in this portfolio have an average price-earnings (p/e) ratio of 33 and a median market capitalization of $650 million. The portfolio's equity holdings can be categorized as small-cap and value-oriented.

Kjeld Thygesen has managed this fund for the past five years. There are no other funds within the fund family. Overall, the fund's risk-adjusted performance can be described as fair.

Tax Minimization

During the past five years, a $10,000 initial investment grew to $17,260 after taxes, assuming a 39.6 percent income tax bracket (state and federal combined) and a capital gains rate of 28 percent. This means that investors in this fund were able to preserve 89 percent of their total returns. Compared to other equity funds, this fund's tax savings are considered to be very good. Over the past year, Midas had a twelve-month yield of zero.

Expenses

Midas's expense ratio is 1.6 percent; it has averaged 2.0 percent annually over the past three calendar years. The average expense ratio for the 95 funds in this category is 1.7 percent. This fund's turnover rate over the past year has been 23 percent, while its peer group average has been 95 percent.

Summary

Midas is one of two gold or metals funds to make this book. It is the clear winner when it comes to total return and tax minimization. This is a one-fund family that has certainly distinguished itself. This is a tough category to do well in and Midas has managed to overcome the industry group's risk and return characteristics. The fund is to be highly commended.

Profile

minimum initial investment $1,000	*IRA accounts available* . . . . yes
subsequent minimum investment . . . $50	*IRA minimum investment* $500
available in all 50 states . . . . yes	*date of inception* . . . . Jan. 1986
telephone exchanges . . . . yes	*dividend/income paid* . . . . annually
number of other funds in family 0	*quality of annual reports* . . . . excellent

Scudder Gold

Scudder Funds
Two International Place
Boston, MA 02110
(800) 225-2470

total return	★ ★ ★ ★ ★
risk reduction	★ ★ ★ ★
management	★ ★ ★
tax minimization	★
expense control	★ ★ ★ ★
symbol SCGDX	17 points
up-market performance	excellent
down-market performance	excellent
predictability of returns	fair

Total Return

Over the past five years, Scudder Gold has taken $10,000 and turned it into $16,850 ($12,110 over three years). This translates into an average annual return of 11 percent over the past five years and 7 percent over the past three years. Over the past five years, this fund has outperformed 55 percent of all mutual funds; within its general category it has also done better than 55 percent of its peers. Metals/natural resources funds have averaged 9 percent annually over these same five years.

Risk/Volatility

Over the past five years, Scudder Gold has been safer than 86 percent of all metals/natural resources funds. Over the past decade, the fund has had four negative years, while the S&P 500 has had one (off 3 percent in 1990). The fund has underperformed the S&P 500 six times in the last eight years.

	last 5 years		last 8 years	
worst year	-9%	1992	-17%	1990
best year	59%	1993	59%	1993

In the past, Scudder Gold has done better than 80 percent of its peer group in up markets and outperformed 95 percent of its competition in down markets. Consistency, or predictability, of returns for Scudder Gold can be described as fair.

Management

There are eighty stocks in this $190 million portfolio. The average metals/natural resources fund today is $129 million in size. Close to 84 percent of the fund's holdings are in stocks. The stocks in this portfolio have an average price-earnings (p/e) ratio of 38 and a median market capitalization of $750 million. The portfolio's equity holdings can be categorized as small-cap and value-oriented.

Hoes and Wallace have managed this fund for the past five years. There are thirty-one funds besides Gold within the Scudder fund family. Overall, the fund family's risk-adjusted performance can be described as good.

Tax Minimization ★

During the past five years, a $10,000 initial investment grew to $15,020 after taxes, assuming a 39.6 percent income tax bracket (state and federal combined) and a capital gains rate of 28 percent. This means that investors in this fund were able to preserve 76 percent of their total returns. Compared to other equity funds, this fund's tax savings are considered to be poor. Over the past year, Scudder Gold had a twelve-month yield of zero.

Expenses

Scudder Gold's expense ratio is 1.5 percent; it has averaged 1.6 percent annually over the past three calendar years. The average expense ratio for the 95 funds in this category is 1.7 percent. This fund's turnover rate over the past year has been 30 percent, while its peer group average has been 95 percent.

Summary

Scudder Gold is one of only two metals funds to make this book. It is also the safer of the two. Achieving very good return figures for a gold fund while being more conservative than close to 90 percent of your peers is not an easy accomplishment. Look for other Scudder funds in this book.

Profile

minimum initial investment . . . . . $2,500   *IRA accounts available* . . . . yes
subsequent minimum investment . . $100   *IRA minimum investment* $1,000
available in all 50 states. . . . . yes   *date of inception* . . . . Sept. 1988
telephone exchanges. . . . . yes   *dividend/income paid* . . . . annually
number of other funds in family 31   *quality of annual reports* . . . . excellent

State Street Research Global Resources A

State Street Research Group
One Financial Center
Boston, MA 02111
(800) 882-0052

total return	★ ★ ★ ★ ★
risk reduction	★ ★
management	★ ★ ★ ★
tax minimization	★ ★ ★ ★ ★
expense control	★ ★ ★
symbol SSGRX	19 points
up-market performance	very good
down-market performance	fair
predictability of returns	good

Total Return   ★ ★ ★ ★ ★

Over the past five years, State Street Research Global Resources A has taken $10,000 and turned it into $29,320 ($19,610 over three years). This translates into an average annual return of 24 percent over the past five years and 25 percent over the past three years. Over the past five years, this fund has outperformed 95 percent of all mutual funds; within its general category it has also done better than 95 percent of its peers. Metals/natural resources funds have averaged 9 percent annually over these same five years.

Risk/Volatility   ★ ★

Over the past five years, State Street Research Global Resources A has been safer than 60 percent of all metals/natural resources funds. Over the past decade, the fund has had two negative years, while the S&P 500 has had one (off 3 percent in 1990). The fund has underperformed the S&P 500 four times in the last six years.

	last 5 years		last 6 years	
worst year	-4%	1994	-18%	1991
best year	70%	1996	70%	1996

In the past, State Street Research Global Resources A has done better than 65 percent of its peer group in up markets but only 35 percent of its competition in down markets. Consistency, or predictability, of returns for State Street Research Global Resources A can be described as good.

Management   ★ ★ ★ ★

There are 100 stocks in this $80 million portfolio. The average metals/natural resources fund today is $129 million in size. Close to 92 percent of the fund's holdings are in stocks. The stocks in this portfolio have an average price-earnings (p/e) ratio of 29 and a median market capitalization of $830 million. The portfolio's equity holdings can be categorized as small-cap and value-oriented.

Daniel J. Rice has managed this fund for the past seven years. There are seventy-four funds besides Global Resources A within the State Street Research Group. Overall, the fund family's risk-adjusted performance can be described as fair.

Tax Minimization   ★ ★ ★ ★ ★
During the past five years, a $10,000 initial investment grew to $28,640 after taxes, assuming a 39.6 percent income tax bracket (state and federal combined) and a capital gains rate of 28 percent. This means that investors in this fund were able to preserve 99 percent of their total returns. Compared to other equity funds, this fund's tax savings are considered to be excellent. Over the past year, State Street Research Global Resources A had a twelve-month yield of zero.

Expenses   ★ ★ ★
State Street Research Global Resources A's expense ratio is 1.8 percent; it has averaged 1.8 percent annually over the past three calendar years. The average expense ratio for the 95 funds in this category is 1.7 percent. This fund's turnover rate over the past year has been 92 percent, while its peer group average has been 95 percent.

Summary
State Street Research Global Resources A is one of only two natural resources funds to make the book. It is the best when it comes to total returns and maintaining those returns on an after-tax basis. State Street Research is well known as a high-class money management company for institutions. In recent years it has made a welcome push into the retail markets—making it more readily available to the masses.

Profile
minimum initial investment $2,500	*IRA accounts available* . . . . yes
subsequent minimum investment . . . $50	*IRA minimum investment* $2,000
available in all 50 states. . . . . yes	*date of inception* . . . . March 1990
telephone exchanges. . . . . yes	*dividend/income paid* . . . . annually
number of other funds in family. 74	*quality of annual reports* . . . . excellent

Vanguard Specialized Energy
Vanguard Group
Vanguard Financial Center
P.O. Box 2600
Valley Forge, PA 19482
(800) 662-7447

total return	★ ★ ★ ★
risk reduction	★ ★ ★
management	★ ★ ★ ★
tax minimization	★ ★ ★ ★
expense control	★ ★ ★ ★ ★
symbol VGENX	20 points
up-market performance	very good
down-market performance	very good
predictability of returns	very good

Total Return   ★ ★ ★ ★
Over the past five years, Vanguard Specialized Energy has taken $10,000 and turned it into $23,860 ($16,820 over three years and $31,870 over the past ten years). This translates into an average annual return of 19 percent over the past five years, 19 percent over the past three years, and 12 percent for the decade. Over the past five years, this fund has outperformed 85 percent of all mutual funds; within its general category it has done better than 90 percent of its peers. Metals/natural resources funds have averaged 9 percent annually over these same five years.

Risk/Volatility   ★ ★ ★
Over the past five years, Vanguard Specialized Energy has been safer than 69 percent of all metals/natural resources funds. Over the past decade, the fund has had two negative years, while the S&P 500 has had one (off 3 percent in 1990). The fund has underperformed the S&P 500 four times in the last ten years.

	last 5 years		last 10 years	
worst year	-2%	1994	-2%	1994
best year	34%	1996	43%	1989

In the past, Vanguard Specialized Energy has done better than 70 percent of its peer group in up markets and outperformed 75 percent of its competition in down markets. Consistency, or predictability, of returns for Vanguard Specialized Energy can be described as very good.

Management   ★ ★ ★ ★
There are seventy stocks in this $1.0 billion portfolio. The average metals/natural resources fund today is $129 million in size. Close to 92 percent of the fund's holdings are in stocks. The stocks in this portfolio have an average price-earnings (p/e)

ratio of 25 and a median market capitalization of $3.6 billion. The portfolio's equity holdings can be categorized as mid-cap and value-oriented.

Ernst H. von Metzsch has managed this fund for the past thirteen years. There are sixty-four funds besides Specialized Energy within the Vanguard Group. Overall, the fund family's risk-adjusted performance can be described as good.

Tax Minimization

During the past five years, a $10,000 initial investment grew to $21,440 after taxes, assuming a 39.6 percent income tax bracket (state and federal combined) and a capital gains rate of 28 percent. This means that investors in this fund were able to preserve 89 percent of their total returns. Compared to other equity funds, this fund's tax savings are considered to be very good. Over the past year, Vanguard Specialized Energy had a twelve-month yield of 1.0 percent.

Expenses

Vanguard Specialized Energy's expense ratio is 0.4 percent; it has averaged 0.3 percent annually over the past three calendar years. The average expense ratio for the 95 funds in this category is 1.7 percent. This fund's turnover rate over the past year has been 15 percent, while its peer group average has been 95 percent.

Summary

Vanguard Specialized Energy is one of only two natural resources funds to make this book. It is also the top point earner. This is one of the very few funds that has done a very good job in both up and down markets. It is also a consistent performer. The fund scores well in every respect, particularly in the area of minimizing shareholder costs.

Profile

minimum initial investment $3,000	*IRA accounts available* . . . . yes
subsequent minimum investment . . $100	*IRA minimum investment* $1,000
available in all 50 states. . . . . yes	*date of inception*. . . . . May 1984
telephone exchanges. . . . . yes	*dividend/income paid* . . . . annually
number of other funds in family 64	*quality of annual reports* . . . . excellent

Money Market Funds

Money market funds invest in securities that mature in less than one year. They are made up of one or more of the following instruments: Treasury bills, certificates of deposit, commercial paper, repurchase agreements, Euro-dollar CDs, and notes. There are four different categories of money market funds: all-purpose, government-backed, federally tax-free, and doubly tax-exempt.

All-purpose funds are the most popular and make up the bulk of the money market universe. Fully taxable, they are composed of securities such as CDs, commercial paper, and T-bills.

Government-backed money funds invest only in short-term paper, directly or indirectly backed by the U.S. government. These funds are technically safer than the all-purpose variety, but only one money market fund has ever defaulted (a fund set up by a bank for banks). The yield on government-backed funds is somewhat lower than that of its all-purpose peers.

Federally tax-free funds are made up of municipal notes. Investors in these funds do not have to pay federal income taxes on the interest earned. The before-tax yield on federally tax-free funds is certainly lower than that of all-purpose and government-backed funds, but the after-tax return can be greater for the moderate- or high-tax-bracket investor.

Double-tax-exempt funds invest in the municipal obligations of a specific state. You must be a resident of that state in order to avoid paying state income taxes on any interest earned. Nonresident investors will still receive a federal tax exemption.

All money market funds are safer than any other mutual fund or category of funds in this book. They have a perfect track record (if you exclude the one money market fund set up for banks)—investors can only make money in these interest-bearing accounts. The rate of return earned in a money market depends upon the average maturity of the fund's paper, the kinds of securities held, the quality rating of that paper, and how efficiently the fund is operated. A lean fund will almost always outperform a similar fund with high operating costs.

Investments such as United States Treasury bills and, for all practical purposes, money market funds, are often referred to as "risk-free." These kinds of investments are free from price swings and default risk because of their composition. However, as we have come to learn, there is more than one form of risk. Money market funds should never be considered as a medium- or long-term investment. The *real return* on this investment is poor. An investment's real return takes into account the effects of inflation and income taxes. During virtually every period of time, the after-tax, after-inflation return on all money market funds has been near zero or even negative.

Over the past fifty years, United States Treasury bills—an index often used as a substitute for money market funds—have outperformed inflation on average 62 percent of the time over one-year periods, 74 percent of the time over five-year periods, 71 percent of the time over ten-year periods, and 100 percent over any given twenty-year period of time. These figures are not adjusted for income taxes. Money market funds have rarely, if ever, outperformed inflation on an *after-tax* basis when looking at three-, five-, ten-, fifteen-, or twenty-year holding positions.

Investors often look back to the good old days of the early 1980s, when money market funds briefly averaged 18 percent, and wish such times would come again. Well, those were not good times. During the early 1980s the top tax bracket, state and federal combined, was 55 percent. If you began with an 18-percent return and deducted taxes, many taxpayers saw their 18-percent return knocked down to about 9 percent. This may look great, especially for a "risk-free" investment, but we are not through yet. During the partial year in which money market accounts paid 18 percent, inflation was 12 percent. Now, if you take the 9-percent return and subtract 12 percent for inflation; the real return was actually –3 percent for the year. So much for the good old days.

Money market funds are the best place to park your money while you are looking at other investment alternatives or if you will be using the money during the next year. These funds can provide the convenience of check writing and a yield that is highly competitive with interest rates in general. These incredibly safe funds should only be considered for short-term periods or for regular expenditures, the way you would use a savings or checking account.

Since money market funds only came into existence for the general public in the mid-1970s, Treasury bills are often used as a substitute by those who wish to analyze the performance of these funds over a long period of time. The results are instructive. Since 1947, a dollar invested in T-bills grew to $10.90 by the end of 1996. By the end of 1996, you would have needed $7.38 to equal the purchasing power of $1 at the beginning of 1947.

To give you a better sense of the cumulative effects of inflation, consider what a $100,000 investment in a money market fund would have to yield at the beginning of 1997 to equal the same purchasing power as the interest (or yield) from a $100,000 investment in a money market fund twenty years ago (1977). At the beginning of 1997, for instance, a $100,000 account held since 1977 would need to generate $10,900 to equal the same purchasing power as a $100,000 account yielding approximately 4 percent in 1977 (the average interest rate for money market accounts that year). The reality, however, is that at the beginning of 1997, money market funds were yielding 5 percent ($5,000 a year vs. the $10,900 that would be required to maintain purchasing power).

You may have avoided stock investing in the past because "stocks are too risky." Yet, it all depends upon how you define risk. As an example, in 1969 a $100,000 CD generated enough interest ($7,900) to buy a new, "fully loaded" Cadillac ($5,936) plus take a week-long cruise. As of the beginning of 1997, that same $100,000 CD would not generate enough income (CD rates were 4.95%) to buy 1/8th of the Cadillac ($4,950 vs. $43,000 for the cost of a 1997 Cadillac Hardtop Sedan De Ville).

As a risk-reduction tool, the addition of a money market fund may be a worthwhile strategy. For the period between 1960 and 1996, a 50–50 mix of stocks and cash delivered 79% of the S&P's return, with half the volatility. A more aggressive mix of 60% stocks and 40% cash yielded 84% of the S&P's gains, with just 60% of the risk (as measured by standard deviation).

Over the past three years, United States Treasury bills—again, similar in return to money market funds—have had an average compound return of 5 percent per year. The *annual return* for the past five years has been 4.2 percent; 5.5 percent for the past ten years, 6.5 percent for the last fifteen years, and 7.3 percent for the last twenty years (all periods ending 12/31/96). The standard deviation for money market funds is lower than any other mutual fund category. This means that these funds have had less return variances than any other group. Close to 1,300 funds make up the money market category. Total market capitalization of this category is over $900 billion.

Income Risk from Money Market Accounts

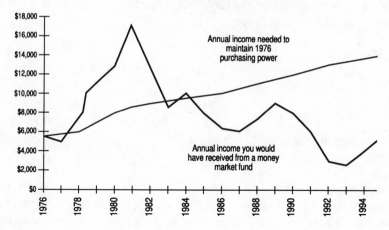

Aetna Money Market Select

Aetna
242 Trumbull St.
Hartford, CT 06103
(800) 367-7732

risk reduction	★ ★ ★ ★ ★
management	★ ★ ★ ★ ★
current income	★ ★ ★ ★ ★
expense control	★ ★ ★ ★ ★
symbol ATNXX	20 points

Total Return   ★ ★ ★ ★ ★

Over the past five years, Aetna Money Market Select has taken $10,000 and turned it into $12,570 ($11,744 over three years). This translates into an average annual return of 4.7% over five years and 5.5% over the past three years. This is the number 6 performing taxable money market fund over the past five years and number 25 for the last three years.

Risk/Volatility   ★ ★ ★ ★ ★

During the last three years, the fund's standard deviation has been 0.12%.

	last 5 years		since inception	
worst year	3.3%	1993	3.3%	1993
best year	6.0%	1995	6.0%	1995

Management   ★ ★ ★ ★ ★

The average maturity of the paper in the portfolio is approximately 42 days. The fund has been managed by Jeanne Wong-Boehm since its December 1991 inception.

Expense Control   ★ ★ ★ ★ ★

The expense ratio for this $300 million fund is 0.3%. This means that for every $1,000 invested, $3 goes to paying overhead.

Summary

Aetna Money Market Select is highly recommended.

Profile

minimum initial investment $1,000	*IRA accounts available* . . . . yes
subsequent minimum investment . . $100	*IRA minimum investment* . . . . n/a
available in all 50 states. . . . . yes	*IRA minimum additions* . . . . n/a
telephone exchanges. . . . . yes	*dividend/income paid.* . . . . monthly
number of other funds in family 18	*quality of annual reports* . . . . n/a

Dreyfus Basic Money Market

Dreyfus
200 Park Avenue, 7th Floor
New York, NY 10166
(800) 645-6561

risk reduction	★ ★ ★ ★ ★
management	★ ★ ★ ★ ★
current income	★ ★ ★ ★ ★
expense control	★ ★ ★ ★ ★
symbol DBAXX	20 points

Total Return ★ ★ ★ ★ ★

Over the past five years, Dreyfus Basic Money Market has taken $10,000 and turned it into $12,585 ($11,733 over three years). This translates into an average annual return of 4.7% over five years and 5.5% over the past three years. This is the number 3 performing taxable money market fund over the past five years and number 8 for the last three years.

Risk/Volatility ★ ★ ★ ★ ★

During the last three years, the fund's standard deviation has been 0.14%. Over the past year, Dreyfus Basic Money Market has had a yield as high as 5.5% and a low of 5.0%.

	last 5 years		since inception	
worst year	3.4%	1993	3.4%	1993
best year	6.1%	1995	6.1%	1995

Management ★ ★ ★ ★ ★

The average maturity of the paper in the portfolio is approximately 67 days. The fund began operations in 1992 and has been managed by Patricia Larkin since June 1994.

Expense Control ★ ★ ★ ★ ★

The expense ratio for this $1.8 billion fund is 0.3%. This means that for every $1,000 invested, $3 goes to paying overhead.

Summary

Dreyfus Basic Money Market is highly recommended.

Profile

minimum initial investment $25,000	*IRA accounts available* . . . . yes
subsequent minimum investment . $1,000	*IRA minimum investment* $5,000
available in all 50 states. . . . . yes	*IRA minimum additions* $1,000
telephone exchanges. . . . . yes	*dividend/income paid*. . . . . monthly
number of other funds in family. 87	*quality of annual reports* . . . . n/a

Dreyfus Basic Municipal Money Market

Dreyfus
200 Park Avenue, 7th Floor
New York, NY 10166
(800) 645-6561

risk reduction	★ ★ ★ ★ ★
management	★ ★ ★ ★ ★
current income	★ ★ ★ ★ ★
expense control	★ ★ ★ ★ ★
symbol DBMXX	20 points

Total Return   ★ ★ ★ ★ ★
Over the past five years, Dreyfus Basic Municipal Money Market has taken $10,000 and turned it into $11,683 ($11,085 over three years). This translates into an average annual return of 3.2% over five years and 3.5% over the past three years. This is the number 3 performing *tax-free* money market fund over the past five years and number 15 for the last three years.

Risk/Volatility   ★ ★ ★ ★ ★
During the last three years, the fund's standard deviation has been 0.13%. Over the past year, Dreyfus Basic Municipal Money Market has had a yield as high as 4.1% and a low of 2.3%.

	last 5 years		since inception	
worst year	2.6%	1993	2.6%	1993
best year	3.9%	1995	3.9%	1995

Management   ★ ★ ★ ★ ★
The average maturity of the paper in the portfolio is approximately 69 days. The fund has been managed since its 1991 inception by Karen Hand.

Expense Control   ★ ★ ★ ★ ★
The expense ratio for this $680 million fund is 0.4%. This means that for every $1,000 invested, $4 goes to paying overhead.

Summary
Dreyfus Basic Municipal Money Market is highly recommended.

Profile

minimum initial investment $25,000	*IRA accounts available.* . . . . no
subsequent minimum investment . $1,000	*IRA minimum investment* . . . . n/a
available in all 50 states. . . . . yes	*IRA minimum additions* . . . . n/a
telephone exchanges. . . . . yes	*dividend/income paid.* . . . . monthly
number of other funds in family 87	*quality of annual reports* . . . . n/a

Fidelity Cash Reserves

Fidelity
82 Devonshire St.
Boston, MA 02109
(800) 544-6666

risk reduction	★ ★ ★ ★ ★
management	★ ★ ★ ★ ★
current income	★ ★ ★ ★ ★
expense control	★ ★ ★ ★ ★
symbol FDRXX	20 points

Total Return   ★ ★ ★ ★ ★

Over the past five years, Fidelity Cash Reserves has taken $10,000 and turned it into $12,397 ($11,662 over three years). This translates into an average annual return of 4.4% over five years and 5.3% over the past three years. This is the number 4 performing taxable money market fund over the past five years and number 6 for the last three years.

Risk/Volatility   ★ ★ ★ ★ ★

During the last three years, the fund's standard deviation has been 0.12%. Over the past year, Fidelity Cash Reserves has had a yield as high as 5.3% and a low of 5.0%.

	last 5 years		last 10 years	
worst year	2.9%	1993	2.9%	1993
best year	5.7%	1995	8.9%	1989

Management   ★ ★ ★ ★ ★

The average maturity of the paper in the portfolio is approximately 70 days. The fund began operations in 1979 and has been managed by John Todd since April 1997.

Expense Control   ★ ★ ★ ★ ★

The expense ratio for this $24 billion fund is 0.5%. This means that for every $1,000 invested, $5 goes to paying overhead.

Summary

Fidelity Cash Reserves is highly recommended.

Profile

minimum initial investment $2,500	*IRA accounts available* . . . . yes
subsequent minimum investment . . $250	*IRA minimum investment* $500
available in all 50 states. . . . . yes	*IRA minimum additions* $250
telephone exchanges. . . . . yes	*dividend/income paid.* . . . . monthly
number of other funds in family 194	*quality of annual reports* . . . . n/a

SEI Daily Income Prime Obligation A

SEI
1 Freedom Valley Drive
Oaks, PA 19456
(800) 342-5734

risk reduction	★ ★ ★ ★ ★
management	★ ★ ★ ★ ★
current income	★ ★ ★ ★ ★
expense control	★ ★ ★ ★ ★
symbol TCPXX	20 points

Total Return   ★ ★ ★ ★ ★

Over the past five years, SEI Daily Income Prime Obligation A has taken $10,000 and turned it into $12,545 ($11,754 over three years). This translates into an average annual return of 4.6% over five years and 5.5% over the past three years. This is the number 11 performing taxable money market fund over the past five years and number 4 for the last three years.

Risk/Volatility   ★ ★ ★ ★ ★

During the last three years, the fund's standard deviation has been 0.11%.

	last 5 years		last 9 years	
worst year	3.1%	1993	3.1%	1993
best year	6.0%	1995	9.4%	1989

Management   ★ ★ ★ ★ ★

The average maturity of the paper in the portfolio is approximately 44 days. The fund has been managed by John Keogh (of Wellington Mgmt. Co.) since its 1987 inception.

Expense Control   ★ ★ ★ ★ ★

The expense ratio for this $2.8 billion fund is 0.2%. This means that for every $1,000 invested, $2 goes to paying overhead.

Summary

SEI Daily Income Prime Obligation A is highly recommended.

Profile

minimum initial investment $1	IRA accounts available . . . . yes
subsequent minimum investment $1	IRA minimum investment . . . . n/a
available in all 50 states. . . . . yes	IRA minimum additions . . . . n/a
telephone exchanges. . . . . yes	dividend/income paid. . . . . monthly
number of other funds in family 43	quality of annual reports . . . . n/a

Strong Municipal Money Market

Strong
P.O. Box 2936
Milwaukee, WI 53201
(800) 368-1030

risk reduction	★ ★ ★ ★ ★
management	★ ★ ★ ★ ★
current income	★ ★ ★ ★ ★
expense control	★ ★ ★ ★ ★
symbol SXFXX	20 points

Total Return   ★ ★ ★ ★ ★
Over the past five years, Strong Municipal Money Market has taken $10,000 and turned it into $11,747 ($11,149 over three years). This translates into an average annual return of 3.3% over five years and 3.7% over the past three years. This is the number 1 performing *tax-free* money market fund over the past five years and number 4 for the last three years.

Risk/Volatility   ★ ★ ★ ★ ★
During the last three years, the fund's standard deviation has been 0.12%. Over the past year, Strong Municipal Money Market has had a yield as high as 3.8% and a low of 3.2%.

	last 5 years		last 10 years	
worst year	2.5%	1993	2.5%	1993
best year	6.1%	1990	4.1%	1995

Management   ★ ★ ★ ★ ★
The average maturity of the paper in the portfolio is approximately 52 days. The fund began operations in 1986 and has been managed by Steve Harrop since March 1991.

Expense Control   ★ ★ ★ ★ ★
The expense ratio for this $2 billion fund is 0.6%. This means that for every $1,000 invested, $6 goes to paying overhead.

Summary
Strong Municipal Money Market is highly recommended.

Profile

minimum initial investment $2,500	*IRA accounts available* . . . . no
subsequent minimum investment . . . $50	*IRA minimum investment* . . . . n/a
available in all 50 states . . . . yes	*IRA minimum additions* . . . . n/a
telephone exchanges . . . . yes	*dividend/income paid* . . . . monthly
number of other funds in family 33	*quality of annual reports* . . . . n/a

Municipal Bond Funds

Municipal bond funds invest in securities issued by municipalities, political subdivisions, and U.S. territories. The type of security issued is either a note or bond, both of which are interest-bearing instruments that are exempt from federal income taxes. There are three different categories of municipal bond funds: national, state-free, and high-yield.

National municipal bond funds are made up of debt instruments issued by a wide range of states. These funds are exempt from federal income taxes only. To determine what small percentage is also exempt from state income taxes, consult the fund's prospectus and look for the weighting of U.S. territory issues (U.S. Virgin Islands, Guam, Puerto Rico), District of Columbia items, and obligations from your state of residence.

State-free funds, sometimes referred to as "double tax-free funds" invest only in bonds and notes issued in a particular state. You must be a legal resident of that state in order to avoid paying state income taxes on the fund's return. For example, most California residents who are in a high tax bracket will only want to consider purchasing a municipal bond fund that has the name "California" in it. Residents of New York who purchase a California tax-free fund will escape federal income taxes but not state taxes.

High-yield tax-free funds invest in the same kinds of issues found in a national municipal bond fund but with one important difference. By seeking higher returns, high-yield funds look for lower-rated or nonrated notes and bonds. A municipality may decide not to obtain a rating for its issue because of the costs involved compared to the relatively small size of the bond or note being floated. Many nonrated issues are very safe. High-yield municipal bond funds are relatively new but should not be overlooked by the tax-conscious investor. These kinds of tax-free funds have demonstrated less volatility and higher return than their other tax-free counterparts.

Prospective investors need to compare tax-free bond yields to *after-tax yields* on corporate or government bond funds. To determine which of these three fund categories is best for you, use your marginal tax bracket, subtract this amount from one, and multiply the resulting figure by the taxable investment. For instance, suppose you were in the 35-percent bracket, state and federal combined. By subtracting this figure from 1, you are left with 0.65. Multiply 0.65 by the fully taxable yield you could get, let us say 9 percent. Sixty-five percent of 9 percent is 5.85 percent. The 5.85 percent represents what you get on a 9-percent investment after you have paid state and federal income taxes on it. This means that if you can get 5.85 percent or higher from a tax-free investment, take it.

Interest paid on tax-free investments is generally lower than interest paid on taxable investments like corporate bonds and bank CDs. But you should compare the yields on tax-free investments to taxable investments only after you have considered the municipal bond fund's tax-free advantage. The result will be the *taxable equivalent yield*—the yield you will have to get on a similar taxable investment to equal the tax-free yield. If the example above was not clear, look at the next table.

1997 federal income tax rates plus tax-free yields
vs. equivalent taxable yields

taxable income single	taxable income joint	marginal tax rate	3% tax-free = what %	4% tax-free = what %	5% tax-free = what %	6% tax-free = what %
$0–$24,650	$0–$41,200	15.0%	3.5%	4.7%	5.9%	7.1%
$24,651–$59,750	$41,201–$99,600	28.0%	4.2%	5.6%	6.9%	8.3%
$59,751–$124,650	$99,601–$151,750	31.0%	4.3%	5.8%	7.2%	8.7%
$124,651–$271,050	$151,751–$271,050	36.0%	4.7%	6.3%	7.8%	9.4%
over $271,050	over $271,050	39.6%	5.0%	6.6%	8.3%	9.9%

As you can see from the table above, if you're in the 36-percent federal tax bracket, a taxable investment would have to yield 7.8 percent to give you the same after-tax income as a tax-free yield of 5.0 percent.

Municipal bond funds are not for investors who are in a low tax bracket. If such investors want to be in bonds, they would be better off in corporates or government issues. Furthermore, municipals should *never* be used in a retirement plan. There is only one way to make tax-free income taxable and that is to put it into an IRA, pension, or profit-sharing plan. Everything that comes out of these plans is fully taxable by the federal government.

Over the past three and five years, the typical municipal bond fund has had an average compounded annual return of 7 and 6 percent respectively. They have averaged a total annual return (current yield plus bond appreciation or minus bond depreciation) of 8 percent over the past ten years and 10 percent annually for the last fifteen years. Municipal bond fund returns have been fairly stable over the past three years, having a standard deviation of 5 percent.

One thousand nine hundred funds make up the municipal bond category. Total market capitalization of all municipal bond funds is $270 billion. Close to 97 percent of a typical municipal bond fund's portfolio is in tax-free bonds, with the balance in tax-free money market instruments. Close to 1,000 of the 1,900 municipal bond funds offered are single-state funds.

The typical municipal bond fund yields 4.7 percent in tax-free income each year. The average weighted maturity is sixteen years. Expenses for this category are 1.0 percent each year.

As you read through the descriptions of the municipal bond funds selected, you will notice a paragraph in each describing the tax efficiency of the portfolio. This may surprise you, since municipal bonds are supposed to be tax-free. Keep in mind that only the *income* (current yield) from these instruments is free from federal income taxes (and often state income taxes, depending on the fund in question and your state of residence). Since bond funds generally have a high turnover rate (which triggers a potential capital gain or loss upon each sale of a security by the portfolio manager), there are capital gains considerations with municipal bonds.

Municipal Bond Funds

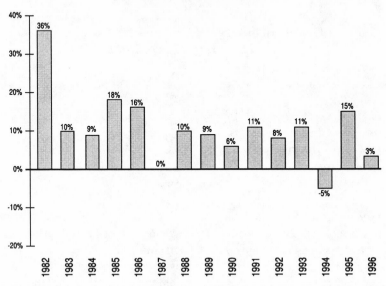

American Century-Benham California Municipal High Yield

American Century Investments
4500 Main Street
P.O. Box 419200
Kansas City, MO 64141-6200
(800) 345-2021

total return	★ ★ ★ ★
risk reduction	★ ★
management	★ ★
current income	★ ★ ★
expense control	★ ★ ★ ★ ★
symbol BCHYX	16 points
up-market performance	very good
down-market performance	good
predictability of returns	good

Total Return   ★ ★ ★ ★

Over the past five years, American Century-Benham California Municipal High Yield has taken $10,000 and turned it into $14,690 ($12,800 over three years and $21,570 over the past ten years). This translates into an average annual return of 8 percent over the past five years, 9 percent over the past three years, and 8 percent for the decade. Over the past five years, this fund has outperformed 45 percent of all mutual funds; within its general category it has done better than 95 percent of its peers. Municipal bond funds have averaged 6 percent annually over these same five years.

During the past five years, a $10,000 initial investment grew to $14,440 after taxes, assuming a 39.6 percent income tax bracket (state and federal combined) and a capital gains rate of 28 percent. This means that investors in this fund were able to preserve 99 percent of their total returns. Compared to other fixed-income funds, this fund offers tax savings that are considered excellent.

Risk/Volatility   ★ ★

Over the past five years, American Century-Benham California Municipal High Yield has been safer than 61 percent of all municipal bond funds. Over the past decade, the fund has had two negative years, while the Lehman Brothers Aggregate Bond Index has had one (off 3 percent in 1994). The fund has underperformed the Lehman Brothers Aggregate Bond Index six times and the Lehman Brothers Municipal Bond Index four times in the last ten years.

	last 5 years		last 10 years	
worst year	-5%	1994	-11%	1987
best year	18%	1995	18%	1995

In the past, American Century-Benham California Municipal High Yield has done better than 75 percent of its peer group in up markets and half of its competition in down markets. Consistency, or predictability, of returns for American Century-Benham California Municipal High Yield can be described as good.

Management   ★ ★
There are one hundred fixed-income securities in this $180 million portfolio. The average municipal bond fund today is $145 million in size. Close to 100 percent of the fund's holdings are in bonds. The average maturity of the bonds in this account is twenty years; the weighted coupon rate averages 6.5 percent. The portfolio's fixed-income holdings can be categorized as long-term, high-quality debt.

Steven Permut has managed this fund for the past ten years. There are forty-seven funds besides California Municipal High Yield within the American Century fund family. Overall, the fund family's risk-adjusted performance can be described as good.

Current Income   ★ ★ ★
Over the past year, American Century-Benham California Municipal High Yield had a twelve-month yield of 5.8 percent. During this same twelve-month period, the typical municipal bond fund had a twelve-month yield that averaged 4.7 percent.

Expenses   ★ ★ ★ ★ ★
American Century-Benham California Municipal High Yield's expense ratio is 0.5 percent; it has averaged 0.5 percent annually over the past three calendar years. The average expense ratio for the 1,900 funds in this category is 1.0 percent. This fund's turnover rate over the past year has been 36 percent, while its peer group average has been 53 percent.

Summary
American Century-Benham California Municipal High Yield is a fine choice for the tax-free investor looking to maximize current income. Even though this fund specializes in lower-rated state and county paper, it is still safer than close to two-thirds of all municipal bond funds.

Profile

minimum initial investment $5,000	*IRA accounts available* . . . . yes
subsequent minimum investment . . . $50	*IRA minimum investment* . . . . n/a
available in all 50 states . . . . no	*date of inception* . . . . Dec. 1986
telephone exchanges . . . . yes	*dividend/income paid* . . . . monthly
number of other funds in family 47	*quality of annual reports* . . . . excellent

Franklin Florida Tax-Free Income I

Franklin Group of Funds
777 Mariners Island Boulevard
San Mateo, CA 94403-7777
(800) 342-5236

total return	★ ★ ★
risk reduction	★ ★ ★ ★
management	★ ★
current income	★ ★ ★
expense control	★ ★ ★ ★ ★
symbol FRFLX	17 points
up-market performance	very good
down-market performance	fair
predictability of returns	very good

Total Return   ★ ★ ★

Over the past five years, Franklin Florida Tax-Free Income I has taken $10,000 and turned it into $14,030 ($12,260 over three years). This translates into an average annual return of 7 percent over the past five years and 7 percent over the past three years. Over the past five years, this fund has outperformed 35 percent of all mutual funds; within its general category it has done better than 75 percent of its peers. Municipal bond funds have averaged 6 percent annually over these same five years.

During the past five years, a $10,000 initial investment grew to $13,940 after taxes, assuming a 39.6 percent income tax bracket (state and federal combined) and a capital gains rate of 28 percent. This means that investors in this fund were able to preserve 100 percent of their total returns. Compared to other fixed-income funds, this fund offers tax savings that are considered excellent.

Risk/Volatility   ★ ★ ★ ★

Over the past five years, Franklin Florida Tax-Free Income I has been safer than 84 percent of all municipal bond funds. Over the past decade, the fund has had one negative year, as has the Lehman Brothers Aggregate Bond Index (off 3 percent in 1994). The fund has underperformed the Lehman Brothers Aggregate Bond Index five times and the Lehman Brothers Municipal Bond Index six times in the last nine years.

	last 5 years		last 9 years	
worst year	-3%	1994	-3%	1994
best year	15%	1995	15%	1995

In the past, Franklin Florida Tax-Free Income I has done better than 75 percent of its peer group in up markets but only 35 percent of its competition in down markets. Consistency, or predictability, of returns for Franklin Florida Tax-Free Income I can be described as very good.

Management ★ ★

There are 315 fixed-income securities in this $1.5 billion portfolio. The average municipal bond fund today is $145 million in size. Close to 100 percent of the fund's holdings are in bonds. The average maturity of the bonds in this account is nineteen years; the weighted coupon rate averages 6.5 percent. The portfolio's fixed-income holdings can be categorized as long-term, high-quality debt.

A team has managed this fund for the past eight years. There are 119 funds besides Florida Tax-Free Income I within the Franklin Templeton Group. Overall, the fund family's risk-adjusted performance can be described as good.

Current Income ★ ★ ★

Over the past year, Franklin Florida Tax-Free Income I had a twelve-month yield of 5.9 percent. During this same twelve-month period, the typical municipal bond fund had a twelve-month yield that averaged 4.7 percent.

Expenses ★ ★ ★ ★ ★

Franklin Florida Tax-Free Income I's expense ratio is 0.6 percent; it has averaged 0.6 percent annually over the past three calendar years. The average expense ratio for the 1,900 funds in this category is 1.0 percent. This fund's turnover rate over the past year has been 12 percent, while its peer group average has been 53 percent.

Summary

Franklin Florida Tax-Free Income I is the only Florida municipal bond fund to appear in this book. Yet, this fund's ratings are so high it is a fund that can be recommended to residents of other states. On a total return basis (which includes appreciation or depreciation of principal as well as current income), this fund has done an excellent job of minimizing taxes.

Profile

minimum initial investment $100	*IRA accounts available* . . . . yes
subsequent minimum investment . . $100	*IRA minimum investment* . . . . n/a
available in all 50 states . . . . no	*date of inception* . . . . Sept. 1987
telephone exchanges. . . . . yes	*dividend/income paid*. . . . . monthly
number of other funds in family 119	*quality of annual reports* . . . . excellent

Franklin High-Yield Tax-Free Income I

Franklin Group of Funds
777 Mariners Island Boulevard
San Mateo, CA 94403-7777
(800) 342-5236

total return	★ ★ ★ ★ ★
risk reduction	★ ★ ★ ★ ★
management	★ ★ ★ ★
current income	★ ★ ★ ★ ★
expense control	★ ★ ★ ★ ★
symbol FRHIX	24 points
up-market performance	excellent
down-market performance	fair
predictability of returns	excellent

Total Return

Over the past five years, Franklin High-Yield Tax-Free Income I has taken $10,000 and turned it into $14,790 ($12,750 over three years and $23,720 over the past ten years). This translates into an average annual return of 8 percent over the past five years, 8 percent over the past three years, and 9 percent for the decade. Over the past five years, this fund has outperformed 45 percent of all mutual funds; within its general category it has done better than 95 percent of its peers. Municipal bond funds have averaged 6 percent annually over these same five years.

During the past five years, a $10,000 initial investment grew to $14,790 after taxes, assuming a 39.6 percent income tax bracket (state and federal combined) and a capital gains rate of 28 percent. This means that investors in this fund were able to preserve 100 percent of their total returns. Compared to other fixed-income funds, this fund offers tax savings that are considered excellent.

Risk/Volatility

Over the past five years, Franklin High-Yield Tax-Free Income I has been safer than 86 percent of all municipal bond funds. Over the past decade, the fund has had one negative year, as has the Lehman Brothers Aggregate Bond Index (off 3 percent in 1994). The fund has underperformed the Lehman Brothers Aggregate Bond Index four times and the Lehman Brothers Municipal Bond Index three times in the last ten years.

	last 5 years		last 10 years	
worst year	-3%	1994	-3%	1994
best year	16%	1995	16%	1995

In the past, Franklin High-Yield Tax-Free Income I has done better than 90 percent of its peer group in up markets but only 35 percent of its competition in down markets. Consistency, or predictability, of returns for Franklin High-Yield Tax-Free Income I can be described as excellent.

Management   ★ ★ ★ ★
There are 800 fixed-income securities in this $4.7 billion portfolio. The average municipal bond fund today is $145 million in size. Close to 100 percent of the fund's holdings are in bonds. The average maturity of the bonds in this account is nineteen years; the weighted coupon rate averages 7.0 percent. The portfolio's fixed-income holdings can be categorized as long-term, high-quality debt.

Kenny and Amoroso have managed this fund for the past seven years. There are 119 funds besides High-Yield Tax-Free Income I within the Franklin Templeton Group. Overall, the fund family's risk-adjusted performance can be described as good.

Current Income   ★ ★ ★ ★ ★
Over the past year, Franklin High-Yield Tax-Free Income I had a twelve-month yield of 6.4 percent. During this same twelve-month period, the typical municipal bond fund had a twelve-month yield that averaged 4.7 percent.

Expenses   ★ ★ ★ ★ ★
Franklin High-Yield Tax-Free Income I's expense ratio is 0.6 percent; it has averaged 0.6 percent annually over the past three calendar years. The average expense ratio for the 1,900 funds in this category is 1.0 percent. This fund's turnover rate over the past year has been 7 percent, while its peer group average has been 53 percent.

Summary
Franklin High-Yield Tax-Free Income I is not only the most highly rated municipal bond fund, its total score makes it the second highest rated fund in the entire book. This fund cannot be recommended highly enough. Other Franklin Templeton funds are also exceptional. Long known for its expertise in tax-free bonds, the fund family does a surprisingly good job with a number of its equity portfolios.

Profile

minimum initial investment $100	*IRA accounts available* . . . . yes
subsequent minimum investment . . . $25	*IRA minimum investment* . . . . n/a
available in all 50 states. . . . . yes	*date of inception* . . . . March 1986
telephone exchanges. . . . . yes	*dividend/income paid*. . . . . monthly
number of other funds in family 119	*quality of annual reports* . . . . excellent

Franklin Pennsylvania Tax-Free Income I

Franklin Group of Funds
777 Mariners Island Boulevard
San Mateo, CA 94403-7777
(800) 342-5236

total return	★ ★ ★
risk reduction	★ ★ ★ ★
management	★ ★ ★
current income	★ ★ ★
expense control	★ ★ ★ ★ ★
symbol FRPAX	18 points
up-market performance	excellent
down-market performance	poor
predictability of returns	very good

Total Return   ★ ★ ★

Over the past five years, Franklin Pennsylvania Tax-Free Income I has taken $10,000 and turned it into $14,030 ($12,290 over three years and $21,790 over the past ten years). This translates into an average annual return of 7 percent over the past five years, 7 percent over the past three years, and 8 percent for the decade. Over the past five years, this fund has outperformed 40 percent of all mutual funds; within its general category it has done better than 80 percent of its peers. Municipal bond funds have averaged 6 percent annually over these same five years.

During the past five years, a $10,000 initial investment grew to $13,990 after taxes, assuming a 39.6 percent income tax bracket (state and federal combined) and a capital gains rate of 28 percent. This means that investors in this fund were able to preserve 100 percent of their total returns. Compared to other fixed-income funds, this fund offers tax savings that are considered excellent.

Risk/Volatility   ★ ★ ★ ★

Over the past five years, Franklin Pennsylvania Tax-Free Income I has been safer than 87 percent of all municipal bond funds. Over the past decade, the fund has had two negative years, while the Lehman Brothers Aggregate Bond Index has had one (off 3 percent in 1994). The fund has underperformed the Lehman Brothers Aggregate Bond Index six times and the Lehman Brothers Municipal Bond Index five times in the last ten years.

	last 5 years		last 10 years	
worst year	-3%	1994	-4%	1987
best year	14%	1995	14%	1995

In the past, Franklin Pennsylvania Tax-Free Income I has done better than 85 percent of its peer group in up markets but virtually none of its competition in down markets. Consistency, or predictability, of returns for Franklin Pennsylvania Tax-Free Income I can be described as very good.

Management   ★ ★ ★

There are 185 fixed-income securities in this $670 million portfolio. The average municipal bond fund today is $145 million in size. Close to 100 percent of the fund's holdings are in bonds. The average maturity of the bonds in this account is eighteen years; the weighted coupon rate averages 7.0 percent. The portfolio's fixed-income holdings can be categorized as long-term, high-quality debt.

A team has managed this fund for the past eight years. There are 119 funds besides Pennsylvania Tax-Free Income I within the Franklin Templeton Group. Overall, the fund family's risk-adjusted performance can be described as good.

Current Income   ★ ★ ★

Over the past year, Franklin Pennsylvania Tax-Free Income I had a twelve-month yield of 5.8 percent. During this same twelve-month period, the typical municipal bond fund had a twelve-month yield that averaged 4.7 percent.

Expenses   ★ ★ ★ ★ ★

Franklin Pennsylvania Tax-Free Income I's expense ratio is 0.6 percent; it has averaged 0.6 percent annually over the past three calendar years. The average expense ratio for the 1,900 funds in this category is 1.0 percent. This fund's turnover rate over the past year has been 22 percent, while its peer group average has been 53 percent.

Summary

Franklin Pennsylvania Tax-Free Income I is one of many members of the Franklin Templeton Group to show its excellence in the municipal bond market. The family has a number of other funds that appear in other categories in this and previous editions of the book. Whenever you are considering tax-free income, start off by contacting the folks at this fine fund family.

Profile

minimum initial investment $100	IRA accounts available . . . . yes
subsequent minimum investment . . . $25	IRA minimum investment . . . . n/a
available in all 50 states. . . . . yes	date of inception. . . . . Dec. 1986
telephone exchanges. . . . . yes	dividend/income paid. . . . . monthly
number of other funds in family 119	quality of annual reports . . . . excellent

SIT Tax-Free Income
Sit Group
4600 Norwest Center 90 South 7th Street
Minneapolis, MN 55402-4130
(800) 332-5580

total return	★ ★ ★ ★
risk reduction	★ ★ ★ ★ ★
management	★ ★ ★ ★ ★
current income	★ ★ ★
expense control	★ ★ ★ ★
symbol SNTIX	21 points
up-market performance	good
down-market performance	very good
predictability of returns	excellent

Total Return   ★ ★ ★ ★

Over the past five years, SIT Tax-Free Income has taken $10,000 and turned it into $14,030 ($12,460 over three years). This translates into an average annual return of 7 percent over the past five years and 8 percent over the past three years. Over the past five years, this fund has outperformed 40 percent of all mutual funds; within its general category it has done better than 85 percent of its peers. Municipal bond funds have averaged 6 percent annually over these same five years.

During the past five years, a $10,000 initial investment grew to $14,020 after taxes, assuming a 39.6 percent income tax bracket (state and federal combined) and a capital gains rate of 28 percent. This means that investors in this fund were able to preserve 98 percent of their total returns. Compared to other fixed-income funds, this fund offers tax savings that are considered excellent.

Risk/Volatility   ★ ★ ★ ★ ★

Over the past five years, SIT Tax-Free Income has been safer than 95 percent of all municipal bond funds. Over the past decade, the fund has had one negative year, as has the Lehman Brothers Aggregate Bond Index (off 3 percent in 1994). The fund has underperformed the Lehman Brothers Aggregate Bond Index four times and the Lehman Brothers Municipal Bond Index six times in the last eight years.

	last 5 years		last 8 years	
worst year	-1%	1994	-4%	1987
best year	13%	1995	13%	1995

In the past, SIT Tax-Free Income has done better than 45 percent of its peer group in up markets and outperformed 75 percent of its competition in down markets. Consistency, or predictability, of returns for SIT Tax-Free Income can be described as excellent.

Management   ★ ★ ★ ★ ★

There are 210 fixed-income securities in this $350 million portfolio. The average municipal bond fund today is $145 million in size. Close to 97 percent of the fund's holdings are in bonds. The average maturity of the bonds in this account is seventeen years; the weighted coupon rate averages 6.0 percent. The portfolio's fixed-income holdings can be categorized as long-term, high-quality debt.

Brilley and Sit have managed this fund for the past eight years. There are nine funds besides Tax-Free Income within the SIT fund family. Overall, the fund family's risk-adjusted performance can be described as good.

Current Income   ★ ★ ★

Over the past year, SIT Tax-Free Income had a twelve-month yield of 5.5 percent. During this same twelve-month period, the typical municipal bond fund had a twelve-month yield that averaged 4.7 percent.

Expenses   ★ ★ ★ ★

SIT Tax-Free Income's expense ratio is 0.8 percent; it has averaged 0.8 percent annually over the past three calendar years. The average expense ratio for the 1,900 funds in this category is 1.0 percent. This fund's turnover rate over the past year has been 25 percent, while its peer group average has been 53 percent.

Summary

SIT Tax-Free Income is not only the safest municipal bond fund in the book, it also has some of the better total return figures. This is one of the few funds whose management can be described as truly great. This is a very small fund that has done an amazing job.

Profile

minimum initial investment $2,000	*IRA accounts available* . . . . yes
subsequent minimum investment . . $100	*IRA minimum investment* $1
available in all 50 states. . . . . yes	*date of inception* . . . . Sept. 1988
telephone exchanges. . . . . yes	*dividend/income paid.* . . . . monthly
number of other funds in family 9	*quality of annual reports* . . . . excellent

Thornburg Intermediate Municipal A

Thornburg Funds
119 East Marcy Street, Suite 202
Santa Fe, NM 87501
(800) 847-0200

total return	★ ★ ★
risk reduction	★ ★ ★ ★
management	★ ★ ★
current income	★ ★
expense control	★ ★ ★
symbol THIMX	15 points
up-market performance	n/a
down-market performance	n/a
predictability of returns	excellent

Total Return ★ ★ ★

Over the past five years, Thornburg Intermediate Municipal A has taken $10,000 and turned it into $14,030 ($12,150 over three years). This translates into an average annual return of 7 percent over the past five years and 7 percent over the past three years. Over the past five years, this fund has outperformed 35 percent of all mutual funds; within its general category it has done better than 75 percent of its peers. Municipal bond funds have averaged 6 percent annually over these same five years.

During the past five years, a $10,000 initial investment grew to $13,950 after taxes, assuming a 39.6 percent income tax bracket (state and federal combined) and a capital gains rate of 28 percent. This means that investors in this fund were able to preserve 100 percent of their total returns. Compared to other fixed-income funds, this fund offers tax savings that are considered excellent.

Risk/Volatility ★ ★ ★ ★

Over the past five years, Thornburg Intermediate Municipal A has been safer than 90 percent of all municipal bond funds. Over the past decade, the fund has had one negative year, as has the Lehman Brothers Aggregate Bond Index (off 3 percent in 1994). The fund has underperformed the Lehman Brothers Aggregate Bond Index and the Lehman Brothers Municipal Bond Index once in the last five years.

	last 5 years		last 5 years	
worst year	-2%	1994	-2%	1994
best year	13%	1995	13%	1995

Consistency, or predictability, of returns for Thornburg Intermediate Municipal A can be described as excellent.

Management   ★ ★ ★

There are 260 fixed-income securities in this $260 million portfolio. The average municipal bond fund today is $145 million in size. Close to 99 percent of the fund's holdings are in bonds. The average maturity of the bonds in this account is eight years; the weighted coupon rate averages 6.5 percent. The portfolio's fixed-income holdings can be categorized as intermediate-term, high-quality debt.

Brian J. McMahon has managed this fund for the past six years. There are fifteen funds besides Intermediate Municipal A within the Thornburg fund family. Overall, the fund family's risk-adjusted performance can be described as good.

Current Income   ★ ★

Over the past year, Thornburg Intermediate Municipal A had a twelve-month yield of 5.0 percent. During this same twelve-month period, the typical municipal bond fund had a twelve-month yield that averaged 4.7 percent.

Expenses   ★ ★ ★

Thornburg Intermediate Municipal A's expense ratio is 1.0 percent; it has averaged 1.0 percent annually over the past three calendar years. The average expense ratio for the 1,900 funds in this category is 1.0 percent. This fund's turnover rate over the past year has been 13 percent, while its peer group average has been 53 percent.

Summary

Thornburg Intermediate Municipal A is a fine choice for the risk-conscious investor. By keeping maturities in the intermediate-term range, management has been able to get the best possible returns with only modest interest-rate risk. Few investors realize that municipal bonds have somewhere between one-third and one-half less risk than similar-maturity U.S. Government securities.

Profile

minimum initial investment $5,000	*IRA accounts available* . . . . yes
subsequent minimum investment . . $100	*IRA minimum investment* . . . . n/a
available in all 50 states. . . . . yes	*date of inception* . . . . July 1991
telephone exchanges. . . . . yes	*dividend/income paid.* . . . . monthly
number of other funds in family 15	*quality of annual reports* . . . . good

United Municipal High Income A

United Group
6300 Lamar Avenue
P.O. Box 29217
Shawnee Mission, KS 66201-9217
(800) 366-5465

total return	★ ★ ★ ★ ★
risk reduction	★ ★ ★ ★
management	★ ★ ★ ★
current income	★ ★ ★ ★
expense control	★ ★ ★ ★
symbol UMUHX	21 points
up-market performance	excellent
down-market performance	very good
predictability of returns	very good

Total Return   ★ ★ ★ ★ ★

Over the past five years, United Municipal High Income A has taken $10,000 and turned it into $14,690 ($12,900 over three years and $22,920 over the past ten years). This translates into an average annual return of 8 percent over the past five years, 9 percent over the past three years, and 9 percent for the decade. Over the past five years, this fund has outperformed 45 percent of all mutual funds; within its general category it has done better than 95 percent of its peers. Municipal bond funds have averaged 6 percent annually over these same five years.

During the past five years, a $10,000 initial investment grew to $14,830 after taxes, assuming a 39.6 percent income tax bracket (state and federal combined) and a capital gains rate of 28 percent. This means that investors in this fund were able to preserve 98 percent of their total returns. Compared to other fixed-income funds, this fund offers tax savings that are considered excellent.

Risk/Volatility   ★ ★ ★ ★

Over the past five years, United Municipal High Income A has been safer than 80 percent of all municipal bond funds. Over the past decade, the fund has had one negative year, as has the Lehman Brothers Aggregate Bond Index (off 3 percent in 1994). The fund has underperformed the Lehman Brothers Aggregate Bond Index six times and the Lehman Brothers Municipal Bond Index five times in the last ten years.

	last 5 years		last 10 years	
worst year	-3%	1994	-3%	1994
best year	17%	1995	17%	1995

In the past, United Municipal High Income A has done better than 95 percent of its peer group in up markets and outperformed 65 percent of its competition in down markets. Consistency, or predictability, of returns for United Municipal High Income A can be described as very good.

Management   ★ ★ ★ ★
There are 160 fixed-income securities in this $430 million portfolio. The average municipal bond fund today is $145 million in size. Close to 98 percent of the fund's holdings are in bonds. The average maturity of the bonds in this account is six years; the weighted coupon rate averages 7.5 percent. The portfolio's fixed-income holdings can be categorized as intermediate-term, low-quality debt.

John M. Holliday has managed this fund for the past eleven years. There are twenty-four funds besides Municipal High Income A within the United fund family. Overall, the fund family's risk-adjusted performance can be described as fair.

Current Income   ★ ★ ★ ★
Over the past year, United Municipal High Income A had a twelve-month yield of 6.2 percent. During this same twelve-month period, the typical municipal bond fund had a twelve-month yield that averaged 4.7 percent.

Expenses   ★ ★ ★ ★
United Municipal High Income A's expense ratio is 0.8 percent; it has averaged 0.8 percent annually over the past three calendar years. The average expense ratio for the 1,900 funds in this category is 1.0 percent. This fund's turnover rate over the past year has been 27 percent, while its peer group average has been 53 percent.

Summary
United Municipal High Income A is a very highly recommended tax-free fund. Its total score, 21 out of 25, also makes it one of the more highly praised funds in the entire book. The fund's total return figures make it and two other municipal bond funds the top performers in the category. And, speaking of total return figures, the tax minimization policy of management is great.

Profile

minimum initial investment $500	*IRA accounts available* . . . . yes
subsequent minimum investment $1	*IRA minimum investment* . . . . n/a
available in all 50 states. . . . . yes	*date of inception* . . . . Jan. 1986
telephone exchanges. . . . . yes	*dividend/income paid.* . . . . monthly
number of other funds in family 24	*quality of annual reports* . . . . good

Vanguard Municipal Intermediate-Term

Vanguard Group
Vanguard Financial Center
P.O. Box 2600
Valley Forge, PA 19482
(800) 662-7447

total return	★ ★ ★
risk reduction	★ ★ ★
management	★ ★
current income	★ ★ ★ ★
expense control	★ ★ ★ ★ ★
symbol VWITX	17 points
up-market performance	very good
down-market performance	very good
predictability of returns	very good

Total Return ★ ★ ★

Over the past five years, Vanguard Municipal Intermediate-Term has taken $10,000 and turned it into $14,030 ($12,130 over three years and $21,590 over the past ten years). This translates into an average annual return of 7 percent over the past five years, 7 percent over the past three years, and 8 percent for the decade. Over the past five years, this fund has outperformed 35 percent of all mutual funds; within its general category it has done better than 75 percent of its peers. Municipal bond funds have averaged 6 percent annually over these same five years.

During the past five years, a $10,000 initial investment grew to $13,780 after taxes, assuming a 39.6 percent income tax bracket (state and federal combined) and a capital gains rate of 28 percent. This means that investors in this fund were able to preserve 97 percent of their total returns. Compared to other fixed-income funds, this fund offers tax savings that are considered excellent.

Risk/Volatility ★ ★ ★

Over the past five years, Vanguard Municipal Intermediate-Term has been safer than 82 percent of all municipal bond funds. Over the past decade, the fund has had one negative year, as has the Lehman Brothers Aggregate Bond Index (off 3 percent in 1994). The fund has underperformed the Lehman Brothers Aggregate Bond Index five times and the Lehman Brothers Municipal Bond Index six times in the last ten years.

	last 5 years		last 10 years	
worst year	-2%	1994	-2%	1994
best year	14%	1995	14%	1995

In the past, Vanguard Municipal Intermediate-Term has done better than 70 percent of its peer group in up markets and outperformed 65 percent of its competition in down markets. Consistency, or predictability, of returns for Vanguard Municipal Intermediate-Term can be described as very good.

Management   ★ ★
There are 690 fixed-income securities in this $6.5 billion portfolio. The average municipal bond fund today is $145 million in size. Close to 87 percent of the fund's holdings are in bonds. The average maturity of the bonds in this account is six years; the weighted coupon rate averages 6.0 percent. The portfolio's fixed-income holdings can be categorized as intermediate-term, high-quality debt.

MacKinnon and Ryon have managed this fund for the past eleven years. There are sixty-four funds besides Municipal Intermediate-Term within the Vanguard fund family. Overall, the fund family's risk-adjusted performance can be described as good.

Current Income   ★ ★ ★ ★
Over the past year, Vanguard Municipal Intermediate-Term had a twelve-month yield of 5.1 percent. During this same twelve-month period, the typical municipal bond fund had a twelve-month yield that averaged 4.7 percent.

Expenses   ★ ★ ★ ★ ★
Vanguard Municipal Intermediate-Term's expense ratio is 0.2 percent; it has averaged 0.2 percent annually over the past three calendar years. The average expense ratio for the 1,900 funds in this category is 1.0 percent. This fund's turnover rate over the past year has been 14 percent, while its peer group average has been 53 percent.

Summary
Vanguard Municipal Intermediate-Term is one of the few funds, in any category, that rates so highly for both bull and bear market performance as well as predictability. Vanguard's legendary cost-cutting are also seen in this fund. This tax-free offering easily beats out the number two municipal bond fund when it comes to expense minimization.

Profile

minimum initial investment $3,000	IRA accounts available . . . . yes
subsequent minimum investment . . $100	IRA minimum investment $1,000
available in all 50 states. . . . . yes	date of inception . . . . Sept. 1977
telephone exchanges. . . . . yes	dividend/income paid. . . . . monthly
number of other funds in family 64	quality of annual reports . . . . excellent

Utility Stock Funds

Utility stock funds look for both growth and income, investing in common stocks of utility companies across the country. Somewhere between a third and half of these funds' total returns come from common stock dividends. Utility funds normally stay away from speculative issues, focusing instead on well established companies with solid histories of paying good dividends. Surprisingly, the goal of most of these funds is *long-term growth*.

Utility, metals, and natural resources funds are the only three sector, or specialty, fund categories in this book. Funds that invest in a single industry, or sector, should be avoided by most investors for two reasons. First, you limit the fund manager's ability to find attractive stocks or bonds if he or she is only able to choose securities from one particular geographic area or industry. Second, the track record of sector funds as a whole is pretty bad. In fact, as a general category, these specialty funds represent the worst of both worlds: above-average risk and substandard returns. If you find the term "aggressive growth" unappealing, then the words "sector fund" should positively appall you.

Utility funds are the one exception. They sound safe and they are safe (-9.0 percent for 1994 notwithstanding). Any category of stocks that relies heavily on dividends generated automatically has a built-in safety cushion. A comparatively high dividend income means that you have to worry less about the appreciation of the underlying issues.

Four factors generally determine the profitability of a utility company: (1) how much it pays for energy, (2) the general level of interest rates, (3) its expected use of nuclear power, and (4) the political climate.

The prices of oil and gas are passed directly on to the consumer, but the utility companies are sensitive to this issue. Higher fuel prices mean that the utility industry has less latitude to increase its profit margins. Thus, higher fuel prices can mean smaller profits and/or dividends to investors.

Next to energy costs, interest expense is the industry's greatest expense. Utility companies are heavily debt-laden. Their interest costs directly affect their profitability. When rates go down and companies are able to refinance their debt, the savings can be staggering. Paying 8 percent interest on a couple of hundred million dollars worth of bonds each year is much more appealing than having to pay 10 percent on the same amount of debt. A lower-interest-rate environment translates into more money being left over for shareholders.

Depending on how you look at it, nuclear power has been an issue or problem for the United States for a few decades now. Other countries seem to have come to grips with the matter, yet we remain divided. Although new power plants have not been successfully proposed or built in this country for several years, no one knows what the future may hold. Venturing into nuclear power always seems to be much more expensive than anticipated by the utility companies and the independent experts they rely on for advice. Because of these uncertainties, mutual fund managers try to seek out utility companies that have no foreseeable plans to develop any or more nuclear power facilities. Whether this will help the nation in the long term remains to be seen, but such avoidance keeps share prices more stable and predictable.

Finally, the political climate is an important concern when calculating whether utility funds should be part of your portfolio. The Public Utilities Commission (PUC) is a political animal and can directly reflect the views of a state's government. Utility bills are something most of us are concerned with and aware of; the powers that be are more likely to be reelected if they are able to keep rate increases to a minimum. Modest, or minimum, increases can be healthy for the utility companies; freezing rates for a couple of years is a bad sign.

Ninety-five funds make up the utilities category. Total market capitalization of this category is close to $23 billion. Over 85 percent of a typical utility fund's portfolio is in common stocks, with the balance in bonds, convertibles, and money market instruments. The typical utilities fund has about 15 percent of its holdings in foreign stocks.

Over the past three years, utility funds have had an average compound return of 15 percent per year; the *annual* return for the past five years has been 12 percent. For the last ten years, these funds have averaged over 10 percent per year; 14 percent per year for the last fifteen years. The standard deviation for growth funds has been 9 percent over the past three years. This means that these funds have been less volatile than any other stock category except equity-income funds, which have exhibited almost identical volatility.

Usually, utility stock prices closely follow the long-term bond market. If the economy surges and long-term interest rates go up, utility stock prices are likely to go down. Utility stocks are also vulnerable to a general stock market decline, although they are considered less risky than other types of common stock because of their dividends and the monopoly position of most utilities. Typically, utilities have fallen about two-thirds as much as other common stocks during market downturns.

Worldwide, there is a tremendous opportunity for growth in this industry. The average per-capita production of electricity in many developing countries is only *one-fifth* that of the United States. The electrical output per capita in the United States is 12,100 kilowatt hours, compared to 2,500 kilowatt hours for developing nations. This disparity may well be on the way out. All over the world, previously underdeveloped countries are making economic strides as they move toward free market systems.

When emerging countries become developed economically, their citizens demand higher standards of living. As a result, their requirements for electricity, water, and telephones tend to rise dramatically. Moreover, many countries are selling their utility companies to public owners, opening a new arena for investors. The net result of all of this for you, the investor, is that fund groups are beginning to offer *global utility funds*. This increased diversification—allowing a fund to invest in utility companies all over the world instead of just in the United States—coupled with tremendous long-term growth potential—should make this a dynamic industry group. Utility funds are a good choice for the investor who wants a hedge against inflation but is still afraid or distrustful of the stock market in general.

Beta, which measures the *market-related risk* of a stock, is only 0.5 percent for utility funds as a group (compared to 1.0 for the S&P 500). This means that when it comes to *stock market risk*, utilities have only 50 percent the risk of the Dow Jones Industrial Average (DJIA) or the S&P 500. Keep in mind, however, that there are other risks, such as rising interest rates, that also need to be considered whenever utilities are being considered.

Utility Stock Funds

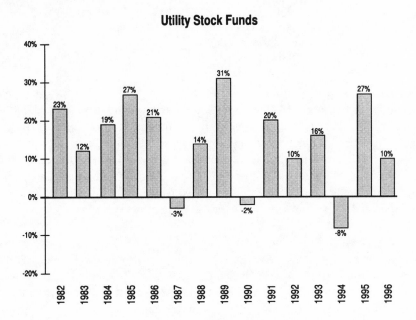

Fidelity Select Utilities Growth

Fidelity Group
82 Devonshire Street
Boston, MA 02109
(800) 544-8888

total return	★ ★ ★ ★
risk reduction	★ ★
management	★ ★ ★
tax minimization	★ ★ ★
expense control	★ ★ ★ ★
symbol FSUTX	16 points
up-market performance	excellent
down-market performance	good
predictability of returns	poor

Total Return   ★ ★ ★ ★

Over the past five years, Fidelity Select Utilities Growth has taken $10,000 and turned it into $19,250 ($16,570 over three years and $35,450 over the past ten years). This translates into an average annual return of 14 percent over the past five years, 18 percent over the past three years, and 13 percent for the decade. Over the past five years, this fund has outperformed 65 percent of all mutual funds; within its general category it has done better than 90 percent of its peers. Utilities funds have averaged 12 percent annually over these same five years.

Risk/Volatility   ★ ★

Over the past five years, Fidelity Select Utilities Growth has only been safer than 15 percent of all utilities funds. Over the past decade, the fund has had two negative years, while the S&P 500 has had one (off 3 percent in 1990). The fund has underperformed the S&P 500 six times in the last ten years.

	last 5 years		last 10 years	
worst year	-7%	1994	-9%	1987
best year	34%	1995	39%	1989

In the past, Fidelity Select Utilities Growth has done better than 90 percent of its peer group in up markets and outperformed 50 percent of its competition in down markets. Consistency, or predictability, of returns for Fidelity Select Utilities Growth can be described as poor.

Management   ★ ★ ★

There are ninety stocks in this $240 million portfolio. The average utilities fund today is $232 million in size. Close to 98 percent of the fund's holdings are in stocks. The stocks in this portfolio have an average price-earnings (p/e) ratio of 20 and a median market capitalization of $22.5 billion. The portfolio's equity holdings can be categorized as large-cap and value-oriented.

John Muresianu has managed this fund for the past five years. There are 164 funds besides Select Utilities Growth within the Fidelity fund family. Overall, the fund family's risk-adjusted performance can be described as good.

Tax Minimization   ★ ★ ★
During the past five years, a $10,000 initial investment grew to $17,060 after taxes, assuming a 39.6 percent income tax bracket (state and federal combined) and a capital gains rate of 28 percent. This means that investors in this fund were able to preserve 80 percent of their total returns. Compared to other equity funds, this fund's tax savings are considered to be fair. Over the past year, Fidelity Select Utilities Growth had a twelve-month yield of 1.3 percent.

Expenses   ★ ★ ★ ★
Fidelity Select Utilities Growth's expense ratio is 1.5 percent; it has averaged 1.4 percent annually over the past three calendar years. The average expense ratio for the 95 funds in this category is 1.4 percent. This fund's turnover rate over the past year has been 31 percent, while its peer group average has been 55 percent.

Summary
Fidelity Select Utilities Growth is part of the elite division at Fidelity. Within the Advisor group, the fund company often utilizes its most respected and seasoned managers. This particular fund is one of only a handful of utilities funds to make this book. The fund outperforms all of its peers during bull markets (which last about four times longer than bear markets).

Profile

minimum initial investment $2,500	*IRA accounts available* . . . . yes
subsequent minimum investment . . $250	*IRA minimum investment* $500
available in all 50 states. . . . . yes	*date of inception*. . . . . Dec. 1981
telephone exchanges. . . . . yes	*dividend/income paid* . . . semi-annually
number of other funds in family 164	*quality of annual reports* . . . . excellent

Fidelity Utilities

Fidelity Group
82 Devonshire Street
Boston, MA 02109
(800) 544-8888

total return	★ ★ ★ ★
risk reduction	★ ★ ★
management	★ ★ ★
tax minimization	★ ★ ★
expense control	★ ★ ★ ★ ★
symbol FIUIX	18 points
up-market performance	very good
down-market performance	very good
predictability of returns	fair

Total Return   ★ ★ ★ ★

Over the past five years, Fidelity Utilities has taken $10,000 and turned it into $19,250 ($15,630 over three years). This translates into an average annual return of 14 percent over the past five years and 16 percent over the past three years. Over the past five years, this fund has outperformed 65 percent of all mutual funds; within its general category it has done better than 85 percent of its peers. Utilities funds have averaged 12 percent annually over these same five years.

Risk/Volatility   ★ ★ ★

Over the past five years, Fidelity Utilities has been safer than just 37 percent of all utilities funds. Over the past decade, the fund has had one negative year, as has the S&P 500 (off 3 percent in 1990). The fund has underperformed the S&P 500 six times in the last nine years.

	last 5 years		last 9 years	
worst year	-5%	1994	-5%	1994
best year	31%	1995	31%	1995

In the past, Fidelity Utilities has done better than 65 percent of its peer group in up markets and outperformed 75 percent of its competition in down markets. Consistency, or predictability, of returns for Fidelity Utilities can be described as fair.

Management   ★ ★ ★

There are 180 stocks in this $1.3 billion portfolio. The average utilities fund today is $232 million in size. Close to 98 percent of the fund's holdings are in stocks. The stocks in this portfolio have an average price-earnings (p/e) ratio of 19 and a median market capitalization of $7.9 billion. The portfolio's equity holdings can be categorized as large-cap and value-oriented.

John Muresianu has managed this fund for the past five years. There are 164 funds besides Utilities within the Fidelity fund family. Overall, the fund family's risk-adjusted performance can be described as good.

Tax Minimization   ★ ★ ★
During the past five years, a $10,000 initial investment grew to $17,000 after taxes, assuming a 39.6 percent income tax bracket (state and federal combined) and a capital gains rate of 28 percent. This means that investors in this fund were able to preserve 81 percent of their total returns. Compared to other equity funds, this fund's tax savings are considered to be fair. Over the past year, Fidelity Utilities had a twelve-month yield of 2.5 percent.

Expenses   ★ ★ ★ ★ ★
Fidelity Utilities's expense ratio is 0.8 percent; it has averaged 0.8 percent annually over the past three calendar years. The average expense ratio for the 95 funds in this category is 1.4 percent. This fund's turnover rate over the past year has been 56 percent, while its peer group average has been 55 percent.

Summary
Fidelity Utilities is one of two Fidelity funds to appear as one of the best utilities funds. This is quite an accomplishment when you consider the fact that only a handful of these sector funds make the book. This particular Fidelity fund sports the lowest expense ratio in its category, which is one of the reasons its total return figures are so good.

Profile
minimum initial investment $2,500	*IRA accounts available* . . . . yes
subsequent minimum investment . . $250	*IRA minimum investment* $500
available in all 50 states. . . . . yes	*date of inception* . . . . Nov. 1987
telephone exchanges. . . . . yes	*dividend/income paid* . . . . quarterly
number of other funds in family 164	*quality of annual reports* . . . . excellent

MFS Utilities A

MFS Family of Funds
500 Boylston Street
Boston, MA 02116
(800) 637-2929

total return	★ ★ ★ ★ ★
risk reduction	★ ★ ★ ★
management	★ ★ ★ ★ ★
tax minimization	★ ★ ★ ★
expense control	★ ★ ★ ★
symbol MMUFX	22 points
up-market performance	n/a
down-market performance	n/a
predictability of returns	good

Total Return   ★ ★ ★ ★ ★
Over the past five years, MFS Utilities A has taken $10,000 and turned it into $22,880 ($18,160 over three years). This translates into an average annual return of 18 percent over the past five years and 22 percent over the past three years. Over the past five years, this fund has outperformed 80 percent of all mutual funds; within its general category it has done better than 95 percent of its peers. Utilities funds have averaged 12 percent annually over these same five years.

Risk/Volatility   ★ ★ ★ ★
Over the past five years, MFS Utilities A has been safer than 68 percent of all utilities funds. Over the past decade, the fund has had one negative year, as has the S&P 500 (off 3 percent in 1990). The fund has underperformed the S&P 500 three times in the last four years.

	last 5 years		last 4 years	
worst year	-5%	1994	-5%	1994
best year	33%	1995	33%	1995

Consistency, or predictability, of returns for MFS Utilities A can be described as good.

Management   ★ ★ ★ ★ ★
There are eighty stocks in this $80 million portfolio. The average utilities fund today is $232 million in size. Close to 80 percent of the fund's holdings are in stocks. The stocks in this portfolio have an average price-earnings (p/e) ratio of 16 and a median market capitalization of $2.8 billion. The average maturity of the bonds in this account is eleven years; the weighted coupon rate averages 9.0 percent. The portfolio's equity holdings can be categorized as mid-cap and value-oriented. The portfolio's fixed-income holdings can be categorized as long-term, high-quality debt.

Maura Shaughnessy has managed this fund for the past five years. There are 108 funds besides Utilities A within the MFS fund family. Overall, the fund family's risk-adjusted performance can be described as fair.

Tax Minimization   ★ ★ ★ ★
During the past five years, a $10,000 initial investment grew to $19,580 after taxes, assuming a 39.6 percent income tax bracket (state and federal combined) and a capital gains rate of 28 percent. This means that investors in this fund were able to preserve 82 percent of their total returns. Compared to other equity funds, this fund's tax savings are considered to be good. Over the past year, MFS Utilities A had a twelve-month yield of 3.4 percent.

Expenses   ★ ★ ★ ★
MFS Utilities A's expense ratio is 1.1 percent; it has averaged 0.9 percent annually over the past three calendar years. The average expense ratio for the 95 funds in this category is 1.4 percent. This fund's turnover rate over the past year has been 137 percent, while its peer group average has been 55 percent.

Summary
MFS Utilities A is easily the most highly rated utilities fund in the book. And, with such a high total point score, this is one of the most highly rated funds in any category. The fund's strongest areas are in management and total return. This is simply a great utilities fund.

Profile
minimum initial investment $1,000	*IRA accounts available* . . . . yes
subsequent minimum investment . . . $50	*IRA minimum investment* $250
available in all 50 states. . . . . yes	*date of inception* . . . . Jan. 1992
telephone exchanges. . . . . yes	*dividend/income paid.* . . . . monthly
number of other funds in family 108	*quality of annual reports* . . . . good

Putnam Utilities Growth and Income A

Putnam Funds
One Post Office Square
Boston, MA 02109
(800) 225-1581

total return	★ ★ ★
risk reduction	★ ★ ★ ★
management	★ ★ ★ ★
tax minimization	★ ★
expense control	★ ★ ★ ★
symbol PUGIX	17 points
up-market performance	n/a
down-market performance	n/a
predictability of returns	very good

Total Return   ★ ★ ★
Over the past five years, Putnam Utilities Growth and Income A has taken $10,000
and turned it into $18,420 ($16,470 over three years). This translates into an average
annual return of 13 percent over the past five years and 18 percent over the past
three years. Over the past five years, this fund has outperformed 60 percent of all
mutual funds; within its general category it has done better than 75 percent of its
peers. Utilities funds have averaged 12 percent annually over these same five years.

Risk/Volatility   ★ ★ ★ ★
Over the past five years, Putnam Utilities Growth and Income A has been safer
than 81 percent of all utilities funds. Over the past decade, the fund has had one
negative year, as has the S&P 500 (off 3 percent in 1990). The fund has underperformed the S&P 500 five times in the last six years.

	last 5 years		last 6 years	
worst year	-7%	1994	-7%	1994
best year	31%	1995	31%	1995

Consistency, or predictability, of returns for Putnam Utilities Growth and
Income A can be described as very good.

Management   ★ ★ ★ ★
There are 130 stocks in this $620 million portfolio. The average utilities fund today
is $232 million in size. Close to 83 percent of the fund's holdings are in stocks. The
stocks in this portfolio have an average price-earnings (p/e) ratio of 17 and a
median market capitalization of $2.7 billion. The portfolio's equity holdings can be
categorized as mid-cap and value-oriented.

Sheldon N. Simon has managed this fund for the past seven years. There are
120 funds besides Utilities Growth and Income A within the Putnam fund family.
Overall, the fund family's risk-adjusted performance can be described as good.

Tax Minimization   ★ ★

During the past five years, a $10,000 initial investment grew to $16,360 after taxes, assuming a 39.6 percent income tax bracket (state and federal combined) and a capital gains rate of 28 percent. This means that investors in this fund were able to preserve 79 percent of their total returns. Compared to other equity funds, this fund's tax savings are considered to be fair. Over the past year, Putnam Utilities Growth and Income A had a twelve-month yield of 3.6 percent.

Expenses   ★ ★ ★ ★

Putnam Utilities Growth and Income A's expense ratio is 1.1 percent; it has averaged 1.1 percent annually over the past three calendar years. The average expense ratio for the 95 funds in this category is 1.4 percent. This fund's turnover rate over the past year has been 65 percent, while its peer group average has been 55 percent.

Summary

Putnam Utilities Growth and Income A is just one of many Putnam funds to appear in this book. A few years ago, the upper management at Putnam made some rather dramatic changes that all appear to have worked out well. The fund family is now one of the most highly regarded in the entire industry of over 8,000 mutual funds.

Profile

minimum initial investment $500	*IRA accounts available* . . . . yes
subsequent minimum investment . . . $50	*IRA minimum investment* $250
available in all 50 states. . . . . yes	*date of inception* . . . . Nov. 1990
telephone exchanges. . . . . yes	*dividend/income paid* . . . . quarterly
number of other funds in family 120	*quality of annual reports* . . . . excellent

World Bond Funds

Global, or world, funds invest in securities issued all over the world, including the United States. A global bond fund usually invests in bonds issued by stable governments from a handful of countries. These funds try to avoid purchasing foreign government debt instruments from politically or economically unstable nations. Foreign, also known as international, bond funds invest in debt instruments from countries other than the United States.

International funds purchase securities issued in a foreign currency, such as the Japanese yen or the British pound. Prospective investors need to be aware of the potential changes in the value of the foreign currency relative to the U.S. dollar. As an example, if you were to invest in U.K. pound–denominated bonds with a yield of 15 percent and the British currency appreciated 12 percent against the U.S. dollar, your total return for the year would be 27 percent. If the British pound declined by 20 percent against the U.S. dollar, your total return would be –5 percent (15 percent yield minus 20 percent).

Since foreign markets do not necessarily move in tandem with U.S. markets, each country represents varying investment opportunities at different times. According to Salomon Brothers, current value of the world bond market is estimated to be about $20 trillion (versus about $18 trillion for worldwide stock market capitalization). About 40 percent of this bond marketplace is made up of U.S. bonds; Japan ranks a distant second.

Assessing the economic environment to evaluate its effects on interest rates and bond values requires an understanding of two important factors—inflation and supply. During inflationary periods, when there is too much money chasing too few goods, government tightening of the money supply helps create a balance between an economy's cash resources and its available goods. Money supply refers to the amount of cash made available for spending, borrowing, or investing. Controlled by the central banks of each nation, it is a primary tool used to manage inflation, interest rates, and economic growth.

A prudent tightening of the money supply can help bring on disinflation—decelerated loan demand, reduced durable goods orders, and falling prices. During disinflationary times, interest rates also fall, strengthening the underlying value of existing bonds. While such factors ultimately contribute to a healthier economy, they also mean lower yields for government bond investors. A trend toward disinflation currently exists in markets around the world. The worldwide growth in money supply is at its lowest level in twenty years.

As the United States and other governments implement policies designed to reduce inflation, interest rates are stabilizing. This disinflation can be disquieting to the individual who specifically invests for high monthly income. In reality, falling interest rates mean higher bond values, and investors seeking long-term growth or high total returns can therefore benefit from declining rates. Inflation, which drives interest rates higher, is the true enemy of bond investors. It diminishes bond values and, in addition, erodes the buying power of the interest income investors receive.

Income-seeking investors need to find economies where inflation is coming under control, yet where interest rates are still high enough to provide favorable bond yields. An investor who has only U.S. bonds is not taking advantage of such opportunities. If global disinflationary trends continue, those who remain invested only in the United States can lose out on opportunities for high income and total return elsewhere. The gradually decreasing yields on U.S. bonds compel the investor who seeks high income to think globally.

While not all bond markets will peak at the same level, they do tend to follow patterns. Targeting those countries where interest rates are at peak levels and inflation is falling not only results in higher income but also creates significant potential for capital appreciation as rates ultimately decline and bond prices increase.

Each year since 1984, at least three government bond markets have provided yields higher than those available in the United States. With over 60 percent of the world's bonds found outside the United States, investors must look beyond U.S. borders to find bonds offering yields and total returns that meet their investment objectives.

According to Lehman Brothers, over the past ten years, international bonds have outperformed U.S. bonds by an average of 2.5 percent per year. Over the past twenty years, the figure edges up slightly to an average of 2.6 percent. Over the last thirty years, it goes back to 2.5 percent a year.

Even with high income as the primary goal, investors must consider credit and market risk. By investing primarily in mutual funds that purchase government-guaranteed bonds from the world's most creditworthy nations, you can get an extra measure of credit safety for payment of interest and repayment of principal. By diversifying across multiple markets, fund managers can significantly reduce market risk as well. Diversification is a proven technique for controlling market risk.

The long-term success of a global bond manager depends on expertise in assessing economic trends from country to country, as well as protecting the U.S. valuation of foreign holdings. The most effective way to protect the U.S. dollar value of international holdings is through active currency management. Although its effects over a ten-year period are nominal at best, currency fluctuations can substantially help returns over a one-, three-, or five-year period.

In the simplest terms, effective currency management provides exposure to bond markets worldwide, while reducing the effects of adverse currency changes that can lower bond values. If a portfolio manager anticipates that the U.S. dollar will strengthen, he or she can lock in a currency exchange rate to protect the fund against a decline in the value of its foreign holdings. (A strong dollar means that other currencies are declining in value.) This strategy is commonly referred to as hedging the exposure of the portfolio. If, on the other hand, the manager expects the U.S. dollar to weaken, the fund can stay unhedged to allow it to benefit from the increasing value of foreign currencies.

Investing in global bonds gives you the potential for capital appreciation during periods of declining interest rates. An inverse relationship exists between bond values and interest rates. When interest rates fall, as is the case in most bond markets in the world today, existing bond values climb. Conversely, as interest rates rise, the value of existing bonds declines (they are less desirable since "new" bonds have a higher current yield).

Over the past three and five years, global bond funds have had an average compound return of 9 and 6 percent per year respectively; the annual returns for the past ten and fifteen years have been 8 and 13 percent, respectively. The standard deviation for global bond funds has been 8 percent over the past three years. This means that these funds have been less volatile than any equity fund but more volatile than government bond funds (std. deviation of 4). Just 225 funds make up the global bond category. During the last thiry years (ending 12/31/96), a portfolio comprised of 70 percent U.S. bonds and 30 percent non–U.S. bonds exhibited about 15 percent less risk than a pure U.S. bond portfolio and about 40 percent less volatility than a pure foreign bond portfolio. Total market capitalization of this category is over $22 billion.

Global bond funds, particularly those with high concentrations in foreign issues, are an excellent risk-reduction tool that should be utilized by the vast majority of investors.

World Bond Funds

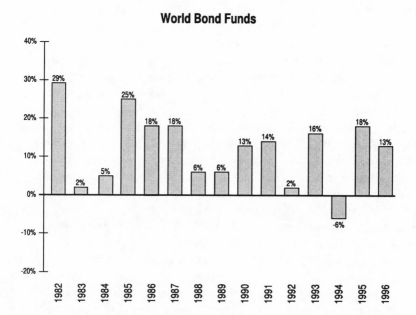

IDS Global Bond A

IDS Group
IDS Tower 10
Minneapolis, MN 55440-0010
(800) 328-8300

total return	★ ★ ★ ★ ★
risk reduction	★ ★ ★
management	★ ★ ★ ★
current income	★ ★ ★
expense control	★ ★ ★ ★ ★
symbol IGBFX	20 points
up-market performance	good
down-market performance	excellent
predictability of returns	good

Total Return   ★ ★ ★ ★ ★

Over the past five years, IDS Global Bond A has taken $10,000 and turned it into $15,390 ($13,050 over three years). This translates into an average annual return of 9 percent over the past five years and 9 percent over the past three years. Over the past five years, this fund has outperformed 45 percent of all mutual funds; within its general category it has done better than 85 percent of its peers. World bond funds have averaged 6 percent annually over these same five years.

During the past five years, a $10,000 initial investment grew to $13,550 after taxes, assuming a 39.6 percent income tax bracket (state and federal combined) and a capital gains rate of 28 percent. This means that investors in this fund were able to preserve 68 percent of their total returns. Compared to other fixed-income funds, this fund offers tax savings that are considered good.

Risk/Volatility   ★ ★ ★

Over the past five years, IDS Global Bond A has only been safer than 35 percent of all world bond funds. Over the past decade, the fund has had one negative year, as has the Lehman Brothers Aggregate Bond Index (off 3 percent in 1994). The fund has underperformed the Lehman Brothers Aggregate Bond Index twice and the Salomon Brother's World Government Bond Index three times in the last seven years.

	last 5 years		last 7 years	
worst year	-5%	1994	-5%	1994
best year	19%	1995	19%	1995

In the past, IDS Global Bond A has done better than half of its peer group in up markets but outperformed 95 percent of its competition in down markets. Consistency, or predictability, of returns for IDS Global Bond A can be described as good.

Management   ★ ★ ★ ★

There are sixty fixed-income securities in this $740 million portfolio. The average world bond fund today is $89 million in size. Close to 96 percent of the fund's holdings are in bonds. The average maturity of the bonds in this account is ten years; the weighted coupon rate averages 8.0 percent. The portfolio's fixed-income holdings can be categorized as intermediate-term, high-quality debt.

Ray S. Goodner has managed this fund for the past eight years. There are twenty-nine funds besides Global Bond A within the IDS fund family. Overall, the fund family's risk-adjusted performance can be described as fair.

Current Income   ★ ★ ★

Over the past year, IDS Global Bond A had a twelve-month yield of 4.7 percent. During this same twelve-month period, the typical world bond fund had a twelve-month yield that averaged 6.1 percent.

Expenses   ★ ★ ★ ★ ★

IDS Global Bond A's expense ratio is 1.2 percent; it has averaged 1.2 percent annually over the past three calendar years. The average expense ratio for the 225 funds in this category is 1.6 percent. This fund's turnover rate over the past year has been 49 percent, while its peer group average has been 234 percent.

Summary

IDS Global Bond A overall ranks as the second best world bond fund in the book. However, it is the number one performer. Part of the fund's success has been due to management's keen eye on expense control and minimal turnover (a potentially large cost that is not reflected in a fund's expense ratio). Management is to be congratulated for doing such a good job. This is one of only global debt funds that receives the highest marks possible for bear market performance, outclassing 95 percent of its peers.

Profile

minimum initial investment $2,000	*IRA accounts available* . . . . yes
subsequent minimum investment . . $100	*IRA minimum investment* $1
available in all 50 states. . . . . yes	*date of inception* . . . . March 1989
telephone exchanges. . . . . yes	*dividend/income paid* . . . . quarterly
number of other funds in family. 29	*quality of annual reports* . . . . good

Kemper Global Income A

Kemper Funds
222 South Riverside Drive
Chicago, IL 60606
(800) 621-1048

total return	★ ★ ★
risk reduction	★ ★ ★ ★
management	★ ★ ★ ★
current income	★ ★ ★ ★
expense control	★ ★ ★
symbol KGIAX	18 points
up-market performance	good
down-market performance	excellent
predictability of returns	good

Total Return

Over the past five years, Kemper Global Income A has taken $10,000 and turned it into $14,030 ($13,000 over three years). This translates into an average annual return of 7 percent over the past five years and 9 percent over the past three years. Over the past five years, this fund has outperformed 35 percent of all mutual funds; within its general category it has done better than 60 percent of its peers. World bond funds have averaged 6 percent annually over these same five years.

During the past five years, a $10,000 initial investment grew to $11,730 after taxes, assuming a 39.6 percent income tax bracket (state and federal combined) and a capital gains rate of 28 percent. This means that investors in this fund were able to preserve 49 percent of their total returns. Compared to other fixed-income funds, this fund offers tax savings that are considered poor.

Risk/Volatility

Over the past five years, Kemper Global Income A has been safer than 64 percent of all world bond funds. Over the past decade, the fund has had two negative years, while the Lehman Brothers Aggregate Bond Index has had one (off 3 percent in 1994). The fund has underperformed the Lehman Brothers Aggregate Bond Index twice and the Salomon Brother's World Government Bond Index four times in the last seven years.

	last 5 years		last 7 years	
worst year	-2%	1992	-2%	1992
best year	20%	1995	23%	1990

In the past, Kemper Global Income A has only done better than 40 percent of its peer group in up markets but outperformed 95 percent of its competition in down markets. Consistency, or predictability, of returns for Kemper Global Income A can be described as good.

Management   ★ ★ ★ ★

There are twenty fixed-income securities in this $80 million portfolio. The average world bond fund today is $89 million in size. Close to 100 percent of the fund's holdings are in bonds. The average maturity of the bonds in this account is six years; the weighted coupon rate averages 7.5 percent. The portfolio's fixed-income holdings can be categorized as intermediate-term, high-quality debt.

Beimford, Jr. and Johns have managed this fund for the past six years. There are sixty-six funds besides Global Income A within the Kemper fund family. Overall, the fund family's risk-adjusted performance can be described as fair.

Current Income   ★ ★ ★ ★

Over the past year, Kemper Global Income A had a twelve-month yield of 6.7 percent. During this same twelve-month period, the typical world bond fund had a twelve-month yield that averaged 6.1 percent.

Expenses   ★ ★ ★

Kemper Global Income A's expense ratio is 1.5 percent; it has averaged 1.5 percent annually over the past three calendar years. The average expense ratio for the 225 funds in this category is 1.6 percent. This fund's turnover rate over the past year has been 276 percent, while its peer group average has been 234 percent.

Summary

Kemper Global Income A is a recommended world bond fund. The fund scores well in every category measured. It ties for number one as the best performer during a bear market. Only a small percentage of investors and advisors understand the benefits provided by foreign debt instruments to an overall portfolio's risk level. Kemper has had more experience in this area than most of its contemporaries.

Profile

minimum initial investment $1,000	*IRA accounts available* . . . . yes
subsequent minimum investment . . $100	*IRA minimum investment* $250
available in all 50 states. . . . . yes	*date of inception* . . . . Oct. 1989
telephone exchanges. . . . . yes	*dividend/income paid*. . . . . monthly
number of other funds in family 66	*quality of annual reports* . . . . excellent

Warburg Pincus Global Fixed Income

Warburg Pincus Funds
466 Lexington Avenue
New York, NY 10017-3147
(800) 927-2874

total return	★ ★ ★ ★ ★
risk reduction	★ ★ ★ ★ ★
management	★ ★ ★ ★ ★
current income	★ ★ ★ ★ ★
expense control	★ ★ ★ ★ ★
symbol CGFIX	25 points
up-market performance	n/a
down-market performance	n/a
predictability of returns	excellent

Total Return   ★ ★ ★ ★ ★

Over the past five years, Warburg Pincus Global Fixed Income has taken $10,000 and turned it into $14,690 ($13,190 over three years). This translates into an average annual return of 8 percent over the past five years and 10 percent over the past three years. Over the past five years, this fund has outperformed 45 percent of all mutual funds; within its general category it has done better than 80 percent of its peers. World bond funds have averaged 6 percent annually over these same five years.

During the past five years, a $10,000 initial investment grew to $13,070 after taxes, assuming a 39.6 percent income tax bracket (state and federal combined) and a capital gains rate of 28 percent. This means that investors in this fund were able to preserve 64 percent of their total returns. Compared to other fixed-income funds, this fund offers tax savings that are considered good.

Risk/Volatility   ★ ★ ★ ★ ★

Over the past five years, Warburg Pincus Global Fixed Income has been safer than 75 percent of all world bond funds. Over the past decade, the fund has had one negative year, as has the Lehman Brothers Aggregate Bond Index (off 3 percent in 1994). The fund has underperformed the Lehman Brothers Aggregate Bond Index and the Salomon Brother's World Government Bond Index four times in the last six years.

	last 5 years		last 6 years	
worst year	-5%	1994	-5%	1994
best year	20%	1993	20%	1993

Consistency, or predictability, of returns for Warburg Pincus Global Fixed Income can be described as excellent.

Management

There are fifty fixed-income securities in this $190 million portfolio. The average world bond fund today is $89 million in size. Close to 69 percent of the fund's holdings are in bonds. The average maturity of the bonds in this account is four years; the weighted coupon rate averages 7.0 percent. The portfolio's fixed-income holdings can be categorized as short-term, high-quality debt.

Christensen and Bhandari have managed this fund for the past six years. There are twenty-nine funds besides Global Fixed Income within the Warburg Pincus fund family. Overall, the fund family's risk-adjusted performance can be described as good.

Current Income

Over the past year, Warburg Pincus Global Fixed Income had a twelve-month yield of 7.1 percent. During this same twelve-month period, the typical world bond fund had a twelve-month yield that averaged 6.1 percent.

Expenses   ★ ★ ★ ★ ★

Warburg Pincus Global Fixed Income's expense ratio is 1.0 percent; it has averaged 1.0 percent annually over the past three calendar years. The average expense ratio for the 225 funds in this category is 1.6 percent. This fund's turnover rate over the past year has been 124 percent, while its peer group average has been 234 percent.

Summary

Warburg Pincus Global Fixed Income is the only fund in the book to receive a perfect score, 25 out of 25. So, not only is this fund considered one of the 100 best, its overall score makes it the best of the best. This is welcome publicity since a world bond portfolio can help an investor get better risk-adjusted returns from his or her portfolio. Foreign bonds are often misunderstood by U.S. investors. More people should check out this fund, given its phenomenal record.

Profile

minimum initial investment $2,500	*IRA accounts available* . . . . yes
subsequent minimum investment . . $100	*IRA minimum investment* $500
available in all 50 states. . . . . yes	*date of inception* . . . . Nov. 1990
telephone exchanges. . . . . yes	*dividend/income paid* . . . . quarterly
number of other funds in family 29	*quality of annual reports* . . . . good

XII.
Summary

Aggressive Growth Funds (10)
1. Baron Asset
2. Fidelity Low-Priced Stock
3. Gabelli Small Cap Growth
4. Gradison Opportunity Value
5. Longleaf Partners Small-Cap
6. Princor Emerging Growth A
7. Royce Micro Cap
8. Royce Premier
9. T. Rowe Price Small Cap Stock
10. Winthrop Small Company Value A

Balanced Funds (9)
11. Flag Investors Value Builder A
12. Founders Balanced
13. Fremont Global
14. Greenspring
15. Income Fund of America
16. Merrill Lynch Global Allocation B
17. Oppenheimer Bond for Growth M
18. Putnam Convertible Income-Growth A
19. SoGen International

Corporate Bond Funds (5)
20. Bond Fund of America
21. FPA New Income
22. IDS Bond A
23. Ivy Bond A
24. Warburg Pincus Fixed Income

Global Equity Funds (14)
25. EuroPacific Growth
26. Fidelity Europe
27. Fidelity Worldwide
28. Founders Worldwide Growth
29. GAM International A
30. Janus Worldwide
31. Managers International Equity
32. MFS World Equity B
33. New Perspective
34. Oppenheimer Quest Global Value A
35. Putnam Global Growth A
36. Scudder Global
37. Templeton Developing Markets I
38. Templeton Growth I

Government Bond Funds (6)
39. Asset Management Adjustable Rate
40. Fidelity Spartan Limited Maturity Government
41. Lexington GNMA Income
42. SIT U.S. Government Securities
43. Smith Breeden Short Duration Government Series
44. Vanguard Fixed-Income Securities Short-Term Federal Bond

Growth Funds (13)
45. Fidelity Advisor Growth Opportunities T
46. Fidelity Destiny II

47. Gradison Established Value
48. Guardian Park Avenue
49. Mairs & Power Growth
50. MAP-Equity
51. Maxus Equity
52. Oakmark
53. Sound Shore
54. Strong Schafer Value
55. T. Rowe Price Spectrum Growth
56. Third Avenue Value
57. Torray

Growth & Income Funds (13)
58. AARP Growth and Income
59. Babson Value
60. Dodge & Cox Stock
61. Excelsior Income & Growth
62. Fundamental Investors
63. Homestead Value
64. Merrill Lynch Basic Value A
65. Scudder Growth and Income
66. T. Rowe Price Equity-Income
67. T. Rowe Price Growth & Income
68. Van Kampen American Capital Equity-Income A
69. Victory Diversified Stock A
70. Washington Mutual Investors

High-Yield Funds (5)
71. Franklin AGE High Income I
72. MainStay High-Yield Corporate Bond B
73. Northeast Investors
74. Oppenheimer Champion Income A
75. Seligman High-Yield Bond A

Metals and Natural Resources Funds (4)
76. Midas
77. Scudder Gold
78. State Street Research Global Resources A
79. Vanguard Specialized Energy

Money Market Funds (6)
80. Aetna Money Market Select
81. Dreyfus Basic Money Market
82. Dreyfus Basic Municipal Money Market
83. Fidelity Cash Reserves
84. SEI Daily Income Prime Obligation A
85. Strong Municipal Money Market

Municipal Bond Funds (8)
86. American Century-Benham California Municipal High Yield
87. Franklin Florida Tax-Free Income I
88. Franklin High-Yield Tax-Free Income I
89. Franklin Pennsylvania Tax-Free Income I
90. SIT Tax-Free Income
91. Thornburg Intermediate Municipal A
92. United Municipal High Income A
93. Vanguard Municipal Intermediate-Term

Utility Stock Funds (4)
94. Fidelity Select Utilities Growth
95. Fidelity Utilities
96. MFS Utilities A
97. Putnam Utilities Growth and Income A

World Bond Funds (3)
98. IDS Global Bond A
99. Kemper Global Income A
100. Warburg Pincus Global Fixed Income

Appendix A
Glossary of Mutual Fund Terms

Advisor—The organization employed by a mutual fund to give professional advice on the fund's investments and asset management practices (also called the "investment advisor").

Asked or Offering Price—The price at which a mutual fund's shares can be purchased. The asked, or offering, price means the current net asset value per share plus sales charge, if any.

Bid or Sell Price—The price at which a mutual fund's shares are redeemed (bought back) by the fund. The bid or redemption price usually means the current net asset value per share.

Board Certified—Designation given to someone who has become certified in: insurance, estate planning, income taxes, securities, mutual funds, or financial planning. To obtain additional information about the board certified programs or to get the name of a board certified advisor in your area, call (800) 848-2029.

Bottom Up—Refers to a type of security analysis. Management that follows the bottom-up approach is more concerned with the company than with the economy in general. (For a contrasting style, see **Top Down**.)

Broker/Dealer—A firm that buys and sells mutual fund shares and other securities to the public.

Capital Gains Distributions—Payments to mutual fund shareholders of profits (long-term gains) realized on the sale of the fund's portfolio securities. These amounts are usually paid once a year.

Capital Growth—An increase in the market value of a mutual fund's securities, as reflected in the net asset value of fund shares. This is a specific long-term objective of many mutual funds.

CFA—Also known as Chartered Financial Analyst, this is a highly desirable designation for managers who select securities for sale or purchase. The CFA program takes at least three years to complete. Each of the three parts is considered quite difficult.

CFS—Also known as Certified Fund Specialist, this is the only designation awarded to brokers, financial planners, CPAs, insurance agents, and other investment advisors who either recommend or sell mutual funds. Fewer than 2,500 people across the country have passed this certification program. To obtain additional information about the CFS program or to get the name of a CFS in your area, call (800) 848-2029.

CPI—The Consumer Price Index (CPI) is the most commonly used yardstick for measuring the rate of inflation in the United States.

Custodian—The organization (usually a bank) that keeps custody of securities and other assets of a mutual fund.

Diversification—The policy of all mutual funds to spread investments among a number of different securities in order to reduce the risk inherent in investing.

Dollar-Cost Averaging—The practice of investing equal amounts of money at regular intervals regardless of whether securities markets are moving up or down. This procedure reduces average share costs to the investor, who acquires more shares in the periods of lower securities prices and fewer shares in periods of higher prices.

EAFE—An equity index (EAFE stands for Europe, Australia, and the Far East) used to measure stock market performance outside of the United States. The EAFE is a sort of S&P 500 Index for overseas or foreign stocks. As of the middle of 1997, the EAFE was weighted as follows: 59.5% Europe, 28.8% Japan, 10.6% Pacific Rim, and 1.1% "other".

Exchange Privilege—An option enabling mutual fund shareholders to transfer their investment from one fund to another within the same fund family as their needs or objectives change. Typically, funds allow investors to use the exchange privilege several times a year for a low fee or no fee per exchange.

Investment Company—A corporation, trust, or partnership that invests pooled funds of shareholders in securities appropriate to the fund's objective. Among the benefits of investment companies, compared to direct investments, are professional management and diversification. Mutual funds (also known as open-ended investment companies) are the most popular type of investment company.

Investment Objective—The goal that the investor and mutual fund pursue together (e.g., growth of capital or current income).

Large-Cap Stocks—Equities issued by companies with a net worth of at least several billion dollars.

Long-Term Funds—An industry designation for funds that invest primarily in securities with remaining maturities of more than one year. In this book the term means fifteen years or more. Long-term funds are broadly divided into bond and income funds.

Management Fee—The amount paid by a mutual fund to the investment advisor for its services. The average annual fee industrywide is about 0.5 percent of fund assets.

Mutual Fund—An investment company that pools money from shareholders and invests in a variety of securities, including stocks, bonds, and money market instruments. A mutual fund stands ready to buy back (redeem) its shares at their current net asset value; this value depends on the market value of the fund's portfolio securities at the time of redemption. Most mutual funds continuously offer new shares to investors.

Net Asset Value Per Share—The market worth of one share of a mutual fund. This figure is derived by taking a fund's total assets—securities, cash, and any accrued earnings—deducting liabilities, and dividing by the number of shares outstanding.

No-Load Fund—A mutual fund selling its shares at net asset value without the addition of sales charges.

Portfolio—A collection of securities owned by an individual or an institution (such as a mutual fund). A fund's portfolio may include a combination of stocks, bonds, and money market securities.

Prospectus—The official booklet that describes a mutual fund, which must be furnished to all investors. It contains information required by the U.S. Securities and Exchange Commission on such subjects as the fund's investment objectives, services, and fees. A more detailed document, known as "Part B" of the prospectus or the "Statement of Additional Information," is available at no charge upon request.

Redemption Price—The amount per share (shown as the "bid" in newspaper tables) that mutual fund shareholders receive when they cash in the shares. The value of the shares depends on the market value of the fund's portfolio securities at the time. This value is the same as net asset value per share.

Reinvestment Privilege—An option available to mutual fund shareholders in which fund dividends and capital gains distributions are automatically turned back into the fund to buy new shares, without charge (meaning no sales fee or commission), thereby increasing holdings.

Russell 2000—An index which represents 2,000 small domestic companies (less than 8 percent of the U.S. equity market).

Sales Charge—An amount charged to purchase shares in many mutual funds sold by brokers or other sales agents. The maximum charge is 8.5 percent of the initial investment; the vast majority of funds now have a maximum charge of 4.75 percent or less. The charge is added to the net asset value per share when determining the offering price.

Short-Term Funds—An industry designation for funds that invest primarily in securities with maturities of less than one year; the term means five years or less in this book. Short-term funds include money market funds and certain municipal bond funds.

Small-Cap Stocks—These are equities (stocks) issued by corporations that you and I might consider large, but the marketplace considers small. Some financial writers consider a company with a capitalization of $500 million or less to be small-cap; other writers have a cut-off point of $1 billion or less.

Top Down—Refers to a type of security analysis. Management that follows the top-down approach is very concerned with the general level of the economy and any fiscal policy being followed by the government.

Transfer Agent—The organization employed by a mutual fund to prepare and maintain records relating to the accounts of its shareholders. Some funds serve as their own transfer agents.

12b-1 Fee—The distribution fee charged by some funds, named after a federal government rule. Such fees pay for marketing costs, such as advertising and dealer compensation. The fund's prospectus outlines 12b-1 fees, if applicable.

Underwriter—The organization that acts as the distributor of a mutual fund's shares to broker/dealers and investors.

Withdrawal Plan—A program in which shareholders receive payments from their mutual fund investments at regular intervals. Typically, these payments are drawn first from the fund's dividends and capital gains distributions, if any, and then from principal (share balance), as needed.

■ ■ ■

The Securities Act of 1933 requires a fund's shares to be registered with the Securities and Exchange Commission (SEC) prior to their sale. In essence, the Securities Act ensures that the fund provides potential investors with a current prospectus. This law also limits the types of advertisements that may be used by a mutual fund.

The Securities Exchange Act of 1934 regulates the purchase and sale of all types of securities, including mutual fund shares.

The Investment Advisors Act of 1940 is a body of law that regulates certain activities of the investment advisors to mutual funds.

The Investment Company Act of 1940 is a highly detailed regulatory statute applying to mutual fund companies. This act contains numerous provisions designed to prevent self-dealing by employees of the mutual fund company, as well as other conflicts of interest. It also provides for the safekeeping of fund assets and prohibits the payment of excessive fees and charges by the fund and its shareholders.

Appendix B
Who Regulates Mutual Funds?

Mutual funds are highly regulated businesses that must comply with some of the toughest laws and rules in the financial services industry. All funds are regulated by the U.S. Securities and Exchange Commission (SEC). With its extensive rule-making and enforcement authority, the SEC oversees mutual fund compliance chiefly by relying on four major federal securities statutes mentioned in Appendix A.

Fund assets must generally be held by an independent custodian. There are strict requirements for fidelity bonding to ensure against the misappropriation of shareholder monies. In addition to federal statutes, almost every state has its own set of regulations governing mutual funds.

Although federal and state laws cannot guarantee that a fund will be profitable, they are designed to ensure that all mutual funds are operated and managed in the interests of their shareholders. Here are some specific investor protections that every fund must follow:

- Regulations concerning what may be claimed or promised about a mutual fund and its potential.
- Requirements that vital information about a fund be made readily available (such as a prospectus, the "Statement of Additional Information," also known as "Part B" of the prospectus, and annual and semiannual reports).
- Requirements that a fund operate in the interest of its shareholders, rather than any special interests of its management.
- Rules dictating diversification of the fund's portfolio over a wide range of investments to avoid too much concentration in a particular security.

Appendix C
Dollar-Cost Averaging

Investors often believe that the market will go down as soon as they get in. For these people, and anyone concerned with reducing risk, the solution is dollar-cost averaging.

Dollar-cost averaging is a simple yet effective way to reduce risk, whether you are investing in stocks or bonds. The premise behind dollar-cost averaging (DCA) is that if several purchases of a fund are made over an extended period of time, the unpredictable highs and lows will average out. The investor ends up with buying some shares at a comparatively low price, others at perhaps a much higher price.

DCA assumes that investors are willing to sacrifice the possibility of having bought all of their shares at the lowest price, in return for knowing that they did not also buy every share at the highest price. In short, we are willing to accept a compromise—a sort of *risk-adjusted* decision.

DCA is based on investing a fixed amount of money in a given fund at specific intervals. Typically, an investor will add a few hundred dollars at the beginning of each month into the XYZ mutual fund. DCA works best if you invest and continue to invest on an established schedule, *regardless of price fluctuations*. You will be buying more shares when the price is down than when it is up. Most investors do not mind buying shares when prices are increasing, since this means that their existing shares are also going up. When this program is followed, losses during market declines are limited, while the ability to participate in good markets is maintained.

Another advantage of DCA is that it increases the likelihood that you will follow an investment program. As with other aspects of our life, it is important to have goals. However, DCA is not something that should be universally recommended. Whether or not you should use dollar-cost averaging depends upon your risk level.

From its beginnings well over one hundred years ago, there has been an upward bias in the performance of the stock market. More often than not, the market goes up, not down. Therefore, it hardly makes sense to apply dollar-cost averaging to an investment vehicle, knowing that historically one would be paying a higher and higher price per share over time.

Studies done by the Institute of Business & Finance (800-848-2029) show that over the past fifty years, a dollar-cost averaging program produced inferior returns compared to a lump-sum investment. The Institute's studies conclude the following: (1) a DCA program is a good idea for a conservative investor (the person or couple who gives more weight or importance to risk than reward); (2) for investor's whose risk level is anything but conservative, an immediate, one-time investment resulted in better returns the great majority of the time; and (3) there have certainly been periods of time when a DCA program would have benefitted even the extremely aggressive investor—but such periods have not been very common over the past half century and have been quite rare over the past twenty, fifteen, ten, five, and three years.

Example of Dollar-Cost Averaging
($1,000 invested per period)

Period (1)	Cost per share (2)	Number of shares bought with $1,000 (3)	Total shares owned (4)	Total amount invested (5)	Current value of shares (2) x (4) (6)	Net gain or loss (percentage) (6) / (5) (7)
1	$100	10.0	10.0	$1,000	$1,000	0
2	$80	12.5	22.5	$2,000	$1,800	−10.0%
3	$70	14.3	36.8	$3,000	$2,576	−14.1%
4	$60	16.7	53.5	$4,000	$3,210	−19.7%
5	$50	20.0	73.5	$5,000	$3,675	−26.5%
6	$70	14.3	87.8	$6,000	$6,146	+2.4%
7	$80	12.5	100.3	$7,000	$8,024	+14.6%
8	$100	10.0	110.3	$8,000	$11,030	+37.9%

Appendix D
Systematic Withdrawal Plan

A systematic withdrawal plan (SWP) allows you to have a check for a specified amount sent monthly or quarterly to you, or anyone you designate, from your mutual fund account. There is no charge for this service.

This method of getting monthly checks is ideal for the income-oriented investor. It is also a risk reduction technique—a kind of dollar-cost averaging in reverse. A set amount is sent to you each month. In order to send you a check for a set amount, shares of one or more of your mutual funds must be sold, which, in turn, will most likely trigger a taxable event, but only for those shares redeemed.

When the market is low, the number of mutual fund shares being liquidated will be higher than when the market is high, since the fund's price per share will be lower. If you need $500 a month and the fund's price is $25.00 per share, 20 shares must be liquidated; if the price per share is $20.00 per share, 25 shares must be sold.

Shown below is an example of a SWP from the Investment Company of America (ICA), a conservative growth and income fund featured in previous editions of this book. The example assumes an initial investment of $100,000 in the fund at its inception, the beginning of 1934. A greater or smaller dollar amount could be used. The example shows what happens to the investor's principal over a 62-year period of time (1934 through 1996). It assumes that $10,000 is withdrawn from the fund at the end of the first year. At the end of the first year, the $10,000 withdrawal *is increased by 4 percent each year thereafter* to offset the effects of inflation, which averaged less than 4 percent during this 63-year period. This means that the withdrawal for the second year was $10,400 ($10,000 multiplied by 1.04), for the third year $10,816 ($10,400 x 1.04), and so on.

Compare this example to what would have happened if the money had been placed in an average fixed-income account at a bank. The $100,000 depositor who took out only $9,000 each year would be in a far different situation. His (or her) original $100,000 was fully depleted by the end of 1948. All the principal and interest payments could not keep up with an annual withdrawal of $9,000.

The difference between ICA and the savings account is over $5.8 million. The savings account had a total return of $26,300 (plus distribution of the original $100,000 principal); the ICA account had a total return of $6,012,000 ($2,708,000 distributed over sixty-three years plus a remaining principal, or account balance, of $3,304,000). This difference becomes even more disturbing when you consider that the bank depositor's withdrawals were not increasing each year to offset the effects of inflation. The interest rates used in this example came from the *U.S. Savings & Loan League Fact Book.*

SWP from The Investment Company of America (ICA)
initial investment: $100,000
annual withdrawals of: $10,000 (10%)
the first check is sent: 12/31/34
withdrawals annually increased by: 4%

date	amount withdrawn	value of remaining shares
12/31/34	$10,000	$109,000
12/31/35	$10,400	$185,000
12/31/40	$12,700	$151,000
12/31/45	$15,400	$241,000
12/31/50	$18,700	$204,000
12/31/55	$22,800	$354,000
12/31/60	$27,700	$431,000
12/31/65	$33,700	$612,000
12/31/70	$41,000	$649,000
12/31/75	$50,000	$552,000
12/31/80	$60,700	$762,000
12/31/85	$73,900	$1,225,000
12/31/86	$76,900	$1,415,000
12/31/87	$79,900	$1,411,000
12/31/88	$83,100	$1,515,000
12/31/89	$86,500	$1,872,000
12/31/90	$89,900	$1,794,000
12/31/91	$93,500	$2,170,000
12/31/92	$86,500	$2,224,000
12/31/93	$101,200	$2,379,000
12/31/94	$105,200	$2,277,000
12/31/95	$109,400	$2,865,000
12/31/96	$113,780	$3,900,000

If the ICA systematic withdrawal plan were 9 percent annually instead of 10 percent (but still increased by 4 percent each year to offset the effects of inflation), the investor would have ended up with remaining shares worth $27.9 million, plus withdrawals that totaled $2.4 million.

Next time some broker or banker tells you that you should be buying bonds or CDs for current income, tell them about a systematic withdrawal plan (SWP), a program designed to maximize your income and offset something the CD, T-bill, and bond advocates never mention: inflation.

Appendix E
Load or No-Load—Which Is Right for You?

As the amount of information available on mutual funds continues to grow almost exponentially, the load versus no-load debate has intensified. What makes the issue difficult to evaluate is the continued absence of neutrality on either side. Before you learn the real truth, let us first examine who is advocating what, what their biases are, and how each side argues its point.

A number of publications, including *Money*, *Forbes*, *Fortune*, *Kiplinger Personal Investor*, and *Business Week*, favor the no-load camp. Although these publications appear neutral, they are not. First, each one derives the overwhelming majority of its mutual fund advertisements from funds that charge no commission. Second, all of these publications are trying to increase readership; they are in the business of selling copy, not information. A good way to increase or maintain a healthy circulation is by having their readership rely on them for advice—instead of going to a broker or investment advisor.

On the other side is the financial services industry, whose most vocal load supporters include the brokerage, banking, and insurance industries. That's not much of a surprise. These groups are also biased. Like the publication that only makes money by getting you to purchase a copy or having an editorial board whose policy favors to no-load funds, much of the financial services community supports a sales charge because that is how they are compensated.

No-load proponents argue that a fund that charges any kind of commission or ongoing marketing fee [which is known as a 12(b)1 charge] inherently cannot be as good as a similar investment that has no entry or exit fee or ongoing 12(b)1 charge. On its surface, this argument appears logical. After all, if one investor starts off with a dollar invested and the other starts off with somewhere between 99 and 92 cents (commissions range from 1–8.5 percent; most are in the 3–5 percent range), all other things being equal, the person who has all of his money working for him will do better than someone who has an initial deduction. The press and the no-load funds say that there is no reason to pay a commission because you can do as well or better than the broker or advisor whose job it is to provide you with suggestions and guidance.

The commission-oriented community says you should pay a sales charge because you get what you pay for—good advice and ongoing service. After all, brokers, financial planners, banks that include mutual fund desks, and insurance agents are all highly trained professionals who know things you do not. Moreover, they study the markets on a continuous basis, ensuring that they have more information than any weekend investor. In short, they ask, do you want someone managing your money who has experience and works full-time in this area, or someone such as yourself who has no formal training and whose time and resources are limited?

There is no clear-cut solution. Valid points are raised by both sides. To gain more insight into what course of action (or type of fund) is best for you, let us take a neutral approach. I believe I can give you valid reasons why both kinds of funds make sense, because I have no hidden agenda. True, I am a licensed broker and branch manager of a national securities firm; however, it is also true that the great majority of my compensation is based on a fee for service, meaning that clients who invest solely in no-load funds pay me an annual management fee.

First, you should never pay a commission to someone who knows no more about investing than you do. There is no value added in such a situation, except perhaps during uncertain or negative periods in the market. (This point will be discussed later.) After all, if your broker's advice and mutual fund experience are based solely on the same financial publications you have access to, you are not getting your money's worth by paying a sales charge. I raise this point first because the financial services industry is filled with a tremendous number of inexperienced and ignorant brokers. These people may make a lot of money, but this is usually the result of their connections (they know a lot of people) or marketing skills (they know how to get new business)—neither of which have anything to do with your money.

Brokerage firms, banks, and insurance companies hire stockbrokers based on their sales ability, not their knowledge or analytical ability. The financial analysts at the home office are the ones involved in research and managing money. The fact that your broker has a couple of dozen years' experience in the securities industry or is a vice president may actually be hazardous to your financial health. Extensive experience could mean that the advisor is less inclined to learn about new products or studies, because he already has an established client base. Brokers obtain titles such as "vice president" because they outsell their peers. Contests (awards, trips, prizes, and enhanced payouts) are based on how much is sold, period. There has never been an instance of a brokerage firm, bank, or insurance company giving an award to someone based on knowledge or how well a client's account performed.

Second, if your investment time horizon is less than a couple of years, it is a mistake to pay anything more than a nominal fee, something in the 1-percent range. Even though the advice you are receiving may be great, it is hard to justify a 3- to 5-percent commission over the short haul. Sales charges in this range can only be rationalized if they can be amortized over a number of years. Thus, worthwhile advice becomes a bargain if you stay with the investment, or within the same family of mutual funds, for at least three years.

Third, if you are purchasing a fund that charges a fee, find out what you are getting for your money. Question the advisor; find out about his or her training, experience, education, and designations. Equally important, get a clear understanding as to what you will be receiving on an ongoing basis. What kind of continuing education does the broker engage in (attending conferences, reading books, seeking a designation, and so forth)? Finally, make sure your advisor or broker tells you how your investments will be monitored. It is important to know how often you will be contacted and how a buy, hold, or sell decision will be made.

So far, it looks as if I've been pretty tough on my fellow brokers. Well, believe me, I'm even harder on about 99 percent of those do-it-yourself investors. I have been in this business for close to fifteen years and I can tell you that I have rarely met an investor who was better off on his or her own. Here's why.

First, it is extremely difficult to be objective about your own investments. Decisions based on what you have read from a newsletter or magazine or what you learned at a seminar are often a response to current news, such as trade relations with Japan, the value of the U.S. dollar, the state of the economy, or the direction of interest rates. This kind of knee-jerk reaction has proven to be wrong in most cases.

Mind you, out of fairness to those who manage their own investments, amateurs aren't the only ones who make investment errors. As an example, the majority of the major brokerage firms gave a sell signal just before the war in the Persian Gulf. It turned out that this would have been about the perfect time to buy. E.F. Hutton was forced to merge with another brokerage firm because they incorrectly predicted the direction of interest rates (and lost tens of millions of dollars in their own portfolio).

The mutual fund industry itself deserves a healthy part of the blame, as evidenced by their timing of new funds. Take my advice: When you see a number of new mutual funds coming out with the same timely theme (government plus or optioned-enhanced bond funds in the mid-eighties, Eastern European funds after German reunification, health care funds a few years ago, derivatives and hedge funds last year), run for cover. By the time these funds come out, the party is about to end. Investors who got into these funds often do well for a number of months but soon face devastating declines.

Your favorite financial publications are also to blame. Their advice is based on a herd instinct—What do our readers think? Instead of providing leadership, they simply reinforce what is most likely incorrect information. For example, for over a year after the 1987 stock market crash, the most popular of these mainstream publications, *Money*, had cover stories that recommended (and extolled the virtues of) safe investments. For almost a year and a half after the crash, this magazine was giving out bad advice. When something goes on sale (stocks, in this case) you should be a buyer, not a seller. Since *Money* routinely surveys (or polls) their readers for feature articles, such behavior is understandable (the herd instinct) but not forgivable.

Besides the lack of objectivity and the constant bombardment of what I call "daily noise" (what the market is doing at the moment, comments from the financial gurus, etc.), there is also the question of your competence. Presumably, you and I could figure out how to fix our own plumbing, sew our own clothes, fix the car when it breaks down, or avoid paying a lawyer by purchasing "do-it-yourself" books. The question then becomes whether it is worth going through the learning curve, and, even supposing we are successful, whether the task would have been better accomplished by someone else—perhaps for less money or better use of our own time. I think the answer is obvious. Each of us has our own area or areas of expertise or skill. You and I rely on others either because they know more than we do about the topic or item at hand, or because having someone else help is a more efficient use of our time.

If you're going to seek the services of an investment advisor or broker, it should be because he or she knows more than you do, because he or she is more objective, or because you can make more money doing whatever you do than in taking the time to make complex investment decisions yourself. This is what makes sense. The fact that there are brokers and advisors who put their interests before yours is simply a reality that you must deal with. And the proper way to deal with these conflicts of interest or ignorant counselors is by doing your homework. Ask questions. Just as there are great plumbers, mechanics, lawyers, and doctors, so too are there exceptional investment advisors and brokers. Your job is to find them.

Eliminating load or no-load funds from your investing universe is not the answer. If you are determined never to pay a commission, then you may miss out on the next John Templeton (the Franklin-Templeton family of funds), Peter Lynch (Fidelity Magellan Fund), or Jean-Marie Eveillard (SoGen Funds). You will also miss out on some of the very best mutual fund families: American Funds (large), Fidelity-Advisor (medium), and SoGen (small). A better way to proceed is to try to separate good funds from bad ones. After all, an investor is clearly far better off in a good load fund than in a bad no-load one.

The bottom line is that performance, as well as *risk-adjusted returns*, for load funds often exceeds the returns on no-load funds, and vice versa. The "top ten" list (or whatever number you want to use) for one period may have been dominated by funds that charge a commission, but in just a year or two the top ten list may be heavily populated by mutual funds with no sales charge or commission.

It might seem strange to be questioning the benefits of financial planning when our society places professions like law and accountancy in such high regard. And certainly I am not suggesting that investors should consider only load funds. But with all the load-fund bashing in recent years, it is important to recognize that no-load funds are not the perfect answer for a large percentage of investors. Approaching the mutual fund industry with an us vs. them mentality results in a great deal of misleading information and unfairly discredits the work of skilled financial planners and brokers.

For those investors who have the temperament, time, and expertise and who wish to consider using a no-load fund, the following is a list of the no-load funds in this book:

AARP Growth and Income	Excelsior Income & Growth
Aetna Money Market Select	Fidelity Cash Reserves
American Century-Benham	Fidelity Spartan Limited
California Municipal High Yield	Maturity Government
Asset Management Adjustable	Fidelity Utilities
Rate	Fidelity Worldwide
Babson Value	Flag Investors Value Builder A
Baron Asset	Founders Balanced
Dodge & Cox Stock	Founders Worldwide Growth
Dreyfus Basic Money Market	Fremont Global
Dreyfus Basic Municipal Money	Fundamental Investors
Market	Gabelli Small Cap Growth

Gradison Established Value
Gradison Opportunity Value
Greenspring
Homestead Value
Janus Worldwide
Kemper Global Income A
Lexington GNMA Income
Longleaf Partners Small-Cap
Mairs & Power Growth
Managers International Equity
Maxus Equity
Midas
Northeast Investors
Oakmark
Royce Micro Cap
Royce Premier
Scudder Global
Scudder Gold
Scudder Growth and Income
SEI Daily Income Prime
    Obligation A
SIT Tax-Free Income

SIT U.S. Government
    Securities
Smith Breeden Short Duration
    Government Series
Sound Shore
Strong Municipal Money Market
Strong Schafer Value
T. Rowe Price Equity-Income
T. Rowe Price Growth & Income
T. Rowe Price Small Cap Stock
T. Rowe Price Spectrum Growth
Third Avenue Value
Torray
Vanguard Fixed-Income
    Securities Short-Term
    Federal Bond
Vanguard Municipal
    Intermediate-Term
Vanguard Specialized Energy
Warburg Pincus Fixed Income
Warburg Pincus Global Fixed
    Income

Appendix F
The Best and Worst Days

Many would-be stock investors fear investing at the wrong time—when market prices are *highest*. Suppose you invested $5,000 in the Dow Jones Industrial Average (which is comprised of just thirty stocks) every year for the last twenty years during the month the market peaked. How much would your total investment of $100,000 be worth versus an investment made each year during the month when prices were *lowest*? The results may surprise you.

Month of Market High	Cumulative Investment	Value of Acct. on 12/31	Month of Market Low	Cumulative Investment	Value of Acct. on 12/31
1/77	$5,000	$4,587	11/77	$5,000	$5,089
9/78	10,000	9,447	2/78	10,000	10,986
10/79	15,000	15,669	11/79	15,000	17,329
11/80	20,000	24,067	4/80	20,000	27,336
4/81	25,000	27,803	9/81	25,000	31,593
12/82	30,000	40,340	8/82	30,000	46,123
11/83	35,000	55,804	1/83	35,000	64,227
1/84	40,000	61,756	7/84	40,000	70,640
12/85	45,000	87,473	1/85	45,000	100,625
12/86	50,000	116,182	1/86	50,000	134,155
8/87	55,000	126,246	10/87	55,000	146,411
10/88	60,000	152,367	1/88	60,000	175,787
10/89	65,000	206,575	1/89	65,000	238,498
7/90	70,000	210,081	10/90	70,000	242,607
12/91	75,000	265,895	2/91	75,000	306,962
6/92	80,000	290,645	10/92	80,000	334,857
8/93	85,000	345,084	4/93	85,000	397,164
8/94	90,000	367,517	11/94	90,000	422,428
12/95	95,000	507,898	1/95	95,000	584,861
11/96	$100,000	659,369	1/96	$100,000	759,672

As you can see, even if you had the worst luck in the world, by investing $5,000 at the high point of the market each year, you would still end up with $659,369 after twenty years. This is not as good as having perfect timing (buying at the market low each year), but the difference is certainly not as great as one might first suspect. Perfect timing resulted in an average annual rate of return of 16.35 percent over each of the past twenty years. Investing on each of the worst possible days still resulted in an average annual rate of return of 15.48 percent.

Appendix G
Investing in the Face of Fear

What do you do when the market declines? When the Iraqis invaded Kuwait, the market retreated from fears of rising interest rates and inflation. The Dow Jones Industrial Average (DJIA) had reached a new high on July 16, 1990, at 2999.75, and by August 22, 1990, had fallen to 2560—a decline of almost 15 percent.

For some insight on how to respond to a drop in the market, let us look back at the first Arab oil embargo in 1973. Oil prices tripled, as did the Consumer Price Index and interest rates. And the DJIA fell from 947 on September 30, 1973, to 616 on December 31, 1974, a drop of 35 percent.

Suppose you had placed $10,000 in AIM Weingarten Fund (a fund featured in a previous edition of this book) on September 30, 1973. By December 31, 1974, your investment had dropped in value to $5,725—a decrease of 43 percent. What would you have done with your shares, and how would you have fared?

Let's look at several scenarios:
1.   Sell now! Take the loss and put the money in a bank certificate of deposit.
2.   Wait until the mutual fund breaks even, then sell it, and put the money in a certificate of deposit.
3.   Hold on to your shares. It was a long-term investment, and time will win out.
4.   Invest an additional $10,000 in Weingarten, capitalizing on the opportunity to buy more shares at a lower price.

Which scenario did you choose?
1.   If you sold your AIM Weingarten Fund shares on December 31, 1974 in reaction to the declining market and placed the remaining money in a bank CD, your investment as of June 30, 1997 would have been worth (depending on the interest rate): $20,630 at 6 percent, $25,360 at 7 percent, and $31,140 at 8 percent.
2.   If you had waited for Weingarten's value to return to $10,000, sold the shares on December 31, 1977, and then placed the money in a bank CD, the $10,000 as of June 30, 1997 would have been worth: $30,260 at 6 percent, $36,170 at 7 percent, and $43,160 at 8 percent.
3.   If you had sat tight and left your money in the fund, your $10,000 would have been worth $366,040 as of June 30, 1997.

4(a). If you had an additional $10,000 to invest in Weingarten on December 31, 1974, your $20,000 total investment would have been worth $970,330 as of June 30, 1997.

4(b). Assuming you did not have another $10,000 lump sum to place in Weingarten, but started investing $100 each month beginning December 31, 1974, your total investment of $32,300 would have been worth $694,000 as of June 30, 1997.

Did you end up with $31,140, $366,040, $970,330, or $694,000? Smart money does not panic! When confidence is low and emotion is high, there are opportunities for the smart investor.

Appendix H
Is Bigger Better?

There is constant debate within the financial services community and mutual fund industry as to whether a large fund is better than a small one. According to the *Wall Street Journal*, if you "stick with the fund industry's major players, you're far less likely to end up with a real turkey." According to a study by Morningstar, Inc. (which includes each of the past five calendar years ending 12/31/93 and covers the twenty-five best and worst performers among diversified U.S. stock funds), small is both better and worse.

The Morningstar study indicates that the worst performers, on average, were over 40 percent smaller than the typical mutual fund, which has assets of approximately $500 million. On the other hand, the top twenty-five, for the calendar years from 1989 through 1993, were, on average, 60 percent smaller than the typical fund. In other words, as the study points out, the majority of each extreme came from small fund families. Only 22 percent of the worst performers and 35 percent of the best performers came from the thirty-nine biggest fund groups. In this study, the largest fund families were described as those companies that managed more than $10 billion by the end of 1993. (As a side note, these thirty-nine groups control over 75 percent of all mutual fund assets; total assets for the mutual fund industry are now approximately $2.5 trillion.)

When viewing each of the ten years through 1994, Morningstar divided the domestic stock group (aggressive growth, small company, growth, growth and income, and equity-income) into four groups, based solely on size. On average, the smallest funds, those in the bottom 25 percent, turned in the best results for calendar years 1984, 1991, and 1992. However, the three smallest funds each year showed the biggest losses in nine of those ten years.

There are a number of explanations for these results. As a fund or fund family gets larger, it has the money available to hire a management team with more depth. Smaller fund groups may have management performing multiple jobs, including research and administrative tasks. On a positive note, smaller funds can be more nimble in exploiting investment opportunities.

A small fund is less likely to have to answer to a large investment committee or other to have forms of restriction. This is a double-edged sword, since it often allows the fund's manager to load up heavily on a comparatively small number of issues. This decisiveness sounds good, but if management is wrong, the losses can be substantial.

A favored argument against small funds has to do with economies of scale, specifically, expenses. The average domestic stock fund has expenses that average 1.4 percent annually; a few small funds have yearly costs that range from 6 to 18 percent.

A big fund has other advantages. First, when an existing manager leaves, it is very likely that his or her replacement will be at least pretty good, if not very good. Second, knowledge is power. Big fund groups have large numbers of researchers, traders, analysts, and other support personnel to help out the money managers.

As you can see by the table below, Fidelity, American Funds (Investment Co. of America, Washington Mutual, Income Fund of America, EuroPacific Growth, and New Perspective), and Vanguard dominate the twenty-largest list. The funds are listed in order of largest to smallest; size is in billions of dollars. The returns shown in the final column are annualized.

The 20 Largest Equity Funds (as of 3/31/97)

name of fund	size (in billions)	5-year
Fidelity Magellan Fund	$56	18.3%
Vanguard Index 500	$39	19.6%
Investment Co. of America	$35	17.2%
Washington Mutual	$30	19.4%
Fidelity Growth & Income	$30	20.5%
Fidelity Contrafund	$27	20.1%
Amer. Cent.—20th Century Ultra	$21	21.2%
Fidelity Puritan	$20	16.2%
Vanguard/Windsor	$19	19.0%
Vanguard/Windsor II	$19	19.4%
Vanguard/Wellington	$18	15.8%
EuroPacific Growth	$18	15.5%
Janus Fund	$18	16.0%
Income Fund of America	$18	14.0%
Fidelity Advisor Growth Opportunity T	$18	19.7%
Fidelity Equity-Income	$17	19.8%
Fidelity Equity-Income II	$16	18.6%
Vanguard Institutional Index	$15	19.8%
New Perspective	$15	16.3%
Putnam Fund for Growth & Income A	$15	18.4%
Average stock fund	**$0.2**	**15.6%**
S&P 500 (dividends reinvested)	**—**	**19.8%**

It is difficult to draw any definitive conclusions from this one, somewhat limited, study. However, there are some important inferences or recommendations that can be made. Unless you know what you are doing, stay away from small funds and small mutual fund families—except those mentioned in this book. If you want to do better than the market averages, you may also want to stay away from the very biggest funds, even though there is safety in numbers. One guideline might be to choose mutual funds that have assets that range in size from $400 million to less than $2 billion. And, as always, diversify by category. Do not load up too heavily on a single category (such as growth, small-cap, foreign stock, etc.), no matter how impressive the results or how convincing the study.

Appendix I
U.S. Compared to Foreign Markets

Investing worldwide gives you exposure to different stages of economic market cycles—which has given international investors an advantage in the past. Foreign equities and bonds have generally offered higher levels of short-, intermediate-, and long-term growth than their domestic counterparts. Not once during the past ten years was the U.S. stock market the world's top performer.

Top-Performing World Stock Markets: A Ten-year Review: 1987–1996

year	1st	2nd	3rd	4th	5th
1996	Spain 41.3%	Taiwan 40.3%	Sweden 38%	Hong Kong 33.1%	Ireland 32.0%
1995	Switzerland 44.1%	USA 33.4%	Sweden 33.4%	Spain 29.8%	Netherlands 27.7%
1994	Finland 52.2%	Norway 23.6%	Japan 21.4%	Sweden 18.3%	Ireland 14.5%
1993	Hong Kong 109.9%	Malaysia 107.3%	Finland 81.3%	Singapore 65.5%	New Zealand 62.6%
1992	Hong Kong 27.4%	Switzerland 15.6%	Sing./Malaysia 4.4%	USA 4.2%	France 1.0%
1991	Hong Kong 49.5%	Australia 33.6%	USA 30.1%	Sing./Malaysia 25.0%	New Zealand 18.3%
1990	United Kingdom 10.1%	Hong Kong 9.2%	Austria 6.3%	Norway 0.7%	Denmark -0.9%
1989	Austria 103.9%	Germany 46.3%	Norway 45.5%	Denmark 43.9%	Sing./Malaysia 42.3%
1988	Belgium 53.6%	Denmark 52.7%	Sweden 48.3%	Norway 42.4%	France 37.8%
1987	Japan 43.0%	Spain 41.3%	United Kingdom 35.1%	Canada 13.9%	Denmark 13.2%

The U.S. stock market has ranked among the five top performers only three times in the past ten years. From 1985 through 1994, the U.S. bond market has ranked among the five top performers only three times. During this same period, the U.S. bond market has never claimed the number one spot against other world markets.

Looking at a different time period, a number of foreign markets have outperformed the United States. The table below shows annualized returns for the five-year period ending 3/31/97 (all figures are in U.S. dollars).

Annualized Returns through 3/31/97

country (annualized return)	country (annualized return)
Finland (30.0%)	Sweden (22.2%)
Switzerland (24.2%)	New Zealand (21.4%)
Brazil (23.1%)	Hong Kong (20.7%)
The Netherlands (22.9%)	USA (16.8%)

Top Performing World Bond Markets: 1985–1994

Year	1st	2nd	3rd	4th	5th
1985	France	Germany	Netherlands	UK	Japan
1986	Japan	Germany	Netherlands	Switzerland	France
1987	UK	Japan	Switzerland	Netherlands	Germany
1988	Australia	Canada	**USA**	Japan	UK
1989	Canada	**USA**	France	Germany	Australia
1990	UK	Denmark	France	Switzerland	Netherlands
1991	Australia	Japan	Canada	Sweden	Spain
1992	Japan	Netherlands	Belgium	**USA**	Germany
1993	Japan	New Zealand	UK	Australia	Ireland
1994	Belgium	Austria	Switzerland	New Zealand	Germany

Source: Salomon Brothers World Government Bond Market Index

Against the nine major bond markets in industrialized nations, the U.S. bond market ranked last, with a 9.7 percent average annual U.S. dollar return, compared to France's top-performing 16.0 percent.

Average Annual U.S. Dollar Returns:
9/30/85 – 9/30/95

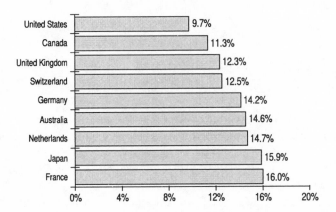

Source: Salomon Brothers World Government Bond Market Index

As of the end of 1995, about 34% of the world government bond market was U.S. debt and 66% of the $6.2 trillion pie was represented by foreign government bonds. Thus, an investor can gain substantial opportunities for diversification by broadening into global bond markets. The table below assumes an initial investment of $10,000 in each of several different government bond markets for the ten years ending 12/31/95. Notice that the U.S. tied for dead last in performance (all figures are in U.S. dollars).

World Bond Market Performance:
Total Returns for 10 Years Ending 12/31/95

country	$10,000 grew to . . .	country	$10,000 grew to . . .
Australia	$48,490	Germany	$31,860
France	$47,570	U.K.	$31,820
Japan	$40,920	Switzerland	$26,700
Italy	$39,810	Canada	$25,100
Netherlands	$38.620	USA	$25,100

Compared to more developed countries, bonds issued in emerging market countries can offer higher yields and strong potential capital *appreciation for the aggressive investor willing to assume additional risk.* The table below shows the top-performing emerging bond market versus returns for the U.S. bond market for each of the past six years (all figures are in U.S. dollars).

Emerging Bond Market vs. U.S. Bond Market

year	emerg. mkt.	USA	year	emerg. mkt.	USA
1996	Ecuador (+67.3%)	+2.7%	1993	Nigeria (+72.5%)	+11.0%
1995	Nigeria (+44.0%)	+18.3%	1992	Philippines (+15.6%)	7.2%
1994	Brazil (+4.8%)	-3.4%	1991	Venezuela (+39.8%)	15.3%

Source: Salomon Brothers World Government Bond Market Index

Growth possibilities that may no longer be present in the United States exist overseas. For example, an Asian phone company with only seven lines per thousand people stands a much greater chance of rapid growth than an established phone company in the United States. Basic businesses such as cement, supermarkets, and appliances are just taking off in developing nations, yet are familiar and relatively easy to analyze. And where national incomes are increasing, demand for checking accounts, car loans, and home mortgages bodes well for bank stocks.

Privatizations often present an opportunity to tap into a monopoly with a growing customer base. Many state-owned industries such as utilities, banks, and railroads are being sold to private investors in countries around the world. Selling these state-operated businesses helps raise revenue, expands equity markets, and attracts foreign investors.

By limiting a portfolio to U.S. stocks, you would have to ignore seventy of the world's ninety largest companies.

Appendix J
Past Performance Compared to Future Returns

Most investors, as well as a large number of brokers, investment advisors, and financial planners, believe that there is a relationship between the past, present, and future performance of a mutual fund. Indeed, the decision as to which mutual fund is purchased usually depends upon its most recent six-month, one-year, five-year, or ten-year track record. The marketing departments at brokerage firms and mutual fund companies reinforce this belief by their constant reference to performance figures in advertisements and brochures.

The reality is that there is virtually no relationship between the past, present, and future performance of an equity fund (aggressive growth, growth, growth and income, international stock, or global equities) or a long-term bond fund (corporate, foreign, government, municipal, or world). A number of studies support this view; in fact, I have never seen a study that disputes it.

During 1994, Lipper Analytical Services, one of the oldest and best known mutual fund tracking services, published a brief report concerning the star-rating system of Morningstar—currently the most frequently quoted source for mutual fund information. According to Lipper, in each of the past four years (1993, 1992, 1991, and 1990), equity funds that had been awarded five stars (the highest rating given by Morningstar) underperformed their respective asset class's average return over the twelve months that followed. Similar conclusions were reached concerning *Business Week*'s analysis of mutual funds. Other studies and reports, some dating back a number of years, reinforce the same point.

In 1991, Yanni Bilkey Investment Consulting Company looked at the *Forbes* mutual fund honor roll. Over seven, rolling five-year periods (1980–1984, 1981–1985, 1982–1986, 1983–1987, 1984–1988, 1985–1989, and 1986–1990), the funds that made the *Forbes'* Honor Roll only once outperformed, as a group, the S&P 500 in the first five-year period—and then only slightly. This same group never outperformed both the index and the average equity fund during any five-year time period.

A 1968 study by Michael Jensen, published in the *Journal of Finance*, concluded that institutional portfolios, regardless of prior track records, were consistent with the principles of random change.

A paper by Edgar Barksdale and William Green, covering close to 150 institutional stock portfolios over all ten-year periods between January 1, 1975, and December 31, 1989 (1975–1984, 1976–1985, 1977–1986, etc.) asked the following question: "How often do equity portfolios that finished in the top 20 percent of the group over the first five years end up finishing in the top half of all portfolios (144) over the second five years?"

The Barksdale-Green study showed an entirely random pattern: institutional portfolios that finished in the top 20 percent in the first years were the least likely (of the remaining groups) to finish even in the top half over the next five years. The results of all six of these ten-year rolling periods was as follows:

performance ranking during first five years	percentage that finished in the top half over the next five years
top 20 percent performers	45%
second 20 percent performers	48%
third 20 percent performers	51%
fourth 20 percent performers	52%
fifth 20 percent performers	50%

Personal Financial Planning magazine updated the Barksdale-Green study in 1994. According to the study's author, Robert Ludwig of SEI Corporation, things have not changed much. Ludwig's study looked at institutional equity account performance figures over five related periods (see table below). As before, the results are quite random.

Percent in the Top Half over Selected Time Periods

performance ranking over prior five-year periods	1986–90 (5 yrs.)	1987–90 (4 yrs.)	1988–90 (3 yrs.)	1989–90 (2 yrs.)	1990 (1 yr.)
top 25%	48%	46%	50%	48%	53%
bottom 25%	50%	51%	40%	52%	41%

According to long-time mutual fund author Roger Gibson, if you have a manager who is beating the market by 2 percent per year, it could take more than seventy years to know, with a 95-percent degree of confidence, whether the performance is based on skill rather than luck.

Appendix K
The Power of Dividends

The table below shows how important common stock dividends can be. The figures assume a one-time investment of $100,000 in the S&P 500 at the beginning of 1977. The table shows that dividends have increased for each of the past twenty years.

Viewed from a different perspective, if you were strictly income-oriented and invested $100,000 in the S&P 500 at the beginning of 1977, you would have received a 4.3 percent return on your investment ($4,300 divided by $100,000). For the 1996 calendar year, this same investment returned 31.2 percent for the year ($31,234 divided by $100,000). These figures assume that dividends received each year were spent and not reinvested. Moreover, these numbers do not include the over *elevenfold* growth of capital (the original $100,000 grew to $1,229,700 without dividends) that also took place.

As a point of comparison for the figures described in the previous paragraph, consider what would have happened if the same investor had invested in a twenty-year U.S. government bond in 1977. By the end of 1996, twenty years later, the original $100,000 worth of bonds would have matured and had an ending value of $100,000. Additionally, the investor would have received approximately 7 percent for each of these twenty years—a far cry from the increased dividend stream and capital appreciation the S&P 500 experienced over the same period. Perhaps more important, the bond investor could have taken his $100,000 at the beginning of 1997 and invested the money for another twenty years, getting a 6.5 percent return for each of those years (versus the S&P 500 investor who just finished receiving over 31.2 percent, based on $100,000, and presumably will be receiving even greater dividend returns for each or most of the next twenty years).

Annual Dividends from $100,000 Invested in the S&P 500

year	S&P 500 dividend	year	S&P 500 dividend
1977	$4,310	1987	$13,286
1978	$4,946	1988	$16,017
1979	$5,647	1989	$17,275
1980	$9,798	1990	$19,824
1981	$7,564	1991	$21,824
1982	$8,112	1992	$22,598
1983	$8,955	1993	$22,725
1984	$10,005	1994	$24,906
1985	$11,893	1995	$26,039
1986	$11,523	1996	$31,234

Appendix L
Growth Stocks vs. Value Stocks

Throughout the different equity sections (e.g., growth, growth and income, global equity, etc.), the end of each stock fund's "Management" paragraph often mentions whether the fund manager seeks out "growth" or "value" issues. The differences and possible consequences of these two forms of equity selection are shown in the table below.

Value means that the stocks are inexpensive relative to their earnings potential. *Growth* refers to stocks of companies whose earnings per share are expected to grow significantly faster than the market average.

As you can see by the table, the performance of these two types of stocks can vary from year to year. On a monthly or quarterly basis, the difference is often much more significant that occurs on an annual basis.

The table below shows performance of the S&P Barra Value Index and the S&P Barra Growth Index (dividends reinvested in both indexes). Over the past twelve years, an investment in both growth stocks and value stocks would have been less volatile than an investment in only one equity style.

Year	Growth Stocks	Value Stocks
1985	33.3%	29.7%
1986	14.5%	21.7%
1987	6.5%	3.7%
1988	12.0%	21.7%
1989	36.0%	26.1%
1990	.2%	−6.9%
1991	38.4%	22.6%
1992	5.1%	10.5%
1993	1.7%	18.6%
1994	3.1%	−.6%
1995	38.1%	37.0%
1996	24.0%	22.0%

Source: S&P 500 Barra Value Index and the S&P 500 Barra Growth Index.

The table below shows the annualized returns of growth versus value funds as categorized by Morningstar. In every single case, growth funds outperformed their value fund counterpart.

Total Returns through 7/31/97

mutual fund category	3 year	5 year	10 year
large growth	27.3%	19.0%	14.4%
large value	24.6%	17.8%	12.2%
mid-cap growth	24.2%	18.1%	13.4%
mid-cap value	22.6%	17.2%	12.1%
small growth	24.4%	18.5%	13.7%
small value	22.3%	18.3%	11.7%

Appendix M
Stock Volatility in Perspective

As of year-end 1996, U.S. households held $20.7 trillion in financial assets, which represents a 50% increase from $13.8 trillion at year-end 1991. Currently, stocks comprise about 40% of household financial assets, up from earlier this decade but still below the level seen in the early 1970s, when interest rates were at comparable levels. And, although there have certainly been quite a few negative years for stocks during the twentieth century, the number of really bad years has been modest (as shown in the following table).

Since 1900, U.S. stocks have had 31 down years, averaging a negative 13.4% return per year—but the 66 positive years have averaged 22.2% annually. Furthermore, the market has had back-to-back negative years only once since World War II.

U.S. Stocks: The Bad Years From 1900 to 1997

up to a 5% loss		5-10% loss		10-25% loss		more than a 25% loss	
1939	-0.4%	1914	-5.11%	1966	-10.1%	1974	-26.5%
1953	-1.0	1977	-7.2	1913	-10.3	1920	-32.9
1934	-1.4	1946	-8.1	1957	-10.8	1937	-35.0
1906	-1.9	1932	-8.2	1941	-11.6	1907	-37.7
1990	-3.2	1929	-8.4	1973	-14.7	1931	-43.3
1923	-3.3	1969	-8.5	1910	-17.9		
1916	-4.2	1901	-8.7	1917	-21.7		
1981	-4.9	1962	-8.7	1903	-23.6		
		1940	-9.8	1930	-24.9		

Since 1900 there have been 54 occassions (not necessarily calendar years) when stocks have "corrected"—meaning that they fell by ten percent or more from their most recent peak. In the past 40 years, there have been fourteen bear markets—drops of fifteen percent or more. The average duration of these fourteen bear markets has been just eight months; in most cases, the market fully recovered in less than one year (the average recovery period was thirteen months).

Sometimes the question is asked, "If the stock market is going down (or "expected" to go down in the near future), why not sit on the sidelines until it passes? The reason you do not want to try and time the stock market is that missing out on just a few good days can make a tremendous difference to a portfolio's performance. According to a study by the University of Michigan, an investor who was on the sidelines during the best 1.2 percent of all trading days from 1963 to 1993 missed 95 percent of the market's gains.

Appendix N
Does Foreign Diversification Really Reduce Risk?

As you can see by the table below, whether you are looking at a purely U.S. portfolio (the S&P 500) or one that has 30 percent of its holdings in foreign stocks (as measured by the EAFE Index), being "global" has done little to enhance returns or reduce risk. The best case for a global portfolio under the heading "average annual return" shows only a 0.2% advantage for the more diversified portfolio (100% stocks). Looking at the "largest 1-year gain", the best one-year period for a global portfolio was a portfolio that was evenly divided between stocks and bonds (25.0% for USA vs. 27.3% for global).

Looking at risk reduction over all one-year calendar periods over the past twenty-five years (ending 12/31/96), the "best" global portfolio only reduced the loss by just 0.6% (100% stock). Looking back at the October 19, 1987 stock market crash, one of the few benefits of owning foreign stocks was that each country bounced back at different times; Japanese stocks took just over a year to recover while U.S. stocks took nineteen months. Evidence suggests that a rising market is local, while a declining market is global. A large decline in U.S. stocks has frequently caused a big loss in foreign markets.

During the 1973–74 bear market, the biggest cumulative loss U.S. stocks have suffered since the Great Depression, the S&P 500 dropped 14.7% in 1973 and 26.4% in 1974. The EAFE (Europe, Australia, Far East) Index fell 14.2% in 1973 and 22.2% in 1974.

By owning just domestic companies, U.S. investors may already be getting quite a bit of international diversification: about 80% of Coca-Cola's profits come from its foreign operations, McDonald's is a similar situation.

The table below covers the twenty-five–year period ending 12/31/96 (all figures are in U.S. dollars).

allocation	average annual return	largest 1-year gain	largest 1-year loss
100% stock	13.7% USA	41.9% USA	-24.5% USA
	3.9% global	40.3% global	-23.9% global
90% stocks/10% bonds	13.3% USA	38.4% USA	-21.4% USA
	13.4% global	37.0% global	-20.8% global
80% stocks/20% bonds	12.8% USA	35.0% USA	-18.3% USA
	12.9% global	33.7% global	-17.8% global
70% stocks/30% bonds	12.3% USA	31.5% USA	-15.2% USA
	12.4% global	31.6% global	-14.8% global
60% stocks/40% bonds	11.8% USA	28.0% USA	-12.2% USA
	11.9% global	29.4% global	-11.8% global

allocation	average annual return	largest 1-year gain	largest 1-year loss
50% stocks/50% bonds	11.3% USA	25.0% USA	-9.1% USA
	11.4% global	27.3% global	-8.7% global
40% stocks/60% bonds	10.7 USA	23.5% USA	-6.0% USA
	10.8% global	23.0% global	-5.7% global
30% stocks/70% bonds	10.2% USA	23.5% USA	-2.9% USA
	10.2% global	23.0% global	-2.7% global
20% stocks/80% bonds	9.6% USA	23.5% USA	-1.6% USA
	9.6% global	22.0% global	-1.2% global
10% stocks/90% bonds	8.9% USA	23.5% USA	-2.0% USA
	8.9% global	22.8% global	-1.8% global
100% bonds	8.3% USA	23.5% USA	-2.4% USA
	8.3% bonds	23.5% global	-2.4% global

Notes:
1. USA = 70% S&P 500 + 30% U.S. small-company stocks
2. Global = 50% S&P 500 + 30% EAFE Index + 20% U.S. small-company stocks
3. Bonds = 70% medium-term government + 30% U.S. T-bills

Appendix O
The Last Fifteen Years

On August 15th, 1997, the U.S. stock market celebrated an unparalleled fifteen-year runup in which the Dow Jones Industrial Average increased nearly elevenfold. During the fifteen years ending July 31, 1997, the Dow averaged 20.8% a year while the S&P 500 had an annualized return of 19.7%. The second-best fifteen-year period for the S&P 500 ended April 1957, with an average annual return of 19.0%.

As good as U.S. stock returns have been, there are a number of other countries that have fared even better during our unparalleled climb (see table below which shows returns for the fourteen major stock markets around the world). Despite some better performers, no other country has created anywhere close to the amount of wealth in the stock market during the recent fifteen-year period. The total valuation of U.S. stocks went from about $1 trillion in 1982 to $10 trillion by July 31, 1997.

Stock Market Performance for the 15 Years Ending July 31, 1997*

country	annualized return	country	annualized return
Netherlands	24.9%	Norway	16.3%
France	21.1%	Germany	16.0%
Belgium	20.6%	Japan	14.1%
Finland	19.9%	Canada	13.8%
U.S.	19.7%	Australia	13.7%
Britain	19.1%	South Africa	13.5%
Switzerland	18.8%	Italy	12.9%
World	17.8%		

* All figures provided by Global Financial Data and shown in U.S. dollars.

When looking at returns from forty-five different countries, it has been the smaller markets that have provided the most excitement (and losses). The Global Financial Data figures shown have also been adjusted to U.S. dollars and do not include dividends.

The Best and Worst Stock Markets
(15-year annualized returns through 7/31/97)

the top 5 markets	the bottom five markets
Peru (35.6%)	Colombia (6.8%)
Mexico (32.6%)	Singapore (6.7%)
Brazil (27.2%)	Kenya (6.0%)
Taiwan (26.3%)	Indonesia (4.8%)
Argentina (23.0%)	South Africa (gold stocks) (-2.2%)

To give you a sense of comparison between August 1997 and August 1982, the table below provides some interesting benchmark figures (all information provided by The Business Picture).

the economy	Aug. 1982	Aug. 1997
unemployment rate	9.8%	4.8%
jobs created	-1,000,000	8,000,000
consumer confidence index	57	130
performance of the Dow		
5-year change	-5%	140%
15-year change	-9%	950%
15-year change adjusted for inflation	-70%	540%
valuation		
dividend yield	6.3%	1.6%
p/e ratio	7	23
ratio of NYSE market value to GDP	0.3	1.1
DJIA to new home prices	.012	.052
DJIA to hourly earnings	105	622
DJIA to gold	2	25
DJIA to commodity prices	3	34
interest rates and inflation		
prime rate	15.0%	8.5%
3-month Treasury bill rate	9.8%	5.1%
30-year Treasury bond yield	13.3%	6.4%
S&P 500 yield	2.1%	3.9%
consumer price index	6.4%	2.3%
producer price index	3.6%	0%
sentiment		
bullish consensus	21	72
net cash flows into mutual funds	-$2 billion	$193 billion
number of investment clubs	4,000	32,000

According to some definitions, the most recent bull market began in October 1990, when the Dow Jones Industrial Average (DJIA) was hovering near the 2,300 mark. Based on that starting date, consider the following statistics (as reported *in* the *Wall Street Journal* on July 17, 1997):

- a bull run of 1,709 trading days
- 9 days unchanged
- a 5,673 point increase in the DJIA
- largest 1-day % gain: 4.6%
- a 240% increase
- largest 1-day gain: 179 points
- 923 up days vs. 777 down days

Appendix P
Asset Categories:
Total Returns for the Last Ten Years

The table below shows the year-by-year returns for eight different asset categories. All of the returns are in U.S. dollars, expressed as perentages, and include the reinvestment of any dividends, interest, and capital gains. The boldface type indicates the best-performing category for the year.

category	'87	'88	'89	'90	'91	'92	'93	'94	'95	'96
S&P 500	5.2	16.8	31.5	-3.2	30.6	7.7	10.0	1.3	**37.5**	23.1
small U.S. stocks	-8.8	24.9	16.2	-19.5	46.1	**18.4**	18.9	-1.8	28.4	16.5
foreign stocks (EAFE)	24.6	28.3	10.5	-23.5	12.1	-12.2	32.6	**7.8**	11.2	6.1
emerging mkt. stocks	13.6	**58.2**	**54.7**	-29.9	17.6	0.3	**67.5**	-0.5	-12.5	7.9
U.S. gov't/ corp. bonds	2.8	7.9	14.5	9.0	16.0	7.4	9.6	-2.9	18.5	3.6
high-yield bonds	5.0	12.5	0.8	-9.6	**46.2**	15.8	17.1	-1.0	19.2	11.1
foreign gov't bonds	**35.2**	2.3	-3.4	**15.3**	16.2	4.8	15.1	6.0	19.6	4.1
U.S. T-bills	5.8	6.8	8.2	7.5	5.4	3.5	3.0	4.3	5.4	5.0

Appendix Q
Alphabetical Index of the Funds

Oppenheimer Quest Global
  Value A
Princor Emerging Growth A
Putnam Convertible Income-
  Growth A
Putnam Global Growth A
Putnam Utilities Growth and
  Income A
Royce Micro Cap
Royce Premier
Scudder Global
Scudder Gold
Scudder Growth and Income
SEI Daily Income Prime
  Obligation A
Seligman High-Yield Bond A
SIT Tax-Free Income
SIT U.S. Government Securities
Smith Breeden Short Duration
  Government Series
SoGen International
Sound Shore
State Street Research Global
  Resources A
Strong Municipal Money Market
Strong Schafer Value

T. Rowe Price Equity-Income
T. Rowe Price Growth & Income
T. Rowe Price Small Cap Stock
T. Rowe Price Spectrum Growth
Templeton Developing Markets I
Templeton Growth I
Third Avenue Value
Thornburg Intermediate
  Municipal A
Torray
United Municipal High Income A
Van Kampen American Capital
  Equity-Income A
Vanguard Fixed-Income
  Securities Short-Term
  Federal Bond
Vanguard Municipal
  Intermediate-Term
Vanguard Specialized Energy
Victory Diversified Stock A
Warburg Pincus Fixed Income
Warburg Pincus Global Fixed
  Income
Washington Mutual Investors
Winthrop Small Company
  Value A

About the Author

Gordon K. Williamson, JD, MBA, MS, CFP, CLU, ChFC, RP is one of the most highly trained investment counselors in the United States. Williamson, a former tax attorney, is a Certified Fund Specialist and branch manager of a national brokerage firm. He has been admitted to the Registry of Financial Planning Practitioners, the highest honor one can attain as a financial planner. He holds the two highest designations in the life insurance industry, Chartered Life Underwriter and Chartered Financial Consultant. He is also a real estate broker with an MBA in real estate.

Mr. Williamson is the founder and Executive Director of the Institute of Business & Finance, a professional education program that leads to the designations "CFS" and "Board Certified" (800/848-2029).

He is also the author of twenty books, including: *Building & Managing an Investment Portfolio, Making the Most of Your 401(k), The 100 Best Annuities You Can Buy, All About Annuities, How You Can Survive and Prosper in the Clinton Years, Investment Strategies under Clinton/Gore, The Longman Investment Companion, Investment Strategies, Survey of Financial Planning, Tax Shelters, Advanced Investment Vehicles and Techniques, Your Living Trust, Sooner Than You Think,* and *Low Risk Investing.* He has been the financial editor of various magazines and newspapers and a stock market consultant for a television station.

Gordon K. Williamson is an investment advisory firm located in La Jolla, California. The firm specializes in financial planning for individuals and institutions ($100,000 minimum account size). Additional information can be obtained by phoning (800) 748-5552 or (619) 454-3938.

Also available from Adams Media Corporation

The 100 Best Stocks You Can Buy, 1998

John Slatter, CFA
ISBN: 1-55850-755-8
$12.95

Slatter chooses stocks in companies that are likely to provide the best return on your investment; companies with innovative marketing, productive research, and years of consistent growth whose stock is selling at a reasonable price. Each of the stocks in *The 100 Best Stocks You Can Buy, 1998* is graded into one of four categories—Income, Conservative Growth, Growth and Income, and Aggressive Growth. Investors with different goals can pick the stocks that best fit their investment strategy. Whether you're looking for blue chips to hold for the long-term or high-tech, high-flyers for short-term profits, *The 100 Best Stocks You Can Buy, 1998* can help you make the right decisions for your investments.

Available Wherever Books Are Sold

If you cannot find these titles at your favorite retail outlet, you may order them directly from the publisher. BY PHONE: Call 1-800-872-5627 (in Massachusetts 781-767-8100). We accept Visa, Mastercard, and American Express. $4.50 will be added to your total order for shipping and handling. BY MAIL: Write out the full titles of the books you'd like to order and send payment, including $4.50 for shipping and handling, to: Adams Media Corporation; 260 Center Street, Holbrook, MA 02343. 30-day money-back guarantee.